INVISIBLE

PUNISHMENT

INVISIBLE PUNISHMENT

The Collateral Consequences of Mass Imprisonment

MARC MAUER AND MEDA CHESNEY-LIND, EDITORS

THE NEW PRESS
NEW YORK

Published in the United States by The New Press, New York, 2002
Distributed by W. W. Norton & Company, Inc., New York

LIBRARY OF CONGRESS CATALOGING-IN-PUBLICATION DATA
Invisible punishment : the collateral consequences of mass imprisonment /
Marc Mauer and Meda Chesney-Lind, editors.
p.   cm.
Includes bibliographical references and index.
ISBN 1-56584-726-1 (hc.)
1. Criminal justice, Administration of—Social aspects—Unites States.
2. Imprisonment—Social aspects—United States.   3. Sentences (Criminal
procedure)—Social aspects—United States.   4. Discrimination in criminal justice
administration—United States.   I. Mauer, Marc.   II. Chesney-Lind, Meda.
HV9950 .I59   2003
365'.6—dc21   200214130

The New Press was established in 1990 as a not-for-profit alternative to the
large, commercial publishing houses currently dominating the book publishing
industry. The New Press operates in the public interest rather than for private gain,
and is committed to publishing, in innovative ways, works of educational, cultural,
and community value that are often deemed insufficiently profitable.

The New Press, 450 West 41st Street, 6th floor, New York, NY 10036
www.thenewpress.com

Printed in the United States of America

2   4   6   8   10   9   7   5   3   1

To my mother, Mildred Mauer, and the memory of my father, Joseph Mauer
—Marc Mauer

To Margaret and Mae, my sisters both in spirit and reality
—Meda Chesney-Lind

Contents

Acknowledgments

D iane Wachtell, our editor at The New Press, approached us with an idea for a book exploring the broad-ranging consequences of America's commitment to imprisonment. No doubt she was reading our minds, since these have been issues of great interest to us in recent years. The project also provided a welcome opportunity for two old friends to collaborate in a way that was both personally and professionally rewarding. Throughout the process, Diane's insightful editing and enthusiasm kept us intellectually sharp and focused. Thanks also to Beth Slovic, Janey Tannenbaum, and others at The New Press for their support and efficiency in the many layers of production and promotion of the book.

Our sincere gratitude goes to all the contributors to the book, each of whom prepared a challenging text and made the editorial process a collegial one in the best sense of the word. Their collective voices are the strength of this volume.

Our respective institutions provided the logistical support necessary for an efficient working environment. Staff of The Sentencing Project aided in the many day-to-day editing and coordinating tasks required to pull together a project of this scope. Thanks in particular to the funders who have supported the organization's work, most notably the Ford Foundation, the John D. and Catherine T. MacArthur Foundation, and the Open Society Institute. Meda wishes to thank her many supportive colleagues at the University of Hawaii, including Konia Freitas, Katherine Irwin, David Johnson, Nancy Marker, David Mayeda, Scott Okamoto, and Vickie Paramore. Meda also thanks her network of academics, policy activists, and practitioners for encouraging a focus on women in prison and the importance of thinking and writing about decarceration as a national priority. Here thanks to Barbara Bloom, Karlene Faith, Russ Immarigeon, Ann McDermott, Andie Moss, Barbara Owen, Joy Pollock, Nicole Hahn Rafter, Paula Schaefer, Vinnie Schiraldi, and Mary Scully Whitaker. Finally, many thanks to the current and former prisoners who have talked to us throughout the years and convinced us of the need for a more humane policy toward those we now imprison.

Helping to provide a healthy balance between work and home on the east coast were Barbara Francisco and Joanna and Daniel Mauer, whose inquisitive spirits and senses of humor always provide just the right environment to keep moving along. And in the Pacific, thanks to Ian Lind for his unfailing support over the years.

INVISIBLE
PUNISHMENT

Introduction

Marc Mauer and Meda Chesney-Lind

Another year goes by in the courtrooms of America. A million defendants are convicted of felony crimes, and 450,000 of them are sentenced to prison. Few of their names or stories are known to us unless we happen to have a personal connection to them. Yet the results of the routine workings of an increasingly massive and punitive criminal justice system have consequences not only for these individuals whose lives are directly touched, but for an extended group of parents, spouses, children, friends, and communities who have committed no crimes but must suffer the largely invisible punishments that are the result of our current approach to criminal justice.

By relying on incarceration as the predominant mode of crime control for the past thirty years, the United States has developed a social policy that can be described only as mass imprisonment. With 2 million Americans behind bars in the nation's prisons and jails, the impact of these policies on American society is more profound than at any previous point in history.

Social scientists have long recognized that all social policies have what might be termed intended and unintended, or "collateral," consequences, and that sorting these out can be complex and a matter of political interpretation. This book provides the first comprehensive examination of what Jeremy Travis has aptly termed "invisible punishments" to describe the effects of policies that have transformed family and community dynamics, exacerbated racial divisions, and posed fundamental questions of citizenship in democratic society. Imprisonment was once primarily a matter of concern for the individual prisoner, but the scale of incarceration today is such that its impact is far broader—first, on the growing number of family members affected financially and emotionally by the imprisonment of a loved one; beyond that, by the way incarceration is now experienced by entire communities in the form of broad-scale economic hardships, increased risk of fatal disease, and marked economic and social risk for the most vulnerable children. And ultimately, a society in which mass imprisonment has become the norm is one in which questions of justice, fairness, and access to resources are being altered in ways hitherto unknown. This collection represents an attempt to frame these issues and explore their wide-ranging impacts on American society.

Nowhere are these effects more highlighted than in the African-American community, where the experience of imprisonment has become almost commonplace among men and increasingly for women as well. More than three-quarters of a million black men are now behind bars, and nearly 2 million are under some form of correctional supervision, including probation and parole. For black males ages twenty-five to thirty-four, at a time in life when they would otherwise be starting families and careers, one of every eight is in prison or jail on any given day. As detailed by Donald Braman and Bruce Western and colleagues, behind these figures lies an experience of profound stress on family relationships, employment prospects, and child-rearing.

The collective portrait of prisoners is very telling. Three-quarters have a history of drug or alcohol abuse, one-sixth a history of mental illness, and more than half the women inmates a history of sexual or physical abuse. Most prisoners are from poor or working-class communities, and two-thirds are racial and ethnic minorities.

For the inmate and his or her family, a variety of collateral consequences are set in motion when he or she is sent off to prison. These begin with the logistical challenges of trying to maintain an intact family in the face of what are often severe economic and emotional hardships. The first obstacle families face is created by the fact that, as Tracy Huling describes, in most states prison policy results in a prisoner population that is primarily urban being housed in rural prisons. In New York State, for example, two thirds of prison inmates are from New York City and are largely housed in upstate rural prisons, many of them hundreds of miles from home.

How does a family of limited means—and most prison families are very much in this category—cope with this distance? For a start, telephone contact is limited. Inmates typically have restrictions placed on their access to telephones, and even when they don't, the ease of communication is often illusory. Prison telephone service remains one of the last bastions of officially sanctioned price gouging. Prisoners are required to place calls collect, allegedly for security reasons, and sweetheart profit deals between phone companies and corrections systems lead to what would be a thirty-five-cent call in the free world becoming a four-dollar collect call to home.

But even at reasonable rates, the limitations of phone contact are but one of many reasons why few marriages survive a long-term prison sentence. Visiting a family member in prison is a significant challenge. First, a low-income city family needs the time and money to make the journey—a reliable car, perhaps an overnight stay in a motel or someone to take care of small children. The visit itself is likely to involve waiting an hour or more in a dingy reception area while the prisoner is tracked down and given a chance to shower. Family members then pass through a metal detector, possibly are searched for drugs, and finally meet their loved one in a crowded visiting room; or, if prison officials deem it necessary, see them only through a Plexiglas window while talking on a telephone. But even when reunited, families can never really leave the reality of the prison. The rules and regulations that define the bureaucracy of the prison even govern when and for how long a husband and a wife may embrace each other.

Communities of color have experienced these family strains for some time, but these problems are magnified by the rapidly rising imprisonment of women. As detailed by Meda Chesney-Lind and Beth Richie, the rate of growth for women in prison has been nearly double that for men over the past two decades, and has been accompanied by profound racial disparities. And for women, the impact of drug policies has been even more dramatic than for men, with one-third of the women in prison currently serving a drug sentence.

These trends mean that we have now entered an era in which substantial proportions of children in minority communities are growing up with a parent behind bars. Two-thirds of the women in prison have one or more minor children. Many women in prison are custodial parents; those who are lucky will have a friend or relative who is able to take on the care of the children while the mother is imprisoned. Those who are not so fortunate will see their children placed in foster care. And as a result of recent legislation (1997) mandating that parental rights can be terminated for children in the care of the state for fifteen months, it will be increasingly likely that the children will be placed for adoption.

For African-American children overall, the family experience of imprisonment is now almost commonplace, with one out of every fourteen having a parent in prison. This represents the experience on a given day; over the course of a year or the duration of childhood the proportion would be far greater. And given the difficulties described above in visiting prisons, more than half of children with a parent in prison have never even visited their parent since his or her incarceration.

Although we can quantify this experience to some degree, what is difficult to measure is the daily impact on children growing up in a neighborhood where prison seems to be almost an inevitable aspect of the maturation process, as Donald Braman describes in his essay. Since current rates of imprisonment dwarf any in the history of democratic nations, we can only speculate about the future impact. But it is not difficult to imagine that neighborhoods beset by social ills are not well served when boys and girls perceive that going to prison may be a more likely prospect than going to college.

Mass imprisonment has had a particularly insidious impact on communities of color due to the curious intersection of criminal justice and political policy making. Most prominent among these is the political disenfranchisement described by Marc Mauer of an estimated 1.4 million African-American males, or 13 percent of the adult African-American population, as a result of felony disenfranchisement laws that strip current or former felons of voting rights. These policies, varying greatly by state, arose originally in the context of the founding of the nation as only white male property holders were given the franchise. In the post-

Reconstruction era in the old Confederacy, these laws were often tailored to target specifically the newly enfranchised black voters. In the modern world, the combined impact of these laws and record rates of incarceration produces a stunning political effect. As implemented in the state of Florida, this policy may well have decided the 2000 U.S. presidential election, with several hundred thousand ex-felons, disproportionately African-American, barred from the ballot box.

Other invisible punishments have increasingly shaped the landscape of the criminal justice system as well. Consider, for example, the collateral consequences imposed on a first-time offender who pleads guilty to felony possession of marijuana. Policy changes of the past two decades now bring a host of such consequences, as described by a task force of the American Bar Association, on the day of sentencing:

> [The] offender may be sentenced to a term of probation, community service, and court costs. Unbeknownst to this offender, and perhaps to any other actor in the sentencing process, as a result of his conviction he may be ineligible for many federally-funded health and welfare benefits, food stamps, public housing, and federal educational assistance. His driver's license may be automatically suspended, and he may no longer qualify for certain employment and professional licenses. If he is convicted of another crime he may be subject to imprisonment as a repeat offender. He will not be permitted to enlist in the military, or possess a firearm, or obtain a federal security clearance. If a citizen, he may lose the right to vote; if not, he becomes immediately deportable.[1]

Looking broadly at the political landscape, the "get tough" movement of the past thirty years has altered our perceptions in ways so profound that one scholar terms it "governing through crime."[2] Where once crime was primarily perceived as a local issue, today there are few election campaigns at any level of office that do not incorporate "the crime issue" as a staple of their platforms. Increasingly, too, it is understood that crime has become a code word for race in American political life, and therefore "tough" talk on crime is a proxy for criminal justice policies that disproportionately control and police African-American communities.

There is nothing inherently wrong with addressing crime as an issue in public policy debate—our violent crime rate is, after all, far out of line with comparable nations. In its practical application in the era of mass imprisonment, though, the nature of this discussion often has increasingly little to do with actually examining the problem and its solutions. We see, for example, the undue influence exerted by rural legislative leaders in convincing state policy makers to expand prison systems by locating them in economically troubled rural communities. In New York State, forty of the forty-one new prisons built since 1983 have been located in rural upstate communities.[3] And, as Judith A. Greene demonstrates, the advent of private prison companies aggressively marketing their wares in the past decade has resulted in questions of liberty and justice now being framed in the context of returns to stockholders.

Much of this expansion is a result of the vigorous campaigning engaged in by leaders of the drug "war" since the early 1980s. Had this effort been conceptualized as a penal institution construction project, one could judge it a sterling success, with the number of Americans serving time or awaiting trial for a drug offense rising tenfold from 40,000 in 1980 to nearly half a million today. One would be hard-pressed to demonstrate that the goal of the policy has been to stem drug abuse among all Americans rather than to wage a war on communities of color, with nearly 80 percent of inmates in state prison for drug offenses being African American or Latino.

The drug war's influence on political decision making and conceptions of civil liberties has been profound as well, as legislators have increasingly adopted ever more punitive measures against those who have been convicted of a drug offense. As Gwen Rubinstein and Debbie Mukamal point out in this book, this has led to the bizarre situation whereby a convicted armed robber or a rapist can apply for higher education or welfare benefits, but a drug offender cannot. And through the guise of asset forfeiture legislation, the presumption of innocence has been ignored as local and federal law enforcement agencies are empowered to seize the property of suspected drug dealers and deposit it in police coffers, even if the suspect is not convicted.

The hardening of public attitudes and public policy in recent years has inadvertently affected our national approach to meeting the needs of victims as well. While ostensibly formulated to control crime and, by implication, to protect potential victims, the "offender-centered" nature of national policy in fact distracts our attention from the needs of victims. Rather than asking the policy question of how to heal the impact of crime and prevent future crime, we instead become focused on how much we can punish the offender. This translates to trying kids as adults, imposing ever-harsher mandatory minimum and "three-strikes" sentences, and imposing the death penalty to a degree hitherto unknown in democratic societies.

Given this orientation, the advances made in the cause of victims' services have been truly impressive. Where once victims received little consideration, virtually every state and county now has some combination of restitution programs, counseling services, and other aids to deal with the emotional and financial trauma of victimization. Yet the political dynamic that has been established is one whereby the interests of victims are pitted *against* the interests of offenders.

The tragedy of this polarization lies in the fact that there is no inherent reason why the two groups need to be seen in opposition. Victims clearly have a set of needs arising from the crime that has been committed against them, but offenders have legitimate needs as well—a fair trial, punishment that fits the crime, and interventions to reduce their future likelihood of reoffending. A "tough on crime" orientation has little room for acknowledging that both parties may have legitimate, albeit distinct, needs and rights. Indeed, if crime victims appear at all on this harsh political landscape, it is often only to plead for the harshest possible penalty for the offender. Victims who seek other ways to heal are frequently marginalized or ignored by a system that purports to dispense justice and heal the wounds of crime.

We would be remiss not to acknowledge that prisons provide some benefits to individuals and society. In some instances, imprisonment may actually bring comfort to the families of offenders themselves. The mother who has done all she can yet is helpless to prevent her son from selling drugs and carrying a gun, may feel that prison provides some temporary relief for the family. And there are some offenders whose life on the streets is so perilous that a prison sentence may bring a respite, even given the high level of violence within prisons themselves.

Prisons also incapacitate certain offenders who would otherwise be committing serious crimes in the community. In extreme cases—the Charles Mansons or the Unabombers of the world—the very real threat of violence is sufficient in itself to justify the isolation of prison.

Incarceration may have some impact on less extreme cases as well. Scholars have attempted to examine the prison-crime relationship over many years, and it is fair to say that the evidence is not conclusive. Among the most recent spate of studies are some that have estimated the impact of the 1990s prison buildup on the declining crime rate. Two scholars using different research methodologies estimated that about one-fourth of the decline in violent crime and homicide could be attributed to rising incarceration.[4]

But is this good news or bad news? Although a 25 percent reduction in crime is quite welcome, it still leaves unexplained three-quarters of the crime drop, not to mention inconsistent results in the late 1980s, when crime rates rose despite a sustained increase in the use of imprisonment. Further, one of these study's authors concludes that a variety of other factors contributed to reducing crime and states that "violent crime *would* have dropped a lot, anyway. Most of the responsibility for the crime drop rests with improvements in the economy, changes in the age structure, or other social factors. Whether the key to further reductions lies in further prison expansions, or (more likely) in further improvements in these other factors remains an open question."[5]

Although the prison-crime relationship is subject to debate, one factor that is not is the near consensus among all serious scholars that fluctuations in crime rates are subject to a host of complex factors. These include individual personality, family dynamics, employment and educational prospects, substance abuse, and, yes, imprisonment.

There is a further complication to the prison-crime analysis as well, one that suggests that the declines of recent years may be more illusory than seems apparent at first. Criminologist Elliott Currie suggests that measuring changes in the crime rate only tells us part of what we need to know. What it fails to do is to calculate what might be termed the "criminality rate," that is, the extent to which we "produce" criminals.[6] The reason for this is that the 2 million Americans behind bars are taken out of the crime equation since they by definition cannot commit crimes (at least outside of prison). Currie likens this to assessing the degree of illness in a society without taking into account sick people in hospitals. Would we say that we've conquered an illness by hospitalizing all people identified with that illness? Of course not, but this is essentially our method of computation for crime. Thus, if one wanted to calculate the total number of identified offenders in a given year, it would be necessary also to include the 2 million persons behind bars[7] to determine the pool of potential lawbreakers.

Examining the collateral consequences of mass incarceration opens up the question of whether these are intended or unintended consequences. One can make a compelling argument for either claim. There have clearly been moments in history when the stated goal of public policy was to imprison a group of people for the purpose of restricting their liberty and freedom of speech. We can recall the internment of Japanese Americans during World War II and the jailing of civil rights protestors in the South. Ongoing and intended consequences of criminal justice policies have included felon voting disenfranchisement statutes adopted in certain Southern states, whereby legislators designated crimes supposedly committed most commonly by blacks to result in the loss of voting rights, but not those offenses believed to be committed primarily by white offenders. These blatantly racist policies have since been changed, but the combined impact of high rates of criminal justice control along with "race neutral" disenfranchisement policies produces rates of exclusion that are eerily similar to the days of the poll tax in some areas.

For other consequences of large-scale incarceration it would be difficult to infer specific intent on the part of policy makers to disempower certain groups or communities, even if that is the actual effect. Consider the transfer of political and financial influence occasioned by the census practice of counting prisoners in the county where they are housed and not their home communities. With a swelling inmate population comprised largely of urban minorities, this has set in motion a significant transfer of resources from urban to rural areas, even though it is unlikely that this was the intent of census officials, who originally established this policy at a time when there were far fewer inmates and the impact of such a policy would have been much more limited.

Examining the individual consequences and attempting to determine their political origins represent only one aspect of an examination of intentionality. Whether or not one believes that these consequences are intended by policy makers, a broader issue concerns the limited vision behind crime control policies and the failure to assess the consequences of these policies, virtually all of which easily could have been foreseen.

In the 1960s, concern with rising crime became identified as an "urban" problem and inescapably a black one in the public mind. Rather than building upon the "war on poverty" that had been inaugurated, however limited in scope, the seeds of the "get tough" movement were planted instead. Indeed, the earliest advocates of this movement, Barry Goldwater and Richard Nixon, explicitly linked the crime issue to the issue of civil rights. Some contend, in fact, that the Republican Party has been pursuing a "Southern strategy" for wresting electoral control of Southern states previously represented by Democrats by appealing to voters' fears of "social unrest" and violent crime—with a major chord being white fear of black street crime.[8] If anything, one can say that the political architects of this "strategy" underestimated its national (not just Southern) appeal.

Crime, and particularly drug-related crime, was a centerpiece of the presidency of an extremely popular Republican president, Ronald Reagan. His successor, George H. W. Bush, arguably owed his election to his "tough on crime" position and the racist deployment of the Willie Horton case against his opponent, then–Massachusetts governor Michael Dukakis. The "war on drugs" launched during these Republican presidencies, and supported in large part by Democrats in Congress and the subsequent Clinton administration, had as its chief hallmark a stepped-up federal role in law enforcement and harsh sentencing policies. As long as the image of a drug abuser was that of a young black man, the arrest and sentencing policies that would be developed would target young crack users and sellers in defined communities, inevitably creating vast racial disparities in the system and distracting public attention away from approaches that emphasized prevention and treatment. And increasingly, as more low-income women became caught up in cycles of poverty, addiction, and dependency, they, too, fell into the criminal justice net created by public policy.

The vast scope of impacts on families and communities could well have been predicted had policy makers taken the time to make such an assessment. But when the subject is crime policy, speed, rather than reflection, is of the essence. Thus, the haste in 1986 when Congress adopted harsh mandatory drug sentencing laws following the death of basketball star Len Bias, the overnight movement that turned "three strikes" from a baseball image to a national crime policy in 1994, and the seeming regularity with which legislators adopt a "crime of the month" campaign. Neither victims nor offenders are well served by such a process.

But the problem is much greater than this if we are still working under the presumption that the criminal justice system is the best or most appropriate venue in which to address behavior that threatens public safety. Rather than investigating the circumstances of families or communities that enhance social solidarity and communicate shared values, a criminal justice–centered policy applies a reactive, and increasingly punitive, approach to the resolution of social conflict. One of the many ironies of this development is that many of the most "anti-Washington" politicians on the national scene are among the first to champion federal directives and incentives for states to build and fill more prisons.

Corrections costs have been the fastest growing segment of state budgets, and this has meant that virtually all other aspects of spending, including funds for education and social welfare, have been affected in order to accommodate prison expansion. This distortion of decision-making detracts from approaches to the problem that could build upon and strengthen the processes by which families and communities contribute to raising children who feel valued and who have a sense of belonging to a community. Whether we are looking at wealthy communities or poor ones, these processes are critical to the healthy functioning of neighborhoods and a reduced propensity for crime.

As we can see from the breadth of issues covered in this book, decisions regarding our national approach to the problem of crime clearly need to be framed in a much broader context than in the past. With the unprecedented expansion of the prison system over three decades has come a complex network of invisible punishments affecting families and communities nationwide.

Ultimately, the impact of mass imprisonment on American society needs to be considered not just in terms of efficacy or benefits but as a moral question as well. Even to the extent that some policy-makers may believe that incarceration is the primary cause of the falling crime rate, this should hardly be cause for celebration. As Vivien Stern notes in her chapter, other nations have demonstrated that it is quite possible to maintain far lower rates of crime and violence without resorting to world record prison building; indeed, most of the rest of the world is moving away from this approach to crime. Americans may continue to lead the world in incarceration, but it comes at a terrible social cost, and increasingly isolates us from the rest of the world.

PART I

Beyond Doing Time:
The Lifetime Consequences
of Imprisonment

1

Invisible Punishment: An Instrument of Social Exclusion

Jeremy Travis[1]

I. BRINGING INVISIBLE PUNISHMENT INTO VIEW

Prisons have this virtue: They are visible embodiments of society's decision to punish criminals. As we punish more people, the number of prisons increases. We can count how many people are in prison, measure the length of the sentences they serve, determine what we spend to keep them there, and conduct empirically grounded analysis of the costs and benefits of incarceration. Because prisons make punishment visible, we can more easily quantify the policy debates over the wisdom of this application of the criminal sanction.

Not all criminal sanctions are as visible as prisons: We punish people in other, less tangible ways. Community corrections is one example. While the number of prisoners has quadrupled over the past two decades, the number of adults under criminal justice supervision through parole and probation agencies has more than tripled.[2] This form of punishment is not as obvious to the public: Probationers and parolees can easily become invisible. Yet, the quantum of punishment meted out through community-based sentences still has discernable bounds. We know the number of people under community supervision. We can measure the length of their sentences. Similarly, we can quantify, and thereby make "visible," the imposition of criminal fines, the collection of restitution, and the forfeiture of assets, three other criminal sanctions that have expanded over recent years.

This chapter focuses on a criminal sanction that is nearly invisible: namely, the punishment that is accomplished through the diminution of the rights and privileges of citizenship and legal residency in the United

States. Over the same period of time that prisons and criminal justice supervision have increased significantly, the laws and regulations that serve to diminish the rights and privileges of those convicted of crimes have also expanded. Yet we cannot adequately measure the reach of these expressions of the social inclination to punish. Consequently, we cannot evaluate their effectiveness, impact, or even "implementation" through the myriad private and public entities that are expected to enforce these new rules. Because these laws operate largely beyond public view, yet have very serious, adverse consequences for the individuals affected, I refer to them, collectively, as "invisible punishment."[3]

They are invisible in a second sense as well. Because these punishments typically take effect outside of the traditional sentencing framework—in other words, are imposed by operation of law rather than by decision of the sentencing judge—they are not considered part of the practice or jurisprudence of sentencing. Through judicial interpretation, legislative fiat, and legal classification, these forms of punishment have been defined as "civil" rather than criminal in nature, as "disabilities" rather than punishments, as the "collateral consequences" of criminal convictions rather than the direct results.[4] Because they have been defined as something other than criminal punishment, scholars, legislators, criminal justice officials, and legal analysts have failed to incorporate them into the debates over sentencing policy that have realigned our criminal justice system over the past quarter century.

Finally, there is a third dimension of invisibility. Although these criminal punishments look like typical legislative enactments, wending their way through the committee process, passage by majority vote, and approval by the executive,[5] their legislative life cycle often follows an unusual course. Unlike sentencing statutes, they are not typically considered by judiciary committees.[6] They are often added as riders to other, major pieces of legislation, and therefore are given scant attention in the public debate over the main event.[7] They are typically not codified with other criminal sanctions. Some exist in the netherworld of the host legislation to which they were attached. Some exist under a separate heading of civil disabilities. Some defy traditional notions of federalism by importing federal penal policy into state sentencing statutes so that a conviction for a state law violation triggers federal consequences. Some apply the restrictions of one state on an offender convicted in another state who chooses to relocate. Little wonder, then, that defense lawyers cannot easily advise their clients of all of the penalties that will flow from a plea of guilty.[8] These punishments are invisible ingredients in the legislative menu of criminal sanctions.

This chapter argues that these punishments should be brought into open view. They should be made visible as critical elements of the sentencing statutes of the state and federal governments. They should be recognized as visible players in the sentencing drama played out in courtrooms every day, with judges informing defendants that these consequences flow from a finding of guilt or plea of guilty. Finally, they should be openly included in our debates over punishment policy, incorporated in our sentencing jurisprudence, and subjected to rigorous research and evaluation.

II. THE CONTEXT AND CONSEQUENCES OF INVISIBLE PUNISHMENT

The idea that convicted offenders should be denied certain rights and benefits of citizenship is certainly not new. In early Roman history, and among some Germanic tribes, the penalty of "outlawry" could be imposed on offenders. The outlaw's wife was deemed a widow, his children orphans; he lost his possessions and was deprived of all rights. In ancient Athens, the penalty of "infamy" could be imposed, meaning the offender was denied the right to attend public assemblies, hold office, make speeches, and serve in the army. Later in the Roman empire, offenders were barred from certain trades. In the medieval era, "civil death" was the consequence of a sentence of life imprisonment, meaning the offenders lost the right to inherit or bequeath property, enter into contracts, and vote.[9]

American legislatures continued this tradition,[10] denying convicted offenders the right to enter into contracts, automatically dissolving their marriages, and barring them from a wide variety of jobs and benefits.[11] Indeed, the Fourteenth Amendment to the United States Constitution explicitly recognizes the power of the states to deny the right to vote to individuals guilty of "participation in rebellion or other crimes."

What is new at the beginning of the twenty-first century is the expansive reach of these forms of punishment. There are simply more of them: After a thirty-year period when these indirect forms of punishment were strongly criticized by legal reformers and restricted by state legislatures, they experienced a surge in popularity beginning in the mid-1980s. And, because of the significant increase in arrests and criminal convictions, they simply apply to more people. More than 47 million Americans (or a quarter of the adult population) have criminal records on file with federal or state criminal justice agencies.[12] An estimated 13 million Americans are either currently serving a sentence for a felony conviction or have been convicted of a felony in the past.[13] This translates into over 6 percent of the adult population having been convicted of a felony crime. The proportion of felony convictions among African-American adult males is even higher. Invisible punishments reach deep into American life.

The new wave of invisible punishments is qualitatively different as well. Taken together, the recent enactments, many of them passed by Congress, chip away at critical ingredients of the support systems of poor people in this country. Under these new laws, offenders[14] can be denied public housing, welfare benefits, the mobility necessary to access jobs that require driving, child support, parental rights, the ability to obtain an education, and, in the case of deportation, access to the opportunities that brought immigrants to this country. For many offenders, the social safety net has been severely damaged.

Why have our policy makers embraced this category of punishment in addition to building more prisons and expanding the reach of criminal justice supervision? We could imagine that the steady buildup of prisons might, by itself, constitute the full articulation of a new punitive attitude of our policy makers and the public they represent. Yet, when we consider the expanded reach of the network of invisible punishment, we detect a social impulse distinct from the robust retributivism that has fueled harsher sentencing policies over the past twenty-five years. When sex offenders are subjected to lifetime parole supervision, drug offenders are denied student loans, families are removed from public housing, and legal immigrants with decades-old convictions are deported from this country, all without judicial review, even the harshest variants of just-deserts theories cannot accommodate these outcomes.

In this brave new world, punishment for the original offense is no longer enough; one's debt to society is never paid. Some commentators, seeing parallels with practices from another era when convicts were sent to faraway lands, refer to this form of punishment as "internal exile." [15] Others liken this extreme labeling to "the mark of Cain," [16] and the effects of these sanctions as relegating the offender to the status of "non-citizen, almost a pariah." [17] The National Council on Crime and Delinquency summarized the effects this way: "Even when the sentence has been completely served, the fact that a man has been convicted of a felony pursues him like Nemesis." [18]

I prefer to focus on the impact of these kinds of punishments on the social fabric. To borrow a phrase now in use by the Labor government in the United Kingdom, these punishments have become instruments of "social exclusion" [19]; they create a permanent diminution in social status of convicted offenders, a distancing between "us" and "them." The principal new form of social exclusion has been to deny offenders the benefits of the welfare state. And the principal new player in this new drama has been the United States Congress. In an era of welfare reform, when Congress dismantled the six-decades-old entitlement to a safety net for the poor, the poor with criminal histories were thought less deserving than others. In an era when Congress has aggressively interjected itself into the criminal justice policy domains traditionally reserved to the states, there was little hesitation in using federal benefits to enhance punishments or federal funds to encourage new criminal sanctions by the states. In an era when the symbolic denunciation of criminals was politically rewarding, the opportunity to deny offenders the largess of the welfare state was just too tempting. In this kind of environment, the people who come through our criminal justice system—mostly poor, urban, minority males, often denied the right to vote by virtue of their felony convictions—have few friends in high places.

The policy goal, then, is to find ways to constrain this form of punishment, to establish limiting principles, and to reverse the movement toward social exclusion. I offer some thoughts on how to accomplish those objectives at the conclusion of the chapter.

III. THE NEW STRAIN OF INVISIBLE PUNISHMENT

A brief review of the ebb and flow of support for collateral sanctions puts our current posture in sharp relief. The high-water mark of the movement to restrain these punishments occurred, not coincidentally, in the middle decades of the twentieth century. During that period, the country witnessed an extraordinary burst of criminal justice reforms. A landmark presidential commission called for a "revolution in the way America thinks about crime."[20] Congress passed the Bail Reform Act of 1968, which reduced pretrial detention for poor people. The Supreme Court issued a series of constitutional rulings granting new rights and protections to those accused of committing a crime. The Model Penal Code was adopted by the American Law Institute. Rehabilitation was understood to be the goal of corrections.

Not surprisingly, reformers in this era focused attention on the collateral consequences of criminal convictions.[21] In its 1955 Standard Probation and Parole Act, the National Council on Crime and Delinquency (NCCD) proposed that an offender's civil rights should be restored upon completion of his criminal sentence. A year later, the National Conference on Parole concluded that "the present law on deprivation of civil rights of offenders is in most jurisdictions an archaic holdover from early times and is in contradiction to the principles of modern correctional treatment."[22] The Act proposed by the NCCD included a provision to allow for the expungement of criminal records, meaning that an individual could be restored to his legal status prior to his conviction.[23]

In 1967, the President's Crime Commission noted that "[t]here has been little effort to evaluate the whole system of disabilities and disqualifications that has grown up. Little consideration has been given to the need for particular deprivations in particular cases."[24] In 1973, the National Advisory Commission on Corrections recommended fundamental changes in voter disqualification statutes, arguing that reintegration required no less: "Loss of citizenship rights . . . inhibits reformative efforts. If corrections is to reintegrate an offender into free society, the offender must retain all attributes of citizenship. In addition, his respect for law and the legal system may well depend, in some measure, on his ability to participate in that system."[25]

In 1981, the American Bar Association (ABA) promulgated the Standards on Civil Disabilities, a document that seems quaint from a contemporary perspective. Asserting that the automatic imposition of civil disabilities on persons convicted of a crime were inconsistent with the goal of reintegration of offenders, the ABA recommended that no such disability be automatically imposed, except those related directly to the offense (for example, revoking the driver's license of a repeated drunk driver); that disabilities be imposed on a case-by-case basis, upon a determination that it was "necessary to advance an important governmental or public interest"; and that they be imposed only for a limited time, and then with adequate avenues for early termination upon appropriate review.[26]

The reform spirit touched state legislatures as well. In the 1960s and 1970s, the number of state laws imposing collateral sanctions declined. The same period witnessed an increase in the number of laws requiring the automatic restoration of an offender's civil rights, either upon completion of his sentence or passage of a certain amount of time. A comprehensive review of all state statutes, conducted in 1986, concluded that "states generally are becoming less restrictive of depriving civil rights of offenders."[27]

The movement to roll back collateral sanctions peaked in the 1980s. Just as sentencing policy generally became more punitive around this time, state legislatures rediscovered collateral sanctions. A new analysis of state statutes, conducted in 1996, documented the reversal.[28] Compared with 1986, there were increases in the number of states (a) permanently denying convicted felons the right to vote (from eleven to fourteen states); (b) allowing termination of parental rights (from sixteen to nineteen); (c) establishing a felony conviction as grounds for divorce (from twenty-eight to twenty-nine); (d) restricting the right to hold public office (from twenty-three to twenty-five); and (e) restricting rights of firearm ownership (from thirty-one to thirty-three).[29]

The largest increase came in the area of criminal registration. In 1986, only eight states required released offenders to register with the local police. Following some well-publicized crimes committed by parolees, a tidal wave of registration laws, spurred on by federal funding, swept across the country.[30] By 1998, every state had enacted legislation requiring that convicted sex offenders register with the police upon release from prison, an increase of forty-two states in twelve years. The duration of sex offender registration requirements range from ten years to life. Twelve states mandate lifetime registration. As of 1998, 280,000 sex offenders were listed in the state registries.[31]

The states also increased the number of occupational bars for people with various criminal convictions. For example, there has been an expansion of the prohibitions against hiring teachers, child care workers, and related professionals with prior criminal convictions. This expansion of legal barriers has been accompanied by an increase in the ease of checking criminal records due to new technologies, expanded access to criminal records, and an increase in the number of employers checking criminal records of prospective employees.[32] One's criminal past became both more public and more exclusionary, limiting the universe of available work.

Congress followed suit, but with a telling twist. As with the state legislatures, Congress ratcheted up the levels of punishment generally, and specifically enhanced the range of collateral consequences for those convicted of violating federal criminal laws. Yet Congress went further. As is illustrated below, Congress created a web of collateral sanctions that transformed a conviction for certain state crimes into ineligibility for federal benefits.[33] Furthermore, it used the power of the federal purse to encourage states to extend the reach of collateral sanctions. Taken together, the laws enacted during this resurgence of collateral sanctions construct substantial barriers to participation in American society. To borrow the phrase from the United Kingdom, the laws became instruments of the social exclusion of people with criminal convictions. Consider the following examples.

The most blatant form of social exclusion is the deportation of criminal aliens, akin to the ancient practice of exile. Foreigners with criminal convictions are generally excluded from admission into the United States, but beginning with the Immigration Reform and Control Act of 1986 and the Illegal Immigration Reform and Immigrant Responsibility Act of 1996, Congress significantly expanded the categories of crimes that would subject an alien to deportation. As a result, the number of deportations of aliens with criminal convictions rose from 7,338 in 1989 to 56,011 in 1998.[34] Congress even authorized deportation for past crimes. (This provision was declared unconstitutional by the Supreme Court in *INS v. St. Cyr* in 2001.[35])

Congress also enacted legislation to cut offenders off from the remnants of the welfare state. The welfare reform law of 1996 ended individual entitlement to welfare and replaced that scheme with block grants to the states known as Temporary Assistance to Needy Families (TANF). One provision of that law requires that states permanently bar individuals with drug-related felony convictions from receiving federally funded public assistance and food stamps during their lifetime.[36] (States can opt out of, or narrow, the lifetime ban, and over half have done so.) The welfare reform law also stipulates that individuals who violate their probation or parole conditions are "temporarily" ineligible for TANF, food stamps or Social Security Income (SSI) benefits, and public housing.[37]

Congress also authorized the exclusion of certain offenders from federally supported public housing. Statutes enacted in the late 1990s permit public housing agencies and providers of Section 8 housing to deny housing to individuals who have engaged in "any drug-related or violent criminal activity or other criminal activity which would adversely affect the health, safety, or right to peaceful enjoyment of the premises [by others]."[38] For those convicted of drug crimes, they can reapply for housing after a three-year waiting period, and must show they have been rehabilitated.[39] Anyone subject to lifetime registration under a state sex offender registration statute is ineligible for federally assisted housing.[40]

Congress cut offenders off from other benefits as well. The Higher Education Act of 1998 suspends the eligibility for a student loan or other assistance for someone convicted of a drug-related offense.[41] (Eligibility can be restored after meeting certain conditions, including two unannounced drug tests.) In the 2000–2001 academic year, about 9,000 students were found to be ineligible under this provision.[42] The Adoption and Safe Families Act of 1997 prohibits individuals with certain criminal convictions from being approved as foster or adoptive parents. It also accelerates the termination of parental rights for children who have been in foster care for fifteen of the most recent twenty-two months.[43]

Finally, Congress used the power of the purse to encourage states to pass laws restricting the rights of offenders. In 1992, Congress passed a law requiring states to revoke or suspend the drivers' licenses of people convicted of drug felonies, or suffer the loss of 10 percent of the state's federal highway funds.[44] Similarly, the 1994 Crime Act required each state to enact a sex offender registration law within three years or lose 10 percent of its federal funding for criminal justice programs.[45] A final example: The Public Housing Assessment System, established by the federal government, creates financial incentives for public housing agencies to adopt strict admission and eviction standards to screen out individuals who engage in criminal behavior.[46]

This recent wave of restrictions creates a formidable set of obstacles to former offenders who want to gain a foothold in modern society. Not only is it harder to find work, drive to work, and get an education, it is harder to exercise the individual autonomy that is taken for granted by others in society—being a parent, living in public housing with one's family, relying on public benefits such as food stamps and welfare assistance, moving freely without notice to the police, and establishing a residence without suffering the rejection of one's neighbors. In his framework for tracing the evolution of the notion of citizenship, Marshall cites the expansion of "civil rights" in the eighteenth century, such as rights to free speech and religion, to own property and enter into contracts; "political rights" in the nineteenth century, such as the right to vote; and "social and welfare rights" in the twentieth century, such as entitlements to shelter, welfare, and food.[47] The strain of invisible punishments that emerged at the end of the twentieth century represented an intrusion into this third dimension to the definition of citizenship. In the modern welfare state, these restrictions of the universe of social and welfare rights amount to a variant on the tradition of "civil death" in which the offender is defined as unworthy of the benefits of society, and is excluded from the social compact.

IV. ASSESSING THE IMPLEMENTATION AND IMPACT OF INVISIBLE PUNISHMENT

Gauging the impact of these invisible punishments is difficult. For some consequences of felony convictions, the analysis is a relatively straightforward task. For example, we know that the laws of forty-eight states and the District of Columbia deny prisoners the right to vote while they are in prison. Therefore, we could survey prisoners, determine how many were registered to vote prior to imprisonment, calculate the likelihood that they would have voted had they not been imprisoned, and project the diminished voter participation attributable to these state laws.[48] In like fashion, one can estimate the impact of statutes denying voting rights to anyone convicted of a felony. One such calculation found that 4 million Americans are now disqualified from voting.[49]

Similarly, one can calculate the number of sex offenders registered with the state, or the number of legal aliens deported following criminal convictions. But what about the impact of the statutes that disqualify criminals from education loans, public housing, welfare benefits, or parental rights? Counting the number of individuals punished through these laws approaches impossibility. The agencies that administer these sanctions are far-flung, have little or no connection with the criminal justice system, may or may not keep records of their decisions, and have no incentive to report on these low-priority exercises of discretion. It is difficult to assess their impact when we have such difficulty evaluating their implementation.

The lack of good data on the reach of invisible punishments raises a more fundamental issue, namely the lack of clarity regarding the purposes of these punishments. When these laws are viewed within the framework of the traditional purposes of punishment—deterrence, prevention, retribution, and incapacitation—they appear quite consistent with those purposes. (It is hard to discern rehabilitative goals in these punishments. In fact, they place barriers to successful rehabilitation and reintegration.) They are clearly intended to deter both the individual offender and others. Many (e.g., sex offender notifications, or narrowly tailored occupational disqualifications) are presumed to have crime prevention effects. They are clearly retributive and convey societal condemnation of antisocial behavior. They also operate as a form of selective incapacitation—for example, by keeping sex offenders away from certain locations and keeping drug offenders away from public housing.[50] Yet, creating a research agenda to measure their effectiveness at achieving these goals would quickly run into the obstacle posed by the paucity of relevant data.

A more fruitful analytical approach might be to evaluate the impact of these punishments at the community level, especially in poor, high-crime communities in this country.[51] This approach commends itself for those punishments designed to cut convicted felons from the network of supports and benefits. For example, if a particular housing authority were to enforce rigorously the three-year ban for individuals convicted of drug-related crimes, what would happen to the families in that housing complex? What would be the impact on the financial assets of poor communities of those states that did not opt out of the lifetime prohibition against individuals with drug-related felony convictions receiving public assistance and food stamps? Arguably, the aggregate effect of this constellation of punishments on the social capital of poor communities could be quite extensive, and with long-lasting consequences for the vitality of families, labor markets, and civic life.[52]

V. THE PARADOX OF PUBLIC SUPPORT FOR PUNISHMENT

How can we explain the rise in this form of punishment? One hypothesis has superficial appeal: The American public has recently become much more punitive, and these legislative enactments, paralleling the increase in imprisonment and other "get tough" policies, simply reflect public opinion. Yet, a closer examination of research on public opinion reveals that the picture is a bit more complicated than that simplistic notion.

Since 1972, the General Social Survey has asked a sample of the American public whether they believed the courts in their communities dealt too harshly or not harshly enough with criminals. Between 1972 and 1980, the portion answering that the courts were too lenient rose from 72 to 90 percent (see Figure 1). Since 1980, however, the rate has been remarkably stable, even declining in 1998 to 80 percent. Over the same period of time, the percentage of Americans who answered that courts were too harsh never exceeded 10 percent. Two conclusions can be drawn from these opinion surveys. First, to the extent that the American public has become more punitive, the increases happened twenty years ago. Second, even after recognizing these fluctuations, one must conclude that Americans have been consistently punitive in their outlook for a long period of time.[53] Between 70 and 90 percent of Americans—a very high rate—think criminals are getting lenient treatment in the courts. Reflecting an even broader view, Zimring, Hawkins, and Kamin observe in *Punishment and Democracy* that "[p]ublic hostility toward criminals is a historical constant in stable democracies and is usually associated with support for punitive treatment of convicted offenders."[54]

Figure 1

Attitudes About the Severity of Courts in Dealing with Crime

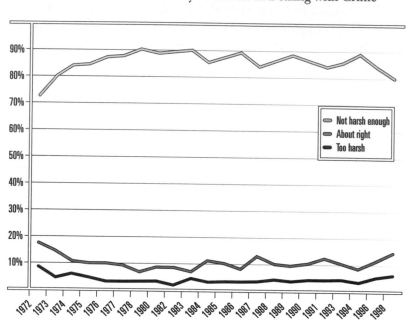

Yet when asked by the Gallup organization which approach they favored for bringing crime rates down in this country—education and jobs to address "the social and economic problems that lead to crime," or "more prisons, police, and judges" to deter crime—we find a different picture of the American mood. In the periodic surveys taken between 1989 and 2000, between one-half and two-thirds of the respondents favored education and jobs, and between one-quarter and two-fifths favored more prisons, police, and judges. When given policy choices, the American public favors prevention over enforcement. As noted by Di-Iulio et al., "even in 'get tough' or 'do justice' periods there has been substantial public support for efforts to keep offenders from turning to crime and to keep ex-offenders from returning to it."[55]

A third source of data adds an important dimension to our understanding of the public mood. In 1965, at the beginning of the escalation of crime rates in America, only 4 percent of Americans polled by the Gallup organization felt that crime was the greatest issue facing the country. By 1994, that percentage had grown to about 50 percent, then declined again to 7 percent by 2001.[56]

So, the public expectations that the government do something about crime laid the groundwork for a change in the political dynamics about crime policy in America. Elected officials, and those aspiring to public office, were compelled to "do something" about crime in order to respond to the demands and expectations of a concerned citizenry. And one thing a legislator can do is pass laws increasing the quantum of punishment. They have shown little reluctance to pass laws increasing prison sentences, at enormous social and fiscal costs. Enacting legislation denying ex-offenders the rights and privileges of citizenship is in many ways much easier. There are no direct costs borne by the taxpayers—on the contrary, there may be savings in public benefits. There are no sentencing commissions to worry about asking tough questions about proportionality or adverse racial impacts. There are no judges who could interpose their own discretion and decide that a particular punishment might not be right for a particular offender. There are no political battles over the siting of prison facilities. So, the political appeal of this strategy is strong, particularly when public posturing over get tough strategies brought political dividends.

VI. THE SHIFTING CONTEXT OF PUNISHMENT POLICY

This shift in the political dynamics of crime policy coincided with—and contributed to—three major realignments in the American political context, two directly related to crime policy, and one indirectly.

First, over the past generation we have witnessed a more fundamental transformation in the locus of our punishment policy from the judicial branch to the legislative branch of government.[57] For most of the twentieth century, American sentencing policy was remarkably constant and consistent, reflected in the framework of indeterminate sentencing. Under this approach, state statutes provided a broad range of possible sentences, leaving the determination of the ultimate sentence to the exercise of discretion by the sentencing judge and parole boards. Beginning in the mid-1970s, this approach came under attack from critics on the political left and right. Liberals thought it vested too much power with judges and parole boards, allowed for disparate treatment of similarly situated defendants, and facilitated racial bias. Conservatives thought it too lenient, open to political manipulation, and deceptive in that long sentences pronounced by courts were shortened by parole boards who granted "early" releases and corrections administrators who awarded good-time credits to hasten departures from prison. The well-known 1974 article finding that "nothing works" in prisoner rehabilitation contributed to the pessimistic mood.[58] With its intellectual and political foundations weakened, the philosophy of indeterminate sentencing lost its dominant position. We have witnessed what Michael Tonry calls the "fragmentation of American sentencing policy" as the legislatures (and, in the case of ballot initiatives, the voters) of the fifty states have created a crazy quilt of widely disparate, legislatively enacted penal policies.[59] The losers in this power shift were the judiciary, whose exercise of sentencing discretion fell into disfavor, and those with expertise in criminal justice policy, whose views were disregarded in favor of politically appealing policy initiatives.[60] The winners were the legislative branch of government, which developed ways to respond to the public's concerns about crime, including "three strikes and you're out" laws, truth-in-sentencing schemes, sentencing commissions designed to constrain judicial discretion, sex offender registration, mandatory minimums, and the abolition of parole boards.

Following in the wake of these fundamental realignments of sentencing policy was the expansion of the universe of invisible punishment.

Unlike prison expansion, these sanctions required little or no expenditures of public funds. Unlike mandatory minimum sentencing statutes, or persistent felon statues like the "three strikes" legislation, these sanctions could not be opposed on the grounds that they would change the calculus of plea bargaining, because they operate outside the courtroom. Attaching them as riders to other pieces of legislation meant they could be enacted outside the traditional judiciary committee review process. Anyone speaking up in opposition could easily be branded as "pro-criminal." Symbolism could easily win the day, at no cost.

Second, we have witnessed the launch of a "war on drugs" with enormous consequences for the operations of the criminal justice system and profound impact on impoverished communities, particularly minority communities. This is not the place to review the effectiveness of those policies, yet one particular feature is noteworthy for this discussion. As seen in Figure 2, the rate of prison admissions for drug offenses of African-American defendants has escalated sharply over the past fifteen years. Recalling that many of the recently enacted invisible punishments target drug offenders with diminished rights, privileges, and benefits, the aggregate consequences of this diminution of citizenship status upon the African-American community reach staggering proportions. To take one example, there are now seven states where lifetime bans on voting for felons mean that one in four African-American men are permanently disenfranchised.[61]

Third, the decade of the 1990s witnessed the culmination of a long campaign to enact fundamental changes in the nation's welfare system. The welfare reform law of 1996 ended the nation's sixty-year commitment to its poor by eliminating the individual entitlement to welfare. This commitment was replaced with the notion of a time-limited eligibility—one could only be a recipient of federal benefits or TANF for a maximum of five years. The rhetoric accompanying this shift had implications for our punishment policy. In his campaign for the presidency, Governor Bill Clinton captured the essence of this shift by saying that those who played by the rules should be able to succeed. The implica-

Figure 2
Prison Drug Admissions by Race, 1983–1998[62]

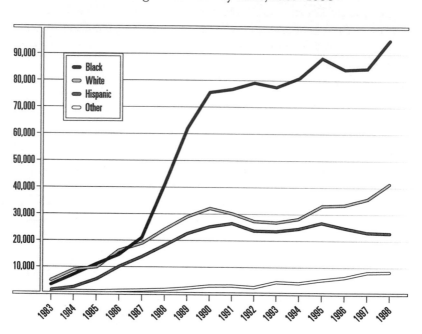

tion is that those who do not play by the rules can be disfavored. A "social contract" concept of citizenship had been replaced with a "civic virtues" concept of citizenship in which the undeserving members of society were increasingly excluded from society's benefits.[63] Felons have clearly not played by the rules; they are hardly deserving; they became prime candidates for a position at the bottom rung of the new regime of federal support for the poor. How could we provide welfare for them, when mothers with small children were on their own after five years?

These three developments have heightened the vulnerability of poor people to the negative effects of invisible punishment. Poor people, minorities, young people, and felons are not well represented in the legislative branches of government that have historically reflected majoritarian wishes. The war on drugs has geometrically extended the reach of the criminal law into poor, minority communities. And the movement from a federally guaranteed safety net to one reflecting assessments of an individual's willingness to abide by society's rules has left those convicted of crimes with little protection.

David Garland has developed a theoretical framework to understand these social forces, which he calls the "preconditions" of more punitive policies. He sets aside the more conventional focus on the politics of crime policy and the shifting ideological debates and posits, instead, that our more punitive policies must be understood by reference to "shifts in social practice and cultural sensibility." He writes that, in the United States and the United Kingdom,

> The field of crime control exhibits two new and distinct lines of governmental action: an *adaptive strategy* stressing prevention and partnership, and a *sovereign state strategy* stressing enhanced control and expressive punishment. These strategies—which are quite different from the penal-welfare policies that preceded them—were formed in response to a new predicament faced by governments in many late-modern societies. This predicament arose because at a certain historical point high rates of crime became a normal social fact, penal-welfare solutions fell into disrepute, and the modern, differentiated criminal justice state was perceived as failing to deliver adequate levels of security.[64]

In this new era, he concludes, "[p]unitive segregation—lengthy sentence terms in no-frills prisons and a marked, monitored existence for those who are eventually released—is increasingly the penal strategy of choice."[65] In our assessment of the universe of invisible punishment, we see the creation of a large population of felons, concentrated in poor, minority communities, who are "marked" and "monitored" and cut off from the supports of modern society. We are creating deeper and longer-lasting distinctions between "us" and "them."

VII. LIMITING THE REACH OF INVISIBLE PUNISHMENT: SOME MODEST SUGGESTIONS

I conclude by offering some thoughts about ways to constrain the impulse to punish those who violate our laws by diminishing their rights and privileges.[66]

Visibility. The first step is to make the punishment visible. This entails three strategies.

1. Truth in Advertising. The first precondition to the reform ideas set forth here is to change the language of the discussion. These are punishments, meaning that they are legislatively authorized sanctions imposed on individuals convicted of criminal offenses. They should be recognized as such.[67]

2. Truth in Legislating. The second step is to require state and federal legislatures to codify the collateral sentences that are scattered throughout their respective statutes. A defendant or his counsel should be able to find, in one place, all of the potential consequences of a criminal conviction. A parallel recommendation is that collateral sentences be reviewed by the legislative committees with jurisdiction over sentencing policies for the state.

3. Truth in Sentencing. The third step is to require that defendants acknowledge their awareness of the potential consequences of a plea of guilty at the arraignment or at the time of sentence following a determination of guilt.[68] One need not recite in open court *all* collateral sentences—that would be impossible. Yet, judges could be required to ask a defendant whether his counsel has explained to him that there *are* collateral consequences, and perhaps list some that might be pertinent to the defendant's situation.[69] It is ironic that the truth-in-sentencing movement, which promotes the notion of certainty of punishment, values open decision making about the terms of punishment, and denigrates the exercise of discretion in sentencing, has not yet discovered that the "secret sentences" that constitute the universe of invisible punishment violate those three principles.

Proportionality. A bedrock principle of our sentencing jurisprudence is the notion that the severity of the criminal sanction should be limited by the seriousness of the offense and relevant attributes of the offender. Sentencing grids, with charge severity on one axis and prior criminal record on the other and limited allowance for departures in mitigation or aggravation, are concrete expressions of this principle. Yet the collateral sanctions under discussion here do not reflect the principle of proportionality. A felon convicted of the lowest felony loses his right to vote, as does a serial murderer. A minor drug offender as well as the major drug dealer can be evicted from public housing. A teenager convicted of statutory rape for consensual intercourse with his underage girlfriend, as well as a repeated child molester, may be subject to lifetime registration. A zero-based review of collateral sanctions by a state's judiciary committee would begin by asking the questions posed in other sentencing contexts: How does this sanction further the purposes of sentencing, to whom should it be applied, and with what consequence? This complicated review might also be carried out by a state's sentencing commission. These quasi-independent entities have a track record of reviewing punishments in an effort to diminish disparities among similarly situated defendants. They could provide similar service to the legislature and the judiciary by developing guidance regarding the imposition of collateral sanctions.

Individualized Justice. Some collateral sanctions may appropriately be automatic. For example, barring convicted felons from jury eligibility automatically may well be reasonable to protect the integrity of criminal trials. But the vast majority of collateral sanctions cannot be justified this way. Within the established legislative ranges, these sanctions should be imposed in ways that tailor the punishment to the circumstances. Is a bar from a particular kind of employment appropriate for a given offender? Does it relate to the offense charged?

Avenues for Relief. Where does a convicted felon turn to challenge the imposition of a collateral sanction? Who tells him what his options are? When a drug offender is barred from living in public housing with his mother, what is his redress? Granted, some of the statutes discussed in this chapter provide avenues for relief—for example, a drug offender denied a student loan may be restored to eligibility after passing two unannounced drug tests. And many states provide for individuals to petition a court for relief from these "civil disabilities." But these are cramped expressions of the notion of legal remedy. Could not a state enact legislation allowing convicted offenders to return to the sentencing court to argue that a collateral sanction should not apply to him? Could a statute allow the offender to bring officials of the housing agency to court to explain why they decided to exclude him from his apartment? Could not the corrections agencies be required to inform offenders of their rights to seek relief?

Embrace the Goal of Reintegration. Remembering Garland's insights about the growth of the punitive state, the most important recommendation—indeed, more a hope—is that the country reverse the current cultural sensibility about those who have violated our laws and adopt a goal of reintegration, not exclusion. We need to find concrete ways to reaccept and reembrace offenders who have paid their debt for their offense.

These reforms of the universe of invisible punishment may not comport with the punitive attitudes found in our political discourse. But they do offer a road map for legislative action. They are rooted in both traditional notions of sentencing philosophy and modern innovations such as truth in sentencing. Even proposing them to the legislature would have this advantage—they would make the universe of these punishments visible and would raise searching questions about why we have chosen these responses to the wrongdoing of our fellow citizens.

2

Welfare and Housing—
Denial of Benefits to Drug Offenders

*Gwen Rubinstein and Debbie Mukamal**

"What do I need to stay off of drugs and out of jail? I need a drug treatment program and a home for me and my kids."

JoAnne, an ex-offender in Pennsylvania[1]

One of the driving forces behind mass imprisonment in the last two decades has been the "war on drugs." The federal government has invested substantially more in programs and policies aimed at supply reduction and law enforcement (more than two-thirds of the drug control budget in any given year) than those aimed at demand reduction, such as treatment. Not surprisingly, the number of Americans incarcerated for drug-related offenses has skyrocketed. Because the war has taken place primarily in the nation's cities, a disproportionate percentage of those affected by these policies are low-income people of color.

As JoAnne's statement so clearly expresses, individuals with alcohol and drug problems, including those with criminal justice histories, need treatment to be able to work and take care of their families. Low-income individuals affected by addiction and criminal records also need access to public benefits—including welfare, food stamps, Medicaid, and public housing—as they learn to live drug- and crime-free in the community. Without these temporary supports, it is unrealistic to expect full recovery without relapse and recidivism. Yet, laws enacted in recent years counterproductively act as barriers to these benefits, virtually (and sadly) ensuring failure for thousands of Americans affected by addiction. This has created a class of impoverished addicts legally unable to gain access to subsistence benefits and other supports and programs that might help them overcome their addictions, find and keep jobs, and avoid further involvement with the criminal justice system.

The irony of public policy in this area is that there exists substantial support for a more compassionate approach to these problems. Law enforcement leaders have recognized for some time that criminal justice responses alone are not likely to solve the nation's drug problem. In a 1996 poll, nearly three-fourths of police chiefs indicated that mandatory minimum sentences for drug possession had been only somewhat effective or were not really the answer to the drug problems in their communities. More than half (59 percent) believed that sentencing drug users to court-supervised treatment programs was more effective than sending them to prison or jail.[2]

Other polls have shown that public support for treatment is strong as well. A 2001 ABC News poll found that Americans, by nearly a three-to-one margin, prefer treatment programs over incarceration for first- and second-time drug offenders.[3]

These sentiments are supported by research documenting that treatment is a cost-effective response to addiction. Every dollar invested in treatment results in savings between $2.50 and $7 in reduced costs of crime and social services. Treatment is also more cost-effective than punishment-oriented drug policies, with estimates that treatment for cocaine addiction is seven times more effective than domestic law enforcement, ten times more effective than interdiction, and twenty-three times more effective than source-country activities.[4]

At the national political level, however, these polls and data are ignored by policy makers in favor of reliance on punishment. Such approaches play on the fears of many Americans that they will be victimized by individuals with drug and alcohol problems, despite the general support for treatment.

This fear fuels discrimination and creates the impression that substance abusers are not worthy of compassion or assistance. These attitudes make individuals with alcohol and drug problems ashamed and afraid to come forward for help, thereby perpetuating the problem. But as General Barry McCaffrey, former director of the White House Office of National Drug Control Policy, has pointed out about the "war on drugs" metaphor, addicted individuals need to be helped, not defeated.[5]

Stigma, discrimination, and unbalanced "get tough" policies have impeded progress toward providing the necessary resources behind treatment, contributing to the persistence of a significant treatment gap. Nationally, available treatment can meet only about half of the demand[6]; for women and low-income individuals, the gap is even larger.

Not only is treatment not widely available in the criminal justice system, but the proportion of inmates receiving treatment has actually declined significantly in recent years. In 1997, less than one-sixth of state and federal prisoners who reported using alcohol or drugs in the month before their offense received *any* treatment while incarcerated,[7] regardless of whether that treatment was appropriate. This was down from the one-third of such prisoners who participated in treatment in 1991.

Two recently enacted policies driven by stigma and "tough" on drugs rhetoric make it particularly difficult for low-income people with drug problems to afford treatment and basic necessities and to find safe and sober housing[8] so they can successfully reintegrate back into the community, live drug- and crime-free, and provide for themselves and their families. This chapter will focus on

- the federal ban on eligibility for welfare and food stamps for individuals with a drug felony conviction; and
- federal laws that require public housing agencies to exclude individuals who engage in drug-related criminal activity.

A PORTRAIT OF DRUG FELONY OFFENDERS

Drug abuse and dependence have driven much of the recent increase in incarceration. At every stage of the criminal justice process, from arrest to conviction to incarceration, most offenders have alcohol and drug problems and/or were under the influence of alcohol or drugs when they committed their offense.

Arrests for drug offenses have nearly tripled since 1980,[9] with more than four-fifths being for possession violations. Although possession arrests have increased significantly during this time, arrests for sale and manufacturing have remained fairly stable.[10]

In 1996 (most recent data available), 365,000 people were convicted of a drug felony—twice as many as were convicted of a violent felony.[11] Drug offenses accounted for 35 percent of felonies in state courts and 41 percent in federal court.[12]

People of color are disproportionately represented among those arrested, tried, convicted, and sentenced to prison for drug offenses. While African Americans make up 13 percent of the nation's monthly drug users, they represent 35 percent of those persons arrested for drug crimes, 53 percent of drug convictions.[13]

Although most drug offenders are men, the number of women convicted of drug offenses is growing steadily. Between 1990 and 1996, drug felony convictions among women increased by 37 percent, compared with an increase of 25 percent for men.[14] Women involved in the criminal justice system because of drugs are likely to be users themselves. A study of twenty-six Pennsylvania women with drug felony convictions found that an overwhelming majority of them had no prior drug conviction, that their felonies were for very small quantities of drugs (often only $5 or $10 worth), and that they had started using drugs to deal with their childhood experiences of physical and sexual abuse.[15]

WELFARE AND FOOD STAMP ELIGIBILITY FOR INDIVIDUALS WITH DRUG FELONY CONVICTIONS

The American welfare system changed dramatically on August 22, 1996, with the signing of the Personal Responsibility and Work Opportunity Reconciliation Act.[16] The law ended the individual entitlement to welfare and replaced it with a block grant to states called Temporary Assistance to Needy Families (TANF), imposed a five-year lifetime limit on benefits, and required welfare recipients to work to receive benefits.

A little-noted provision of the law[17] imposes a lifetime ban on eligibility for TANF assistance and food stamps on individuals with drug felony convictions.[18] Drug use, possession, and distribution are the only types of offenses singled out for sanctions other than welfare fraud (specifically, illegally receiving benefits in two states at the same time).[19] Notably, the welfare fraud ban is limited to ten years. Thus, a person convicted of armed robbery can qualify for TANF assistance after completing a sentence, but someone with a single felony conviction for drug possession cannot.

No one is exempt from the drug felony ban, not even pregnant women, individuals in treatment or recovery, or people with HIV/AIDS. The ban applies only to the individual with the conviction; others in the welfare case, such as children, retain their eligibility.

Women in treatment are keenly aware of this provision. As one woman in treatment in Atlanta reported: "Thank [goodness] all my convictions were before [19]96 or I wouldn't be able to get TANF . . . — even . . . being in treatment, getting my life back together. They don't take that into consideration, that maybe you were astray, and now you're getting your life back together. They don't care. . . . I know there are some women out there struggling, trying to get their life together . . . because there is no way out because of your past."[20]

States can "opt out" of the ban completely or narrow it, but otherwise the ban is permanent and continues regardless of a person's successful job history, participation in drug treatment, avoidance of recidivism, or abstinence from drug use. Ironically, the ban could deny benefits years later to people who have lost their jobs through circumstances beyond their control, such as a recession or economic downturn.

Introduced as an amendment by Senator Phil Gramm (Republican—Texas) during Senate floor debate over welfare reform legislation in July 1996, the ban was originally broader. It applied to all federal means-tested benefits, including Medicaid, and lasted a lifetime for individuals with drug felony convictions, and five years for individuals with misdemeanors. A conference committee later narrowed its scope in final negotiations over the bill.

The Senate debated the ban for a total of two minutes—one minute for Republicans, and one minute for Democrats. Speaking for the ban, Senator Gramm noted that "if we are serious about our drug laws, we ought not to give people welfare benefits who are violating the nation's drug laws."

States have implemented the ban in a variety of ways. As of the end of 2001,[21] twenty-two states left the ban intact, including California and Pennsylvania—two states with relatively large welfare caseloads and prison populations. Another twenty states enforce the ban but have narrowed its scope, with the most common modification being to exempt individuals who are in treatment (or on a waiting list for treatment or have finished treatment or achieved recovery). These states include Florida, Illinois, Iowa, Maryland, Washington, and Wisconsin. Eight states and the District of Columbia have opted out completely—Connecticut, Michigan, New Hampshire, New York, Ohio, Oklahoma, Oregon, and Vermont.

THE BAN'S EFFECTS

The welfare ban acts as a bizarre catch-22 for both treatment providers and consumers. A 1998 survey of twenty women's treatment programs found that, on average, 15 percent of clients on welfare had a drug felony conviction.[22] The ban now denies these women benefits that have traditionally paid for room and board during treatment. In addition, since many states are screening TANF recipients for alcohol and drug problems and referring them to treatment if needed, the ban closes this new pathway into treatment. Without access to subsistence benefits, treatment, and safe and sober housing, it is much less likely that these women will be able to live drug-free in the community and avoid recidivism.

As an ex-offender in Pennsylvania stated: "I have been clean now for three years and six months with G—d's help, and I am trying to stay that way, but with no help for people like me it is very hard not to go back to that way of life. I want people to realize that is why people do time, get out and do it again. They can't survive any other way."[23]

The ban's financial effects have presented challenges for treatment providers as well. Providers in Chicago, Los Angeles, and Atlanta have reported that their clients are eligible for fewer programs (TANF, food stamps, and Medicaid) and for shorter periods of time. These revenue reductions have forced providers to spend more time raising money and put more pressure on program staff to manage larger caseloads with fewer resources.[24]

The 1998 survey found that, among the twenty women's programs, welfare and food stamps accounted for an average of 7 percent of total funding. But programs reported wide variations in funding patterns—five of the programs reported that welfare made up 10 percent or more of their funding, and 10 programs reported receiving no welfare funding at all.[25] Another study (of eight women's residential programs in California) found that providers reported that their loss in monthly revenue ranged from none to as much as 30 percent.[26]

The effects of the ban reach beyond the treatment system and treatment clients, however. If these women cannot receive treatment or find safe and sober housing once they have finished treatment, they are less likely to succeed at recovery and work. The added burden falls on state and local governments in the form of increased public health, child welfare, and criminal justice costs.

PUBLIC HOUSING ELIGIBILITY FOR INDIVIDUALS
WITH DRUG AND CRIMINAL HISTORIES

Like the drug felon ban on eligibility for TANF assistance and food stamps, federal housing laws underwent drastic changes in 1996 that resulted in stringent admission and eviction standards for individuals with drug-related convictions. However, unlike the welfare laws, which were limited to drug offenders, the housing laws allow providers of Section 8 and other federally assisted housing to exclude other individuals with criminal records as well.

Federal housing laws began to target people with criminal records—especially those that were drug-related—as early as 1988. The Anti-Drug Abuse Act of 1988[27] required public housing authorities to include in their leases a clause prohibiting tenants, any member of the household, guest, or other person under the tenant's control from engaging in "criminal activity, including drug-related criminal activity, on or near public housing premises."[28] When such criminal activity occurred while the tenant was living in public housing, the tenant could be evicted.[29]

While earlier legislation provided public housing agencies with legislative authority to exclude individuals with criminal histories from federally assisted housing, the Housing Opportunity Program Extension Act of 1996[30] and the Quality Housing and Work Responsibility Act of 1998[31] created stricter mandates, especially for people with drug backgrounds. In addition, the 1996 law provided the legal foundation for the U.S. Department of Housing and Urban Development's (HUD) "One Strike and You're Out" Initiative, which was intended to clarify and reinforce the new legislation. In his announcement of the new policy, President Clinton explained, "From now on, the rule for residents who commit crime and peddle drugs should be one strike and you're out."[32] The new rule promised to be ". . . the toughest admission and eviction policy that HUD has implemented."[33]

While some local housing authorities were already excluding people with criminal backgrounds, the 1996 and 1998 laws and the "One Strike and You're Out" Initiative served as the basis for creating uniform screening tools, admission standards, and eviction policies toward people with criminal records across public housing agencies around the country. While ostensibly designed to provide a safer environment in public housing, the laws have exacerbated the difficulties faced by drug offenders and others in reintegrating back into their communities after completing their sentences. By imposing lengthy waiting periods on individuals with criminal records before being eligible for admission into public housing, these laws punish those who have paid their debt to society who are maintaining drug- and crime-free lives. In addition, by punishing entire families for the behaviors of a single household member, these policies are harsh and destabilizing to communities. Despite this, in March 2002 the Supreme Court upheld the law in a challenge brought by public housing residents whose family members or guests had engaged in drug-related activity without the tenant's knowledge or beyond the tenant's control.[34]

ADMISSION TO PUBLIC HOUSING

The federal housing laws simplify the background screening process of applicants for public housing by permitting public housing agencies to require that prospective tenants agree to undergo background checks and authorizing law enforcement agencies to provide criminal background information to public housing agencies and providers of Section 8 housing. These checks are also permitted to ensure tenants comply with lease agreements and serve as the basis for eviction decisions. In addition, in order to assess whether the applicant is currently using drugs, public housing agencies may also require prospective tenants to sign consent forms agreeing to grant access to the applicant's drug treatment records.[35]

The 1996 and 1998 laws strengthened the ability of public housing authorities to exclude individuals with drug backgrounds by specifically targeting individuals convicted of drug-related offenses[36] and households with a member who is currently abusing alcohol. Tenants who have been evicted from federally assisted housing because of drug-related criminal activity are ineligible for federally assisted housing for a period of three years.[37]

The new laws also give local authorities discretion to deny admission to applicants with other kinds of criminal records. In particular, they permit, but do not require, local housing authorities to deny public, Section 8, and federally assisted housing to households if a member has engaged in any drug-related or violent criminal activity or any other criminal activity that would adversely affect the health, safety, or right to peaceful enjoyment of the premises by other residents if the criminal activity occurred a "reasonable" time before the person seeks admission. The federal laws do not define how recent a conviction must be to be a "reasonable" basis for denying housing. The local housing authority sets the time frame, and some require individuals with criminal records to wait long periods of time before being eligible to apply for housing.

BASES FOR EVICTION

In addition to strengthening the ability of public housing authorities to screen and deny housing to prospective tenants with criminal records, the 1996 and 1998 legislation also reinforced the ability of local agencies to evict tenants for current criminal behavior. Here again, the law targets individuals engaging in drug-related activity.

First, the law, and regulations implementing the law, give public housing agencies discretion to terminate tenancy if anyone in the household or under the tenant's control engages in drug-related criminal activity. Thus, for example, a grandmother whose drug-using grandson is living with her could be evicted under these provisions.[38] Second, whereas earlier legislation gave public housing authorities the ability to evict individuals for drug-related criminal activity "on or near the premises," the 1996 law changed the statutory language to read "on or off such premises,"[39] thus expanding the scope of activity that could make a tenant subject to eviction. Third, the lease must provide that a public housing agency may evict an entire family when the agency determines that a household member is illegally using a drug or when the agency determines that a pattern of illegal use of a drug interferes with the health, safety, or right to peaceful enjoyment of the premises by other residents.[40]

When considering whether to evict a tenant because of criminal activity, public housing agencies are not required to do so on the basis of

the tenant having actually been arrested or convicted.[41] These regulations also allow, but do not require, public housing agencies to consider
all circumstances regarding the criminal activity, such as the seriousness
of the offense, the extent of the tenant's participation in the activity, and
the effects the eviction would have on other family members.

LOCAL IMPLEMENTATION

Although eviction and denial of admission for criminal and drug-related
activity was technically legal under federal law since 1988, the 1996 and
1998 laws and "One Strike and You're Out" Initiative provided public
housing authorities with legislative and executive cover to implement
strict screening and eviction policies against people with criminal
records, especially those with histories of drug-related criminal activity.

Most public housing agencies around the country have responded to
the Congressional and Executive mandate to get tough on drugs and
crime in public housing. Within a year of the adoption of the 1996 law,
75 percent of the 1,818 housing authorities responding to a HUD survey
indicated they had adopted the "One Strike and You're Out" Initiative's
policies.[42] In the six months after these policies were implemented, the
number of applicants denied public housing because of drug or criminal backgrounds nearly doubled from 9,835 to 19,405.[43] Public housing
agencies are now rewarded with Public Housing Assessment System
points for documenting that they have adopted policies and procedures
to deny admission to and evict individuals who engage in activity considered to be detrimental to the public housing community.[44]

A random sampling of housing authorities illustrates that many exclude applicants with any kind of criminal background, not just those
with drug-related and violent convictions. The policy may be to deny, at
least initially, any applicant whose background check indicates a history
of criminal activity, no matter what kind or how remote the conviction.
Some housing authorities even exclude applicants on the basis of arrest
information. In some instances, local housing authorities will consider—

either during the application process or during the grievance procedure challenging the initial denial—whether the prospective tenant has undergone treatment, how long ago the conviction occurred, and the seriousness of the offense.

THE HOUSING LAWS' EFFECTS

Changes in federal housing policies have had a dramatic effect on the ability of people with criminal records to obtain stable, affordable housing. Because the laws authorize housing authorities to deny or evict entire families for the criminal behavior of a single member, whether for a current or a previous conviction, families who live in public housing cannot allow a relative recently released from prison to live with them without putting the family's tenancy in jeopardy. Without access to decent, stable, and affordable housing, the likelihood of an ex-offender being able to obtain and retain employment and remain drug- and crime-free is significantly diminished.

Moreover, in excluding large numbers of individuals from public housing, these policies put a strain on the shelter system. With nowhere else to turn, people with criminal records often go to community shelters.

Finally, by excluding people with criminal records from public housing, these laws interfere with the ability of families to successfully reunify once a parent has returned from prison. The growing numbers of incarcerated parents—especially women[45]—who are released from prison find it nearly impossible to reunify with their children without secure, stable housing. When coupled with the Adoption and Safe Families Act,[46] which mandates that state child welfare agencies initiate termination proceedings against biological parents if they have not had contact with a child in fifteen of the most recent twenty-two months, the stakes for obtaining housing become even greater.

CONCLUSION

The bans on TANF assistance, food stamps, and public housing are counterproductive public policies for addressing addiction and reintegration of people with criminal histories, since they actually make it more difficult for low-income individuals to afford treatment, obtain food and employment, and find safe and sober housing as they transition back into the community. In continuing efforts to enhance the success of welfare reform, Congress should eliminate the ban on TANF assistance and food stamps to individuals with drug felony convictions. In the absence of federal change, states should adopt legislation to opt out of the ban or narrow its scope.

Local housing authorities should use their discretion to adopt fair and balanced admission and eviction policies that consider individual circumstances and reinforce the community's goals of encouraging people to remain in recovery and facilitating the successful reintegration of returning offenders into the community. Blanket policies that deny decent, safe, and affordable housing to individuals with criminal records and their families for long periods of time create challenges not only for the returning offender and his or her family but for the community that must absorb the criminal justice, shelter, and child welfare costs as well.

Public policy makers should focus their attention on how best to craft policies that give low-income and other individuals with alcohol and drug problems and criminal records incentive to enter treatment, stay in treatment, maintain their recovery, obtain employment, and lead productive lives. Only then will the revolving door between prison and community stop spinning for thousands of nonviolent drug offenders.

3
Mass Imprisonment and the Disappearing Voters

Marc Mauer

On Election Day 2000 in Florida, in the midst of all the dimpled ballots and hanging chads, Thomas Johnson stayed home. Johnson, the African-American director of a Christian residential program for ex-offenders, wanted to vote for George W. Bush, but was prevented by Florida law from doing so. In 1992, Johnson had been convicted of selling cocaine and carrying a firearm without a license in New York. After serving his sentence and moving to Florida in 1996, Johnson found that as an ex-felon he was barred from the voting booth. He was hardly alone in this situation, as at least 200,000 others in Florida who had theoretically "paid their debt to society" were also frozen out of the electoral process.

Nationwide, 4 million Americans either serving a felony sentence or having previously been convicted of a felony were forced to sit out the election.[1] The laws that kept these citizens home could be traced back to the founding of the nation. With the founding "fathers" having granted the vote only to wealthy white male property holders, political participation in the new democracy was extended to just 120,000 of the 2 million free Americans (not counting the more than 1 million slaves and indentured servants) at the time, about 6 percent of the population.[2] The excluded population incorporated women, African Americans, convicted felons, illiterates, and the landless. Except for convicted felons, of course, all these other exclusions have been removed over a period of two hundred years, and we now look back on those barriers with a great deal of national embarrassment.

The exclusion of felons from the body politic derived from the concept of "civil death" that had its origins in medieval Europe. Such a designation meant that a lawbreaker had no legal status, and imposed dishonor and incapacity on one's descendants. The concept was brought to North America by the English in the Colonial period. After the Revolution, some of the English common law heritage was rejected, but the voting disqualifications were maintained by many states. Two hundred years later, every state but Maine and Vermont (which allow prisoners to vote) has a set of laws that restrict the voting rights of felons and former felons. Forty-eight states and the District of Columbia do not permit prison inmates to vote; thirty-two states disenfranchise felons on parole; and twenty-eight disenfranchise felons on probation. In addition, in thirteen states a felony conviction can result in disenfranchisement, generally for life, even after an offender has completed his or her sentence. Thus, for example, an eighteen-year-old convicted of a one-time drug sale in Virginia who successfully completes a court-ordered treatment program and is never arrested again has permanently lost his voting rights unless he receives a gubernatorial pardon.

Although the issue of disenfranchisement would raise questions about democratic inclusion at any point in history, the dramatic escalation of the criminal justice system in the past thirty years has swelled the number of persons subject to these provisions to unprecedented levels. Currently, 2 percent of the adult population cannot vote as a result of a current or previous felony conviction. Given the vast racial disparities in the criminal justice system it is hardly surprising, but shocking nonetheless, to find that an estimated 13 percent of African-American males are now disenfranchised.

The coalescence of disenfranchisement laws and racial exclusion began to be cemented in the post-Reconstruction era following the Civil War. Prior to that not only were blacks in the South obviously unable to vote, but only six Northern states permitted their participation. The newly enfranchised black population in the South was quickly met with resistance from the white establishment. In many states this took the form of the poll tax and literacy requirements being adopted, along with a number of states tailoring their existing disenfranchisement policies with the specific intent of excluding black voters. One scholar describes this as a measure designed to provide "insurance if courts struck down more blatantly unconstitutional clauses."[3]

The disenfranchisement laws adopted in a number of Southern states were not at all subtle, often requiring the loss of voting rights only for those offenses believed to be committed primarily by blacks. In Mississippi, for example, the 1890 constitutional convention called for disenfranchisement for such crimes as burglary, theft, arson, and obtaining money under false pretenses, but not for robbery or murder. In the words of a Mississippi Supreme Court decision several years later, blacks engaged in crime were "given rather to furtive offenses than to the robust crimes of the whites."[4]

Other Southern states—Alabama, Louisiana, South Carolina, and Virginia—followed this pattern as well in their targeting of "furtive offenses." The intent of such policy was made clear by the author of the Alabama provision, who "estimated the crime of wife-beating alone would disqualify sixty percent of the Negroes."[5] Thus, by the convoluted logic of these provisions, a man would be disenfranchised for beating his wife but not for killing her. Alabama's constitution also barred voting for anyone convicted of crimes of "moral turpitude," including a variety of misdemeanors. Here, too, the intent and effect were quite obvious, resulting in ten times as many blacks as whites being disenfranchised, many for nonprison offenses.[6]

These policies were not of fleeting duration. Alabama's disenfranchisement law for offenses of "moral turpitude" was in place until 1985 before finally being struck down by the Supreme Court due to its discriminatory intent and impact. And while Mississippi barred many petty offenders from voting for decades, it did not disenfranchise rapists and murderers until 1968.[7]

While one might debate whether the *intended* effect of disenfranchisement policies today is to reduce minority voting power, it is inescapable that this impact could have been predicted as a logical consequence of the nation's wars on crime and drugs. The fivefold increase in the nation's inmate population since the early 1970s brought about both an absolute increase in numbers as well as a disproportionately greater impact on persons of color. Much of this was because of the inception of the modern-day "war on drugs" in the 1980s, whereby the number of persons incarcerated for a drug offense rose from 40,000 in 1980 to nearly half a million today. Blacks and Latinos now constitute four of every five drug offenders in state prison. A considerable body of research documents that these figures are not necessarily a result of greater drug use in minority communities but rather drug policies that have employed a law enforcement approach in communities of color and a treatment orientation in white and suburban neighborhoods.[8] And the greater the number of minority offenders in the system, the greater the rate of disenfranchisement.

At modest rates of disenfranchisement such a policy is one that is clearly of concern to an individual felon but is unlikely to affect electoral outcomes in any significant number of cases. But at the historic levels that have been achieved in recent decades the issue is no longer one of merely academic interest but is likely to have a profound impact on actual electoral results.

Sociologists Christopher Uggen and Jeff Manza have produced a sophisticated model for estimating the number of disenfranchised voters in each state and the effect of their absence on elections for national office.[9] Uggen and Manza assume that felons and former felons would vote at lower rates than the (already low) national rate but that they would be more likely to vote Democratic, given that they are disproportionately comprised of minorities (an estimated 38 percent African American) and poor and working-class whites. Even with a projected lower turnout, they conclude that disenfranchisement policies have affected the outcome of seven U.S. Senate races from 1970 to 1998, generally in states with close elections and a substantial number of disenfranchised voters. In each case the Democratic candidate would have won rather than the Republican victor. Projecting the impact of these races over time leads them to conclude that disenfranchisement prevented Democratic control of the Senate from 1986 to 2000. While these projections are based on the inclusion of both current and former felons, even permitting just ex-felons to vote would likely have a significant impact as well since they represent more than a third of the disenfranchised population.

Supporters of felon disenfranchisement contend that regardless of their outcome these policies are important for several reasons. One of the significant court decisions, an Alabama case decided in 1884, found that denying the vote to ex-convicts was necessary to preserve the "purity of the ballot box" from the "invasion of corruption" and that "this class should be denied a right, the exercise of which might sometimes hazard the welfare of communities."[10]

In more recent times this rationale has been presented within the context of the "law and order" political climate, being expressed as a fear that convicted felons would presumably cast their vote in such a way as to weaken law enforcement institutions. In a significant New York case in 1967, Judge Friendly wrote that "[I]t can scarcely be deemed unreasonable for a state to decide that perpetrators of serious crimes shall not take part in electing legislators who make the laws, the executives who enforce these, the prosecutors who must try them for further violations, or the judges who are to consider their cases."[11] Or, in the words of one modern-day proponent, "criminal disenfranchisement allows citizens to decide law enforcement issues without the dilution of voters who are deemed . . . to be less trustworthy."[12] In other words, ex-felons would presumably vote for policies that help criminals and thwart the legitimate interests of otherwise law-abiding members of the community. If so, this might set up a conflict between the principle of democratic inclusion and the need for public safety.

But it is clear that in at least some cases, individuals subjected to criminal justice policies that may be overly harsh would be natural and legitimate advocates of political change. An example relates to drug policy. As the "war on drugs" has swelled prison populations and taken a disproportionate toll on minority communities, considerable opposition has developed to mandatory sentencing and related policies. In some neighborhoods, substantial numbers of people are returning home after serving five-year prison terms for low-level drug offenses. Arguably, their voices and votes, along with those of their neighbors, might be successful in electing candidates who support scaling back harsh drug laws. Is there a policy rationale that justifies excluding persons who have experienced the impact of such laws from deliberating about their wisdom?

The prospect of electoral fraud is also sometimes raised as a legitimate concern in regard to felon voting. Although there might be some validity to this argument for felons convicted of electoral fraud, it is hard to imagine why a car thief or a drug seller would be more likely than another citizen to commit such an offense. Since more than 99 percent of felons have *not* been convicted of electoral offenses, this seems to be a rather overbroad concern. And when electoral fraud occurs, it rarely manifests itself in the presence of a voter in the voting booth, but rather through improper counting of ballots or outright bribery. One does not need to be a registered voter to commit these offenses. Ironically, in some states, electoral offenses are classified only as misdemeanors, and therefore persons convicted of these crimes are not subject to disenfranchisement.

Disenfranchisement is sometimes premised on being a legitimate aspect of punishment for a criminal offense, but this is curious in several respects. While all other aspects of sentencing are expected to be proportional to the offense involved and are imposed by a judge on an individual basis, disenfranchisement is a penalty imposed, across the board, on mass murderers and larcenists alike. Further, criminal convictions do not otherwise result in the loss of basic rights. Convicted felons maintain the right to divorce, own property, or file lawsuits. The only restrictions generally placed on these rights are ones that relate to security concerns with a prison. Thus, an inmate may subscribe to *Time* magazine but not to a publication that describes the production of explosive devices. Conflating legitimate punishment objectives with the denial of constitutional rights sets a risky precedent.

Proponents of disenfranchisement suggest that even in the most extreme cases the loss of the right to vote is never truly for a lifetime, since all states maintain a process whereby ex-felons can seek restoration of their rights from the governor. Although this is true in theory, in practice it is often illusory. A number of states impose a waiting period of five or ten years before an ex-felon can even petition to have his or her rights restored. The process of seeking restoration is also often cumbersome and expensive. In Alabama, for example, ex-felons are required to seek a pardon from the Board of Pardons and Paroles, but also to provide a DNA sample to the state.[13] Yet only four counties are set up to administer DNA testing, so an ex-felon might have to travel hundreds of miles to do so. In Mississippi, ex-felons must either secure an executive order from the governor or convince a state legislator to introduce a bill on his or her behalf, obtain a two-thirds vote in the legislature, and have the bill signed by the governor.[14]

Data on the number of former felons who have their rights restored are difficult to come by, but in one recent two-year period, a total of 404 persons in Virginia regained their voting rights at a time when there were more than 200,000 ex-felons in the state.[15] The state of Florida had previously instituted a procedure whereby the Department of Corrections was required to aid released inmates in regaining their voting rights, and as many as 15,000 former felons a year were able to do so in the mid-1980s. But new rules imposed by the state in the early 1990s greatly restrict the number of eligible inmates, with the result that fewer than 1,000 persons a year have their rights restored. Those who are not eligible still have the option of applying for executive clemency, but for many years this process involved completing a twelve-page questionnaire asking about such items as the details of a spouse's previous marriage, existing disabilities, amount of stocks and bonds owned, and a description of "your relationship with your family."[16]

Although the case for disenfranchisement is hardly compelling, two primary arguments suggest that felon disenfranchisement laws are both counterproductive and out of line with evolving international norms. First, disenfranchisement policies are in sharp conflict with the goal of promoting public safety. Whether an offender has been sentenced to prison, probation, or some other status, a primary goal of the criminal justice system and the community should be to reduce the likelihood that the person will reoffend. One means by which this can be accomplished is through instilling a sense of obligation and responsibility to the community. Those persons who feel some connection to their fellow citizens are less likely to victimize others. As former Supreme Court Justice Thurgood Marshall stated, "[Ex-offenders] . . . are as much affected by the actions of government as any other citizen, and have as much of a right to participate in governmental decision-making. Furthermore, the denial of a right to vote to such persons is hindrance to the efforts of society to rehabilitate former felons and convert them into law-abiding and productive citizens."[17]

American disenfranchisement policies are also quite extreme by the standards of other industrialized nations. In no other democracy are convicted offenders who have completed their sentences disenfranchised for life, as is the case in more than a dozen states.[18] Of the handful of nations that restrict voting rights for a period of time after the conclusion of a prison term, those such as Finland and New Zealand do so only for several years and only for electoral offenses or corruption. A number of nations, including ones as diverse as the Czech Republic, Denmark, Israel, Japan, and South Africa, permit inmates to vote as well.

In recent years the increased attention devoted to this issue has resulted in a reconsideration of some of the more extreme policies within the states. In 2000, the governor of Delaware signed into law a measure repealing the state's lifetime ban on ex-felon voting (imposing a five-year waiting period in its place), and the following year New Mexico did away with its lifetime ban as well. Connecticut went further, extending voting privileges to felons currently on probation. And in August 2001, the bipartisan National Commission on Federal Election Reform, cochaired by former presidents Ford and Carter, recommended that states allow for the restoration of voting rights for felons who have completed their sentences. In the wake of the national discussion generated over electoral problems and reforms, we are likely to see a renewed focus on this area of public policy in the coming years.

The irony of the combined impact of American disenfranchisement policies along with the massive expansion of the prison system is that a half century after the beginnings of the civil rights movement, increasing numbers of African Americans and others are losing their voting rights each day. It is long past time for the United States, as the Western democracy with the lowest rate of voter participation, to consider means of bringing more Americans into the electoral process rather than excluding large groups of citizens.

PART II

Distorting Justice

4

Incarceration and the Imbalance of Power

Angela J. Davis

The massive incarceration that has had such a devastating effect on families and communities was the result of a clear and dramatic shift in the focus of criminal justice policy. Although punishment has always been the defining characteristic of criminal law, it is only in the past thirty years that incarceration has become the presumptive method of punishing lawbreakers. This focus on incarceration coincided with a shift toward incapacitation and retribution and away from rehabilitation and deterrence as the preferred goals of the criminal justice system. Instead of utilizing modes of punishment that would rehabilitate, such as treatment, community service, and fines, policy makers have changed the criminal laws and policies in ways that have often mandated lengthy prison terms for many types of criminal offenses.

The criminal justice system itself has been profoundly affected by the drastic increase in incarceration. The shift toward a more retributive, punitive philosophy and the resulting increase in incarceration has prompted significant changes in the policies and practices of all sectors of the system. These changes seemingly have focused on the ever-looming specter of long and harsh prison terms. Indeed, the threat of incarceration seems to drive the system, often causing criminal justice officials to base critical decisions almost entirely on this factor rather than weigh it as one of many issues to be considered in the fair administration of justice.

Although many criminal justice officials play a critical role in the system,[1] the officials who have the greatest influence on the outcome of a criminal case are the prosecutor, the defense attorney, and the judge. Theoretically, justice is administered fairly in the criminal justice system when each of these officials has adequate resources and zealously performs her duties and responsibilities in an ethical manner. However, this fair balance is rarely achieved because of the political nature of many prosecutorial and judicial positions and the woeful lack of funding for public defender and other indigent defense systems.

Most state and local prosecutors and many local judges are elected officials who respond to political pressures and whose everyday decisions are shaped by the desire to be reelected. Thus, instead of performing their duties and responsibilities as prosecutors and judges based solely on what is fair and just in an individual case, far too often they are greatly influenced by how their actions will be portrayed in the media and perceived by the public.

The defense function is also rarely implemented free of political influences. Most people charged with crimes are poor and are represented by court-appointed attorneys—public defenders or individual lawyers in some other indigent defense system.[2] Very few court-appointed attorneys are provided resources commensurate with those of the prosecutor's office. Because they represent people who are unpopular and have very little, if any, influence in the political process,[3] court-appointed attorneys frequently do not have a constituency to effectively lobby for adequate funding. Without adequate funding, these attorneys are often unable to investigate their cases, file appropriate motions, hire experts when needed, or perform the many other responsibilities of a competent and zealous advocate.

In sum, the criminal justice system often malfunctions. Victims and criminal defendants alike complain of unfairness, and the large number of cases encourages assembly-line justice, often dehumanizing the process for everyone involved. The starkest example of this is the plea bargaining process, which accounts for the disposition of over 90 percent of all criminal cases. Class and racial bias, although often unintentional and unconscious, exist at every step of the process.[4] Dissatisfaction with the criminal process abounds.

Although many of the system's defects have existed for years, the philosophic shift toward retribution and harsh punishment and the corresponding, dramatic increase in incarceration have exacerbated many

of the problems and have effected significant and fundamental changes
in the way the system operates. These changes include

1. a significant increase in prosecutorial power;
2. a minimization and weakening of the defense function; and
3. a decrease in judicial discretion and power.

These fundamental changes in the roles of the most important criminal
justice officials only serve to exacerbate many of the system's defects and
the overall concerns about fairness.

INCREASED PROSECUTORIAL POWER

Although always dominant and influential, the prosecutor now essentially controls the criminal justice system. This crucial shift in power is
almost entirely the result of the adoption of mandatory minimum sentencing laws and guidelines reinforced by the prosecutor's wide-ranging
charging power. Of the many duties and responsibilities of the prosecutor, the charging power is the most important and is the essence of her
control over the entire system, especially since the adoption of mandatory minimum laws in most jurisdictions. Prosecutors decide whether to
charge an individual with a criminal offense, and what the charge should
be. Although a police officer arrests an individual when he has probable
cause to believe the individual has committed a criminal offense, he does
not ultimately decide whether the individual will be charged formally.
That decision is left to the prosecutor, who has an almost unlimited
amount of discretion in making this determination. The charging decision is critical, because it determines whether a person will face criminal
charges and ultimately risk the loss of liberty. The prosecutor is in control at this stage, even in jurisdictions where grand juries investigate and
bring charges through the indictment process.[5]

For example, if an individual is arrested because he was in possession
of a quantity of cocaine, the prosecutor has many options. She can dis-

miss the case, even if there is evidence sufficient to prove the case beyond a reasonable doubt. Neither the judge nor any member of the community would have standing to challenge this decision.[6] In fact, few
individuals would be aware of a precharge dismissal, since typically
these decisions are made in the privacy of the prosecutor's office. Because there is never a formal charge before these dismissals, there is
no case before the judge and obviously no need to appoint a defense
attorney.

Even if the prosecutor decides to formally charge the individual, she
has a wide range of discretion, and the decision she makes will determine or at least influence the role of the judge and defense attorney. The
drug offense again provides the perfect example. If an individual is arrested in possession of a quantity of cocaine, the prosecutor's arsenal of
possible charges includes possession of cocaine, possession with intent
to distribute cocaine, and distribution of cocaine. The significance of
this decision cannot be overstated. In most states, possession of cocaine
is a misdemeanor with a maximum penalty of one year in jail, whereas
possession with intent to distribute cocaine and distribution of cocaine
are felonies with mandatory minimum terms of imprisonment.[7] Depending on the statute, the mandatory prison term may be as much as
five or ten years, or even more. If the defendant has prior convictions,
the mandatory term may be much longer.

Most drug statutes do not mandate that the defendant possess a particular amount of the drug before he can be charged with either possession or possession with intent to distribute. Even if the amount is large
enough for a judge or jury to conclude that the defendant possessed it
for the purpose of distribution, the prosecutor may decide to charge the
person with simple possession of cocaine. Conversely, even if the
amount seems relatively small, a prosecutor may charge the person with
possession with intent to distribute if she believes she has evidence that
would prove that the defendant intended to sell that amount. Of course,
this decision is crucial, because if the defendant is convicted, it will determine the status of his liberty. Depending on the laws and the existence
of mandatory jail time, he may be eligible for probation if the charge is

simple possession. If the charge is possession with intent to distribute, distribution, or other drug offenses requiring mandatory time, the judge may be required to sentence him to prison for a mandatory term of years, and that mandatory term may be lengthy.

The highly publicized case of Kemba Smith provides an example. Kemba Smith's boyfriend, Peter Hall, was one of the biggest cocaine dealers on the East Coast in the 1990s. Ms. Smith's involvement with the drug trade was minimal, and by all accounts she acted under the direction and control of Hall, who ordered her to transport money across state lines and perform other tasks that did not directly involve distribution of the illegal drugs. Nonetheless, Ms. Smith was charged with numerous serious offenses. After charging her with these offenses, the prosecutors attempted to make a deal that would involve dismissing most of the charges in exchange for her testimony, but Mr. Hall was murdered before any agreement was reached. Ms. Smith pled guilty to money and drug laundering, drug conspiracy, and lying to federal agents, in exchange for the government's agreement to dismiss other offenses. Despite her minimal involvement in Mr. Hall's drug cartel and substantiated accusations of his physical abuse and threats, she was sentenced to twenty-four and a half years in prison—more prison time than many murderers or rapists receive.[8]

The prosecutor's decision to charge Ms. Smith with these offenses was totally discretionary and not necessarily defensible. Her minimal, indirect involvement in Mr. Hall's drug enterprise arguably warranted less serious charges or perhaps no criminal prosecution at all. But this critical decision was left totally to the prosecutor, whose discretion was almost boundless. Otto Obermaier, a former prosecutor in the U.S. Attorney's Office of the Southern District of New York, describes the charging power this way:

If you push and pull a whole lot you can reach almost any conclusion you want about what you actually charge a person with . . . And that's the whole ballgame. You can call the same act by several names, and each one brings about a different result in prison time.[9]

Of course, there are a number of *legitimate* factors that a prosecutor may consider in making the charging decision. A prosecutor may decide not to charge an arrested individual if, for example, the police officer conducted an illegal search or seizure and she knows that the judge will likely exclude the evidence for that reason.[10] Or the prosecutor may decide not to charge an individual if he is a first offender arrested for possession of a small amount of an illegal drug. The decision to charge an individual with possession or possession with intent to distribute should depend upon the relative evidence, including the amount of the drug and the individual's behavior and actions before the arrest. If the amount of the drug appears to be too large for personal use, the prosecutor might legitimately charge possession with intent to distribute. On the other hand, even if there is a small amount of the illegal drug, if there is evidence that the individual intended to sell it, the prosecutor may legitimately bring the more serious charge.

A prosecutor may also make an arbitrary charging decision or base the decision on totally illegitimate grounds. Because the prosecutor is not required to justify her charging decision to anyone beyond her immediate supervisors, there is no system of checks and balances to assure that this important decision is not tainted by race or class bias. In fact, there are numerous examples that suggest racial bias in the charging decision, either by charging African Americans more harshly than similarly situated whites[11] or by charging individuals more harshly when the victims are white and/or wealthy.[12] Because these decisions are made in the privacy of the prosecution office, it is difficult to discover arbitrary or racially biased decisions. Even when biased decisions are discovered, it is extremely difficult to prove intentional discrimination.[13] In fact, in most instances, the race or class bias is not intentional and is more frequently the result of unconscious and deeply internalized biases that have a racially disparate, and thus harmful, effect. Although unintentional discrimination harms its victims as much as the intentional type, there is no judicial remedy for discriminatory prosecutorial behavior unless the harmed party can prove that it was intentional.

The Armstrong case provides a stark example of a charging decision that appeared to be based on racial bias.[14] The defendants in the case were charged with a number of crack cocaine and gun offenses in federal court in Los Angeles. They claimed unconstitutional selective prosecution based on race, alleging that the U.S. Attorney prosecuted virtually all African Americans charged with crack offenses in federal court and all white crack defendants in state court. The significance of these allegations stemmed from the fact that the federal crack cocaine laws penalized crack trafficking much more harshly than the California state law. Although the defendants presented some evidence to support their claim, the Supreme Court ultimately found the evidence insufficient to prevail, even in their efforts to obtain discovery of information from the prosecutor that may have helped them prove the ultimate claim. The Court required some proof that similarly situated whites could have been prosecuted, but were not—information that is almost impossible for a criminal defendant to obtain given the secret nature of prosecutorial decision making.

The problem of unbridled prosecutorial discretion has had a very unsettling effect on the operation of the criminal justice system since the establishment of mandatory minimum sentencing laws and longer prison terms. Although prosecutors always have wielded a disproportionate amount of power in the criminal justice system, mandatory minimum sentencing laws and the threat of long prison terms have shifted the balance of power in a way that dangerously threatens core principles of fairness and justice. Judges and defense attorneys have always been in a reactive mode vis-à-vis prosecutors, but now the prosecutor's disproportionate control over the prospect of extreme loss of liberty has resulted in a weakening of their respective roles in the adversarial system.

With mandatory minimum sentencing laws and sentencing guidelines that require judges to impose a specific sentence based on limited, charge-based information, prosecutors essentially predetermine the outcome of many cases. Unless the defendant exercises his right to trial and is acquitted of all of the offenses, the prosecutor's charging decision will determine whether he will be incarcerated and how long the term of incarceration will be. Because the mandatory minimum sentencing laws require a specific term of imprisonment upon conviction, the judge has no power to consider mitigating factors at the sentencing hearing.

Although all criminal defendants have the right to a trial, very few exercise this right. Defendants plead guilty in over 90 percent of all criminal cases through the plea bargaining process,[15] which is controlled entirely by the prosecutor. After the prosecutor has charged the defendant with one or more offenses, she may offer the defendant a "deal," agreeing to drop one or more charges if the defendant agrees to plead guilty to one or more charges. Although the defendant may make a counteroffer and attempt to negotiate the best deal possible, the prosecutor must agree to the final terms of the agreement.

The vast majority of criminal defendants engage in plea bargaining because going to trial is risky business. If a defendant is charged with several offenses and each offense carries a lengthy term of imprisonment, the defendant faces the prospect of many years in prison if he is convicted of all charges. If one or more of the offenses carries a mandatory minimum term of imprisonment, that prospect becomes a guarantee. For many defendants, the possibility that a jury or judge may acquit him of the charges is too risky and uncertain. If he accepts a plea offer, he knows how much time he faces and how much time he avoids.

The increase in mandatory minimum sentences and longer prison terms has inflated the importance of the plea bargaining process. The risks associated with having a trial have become too high. Before the mandatory minimum phenomenon, even if a defendant were convicted of all charges, he would at least have the opportunity to try to convince the sentencing judge that he should be given a lenient sentence, or even probation. Mandatory minimum sentencing laws remove that possibility.

David Moe Robinson of Baltimore knows all too well about the risks of going to trial in a case involving mandatory minimum sentencing laws. Mr. Robinson was charged with a number of crack conspiracy and weapons charges. The prosecutors offered him a deal that would require him to tell them about his mother's involvement in the drug ring. Mr. Robinson rejected the deal, which involved dismissal of some of the charges and would have exposed him to a maximum of twenty-four to twenty-seven years in prison. He went to trial, was convicted, and was sentenced to forty-five years in prison. The prosecutors argued that he should have received more.[16]

Some prosecutors take advantage of the power they wield during the plea bargaining process. Many prosecutors engage in "overcharging"— charging the defendant with the offense that carries the greatest penalty, even when she knows she may not be able to prove it at trial. The purpose of this practice is to goad the defendant into pleading guilty to a lesser offense. For example, a prosecutor may charge a defendant with possession with intent to distribute cocaine that may carry a mandatory minimum sentence of five years. Although she may have had enough evidence to convince a grand jury that there was probable cause to believe the defendant committed the offense,[17] she may doubt whether the evidence is sufficient to prove guilt beyond a reasonable doubt at a jury trial. So the prosecutor may offer the defendant a plea to possession of cocaine, a misdemeanor offense that carries a maximum term of one year in jail with the possibility of probation. Even an innocent defendant with an absolute defense to the lesser possession charge might plead guilty to avoid the risk of being convicted of the higher charge after trial and facing a certain five years in prison. These decisions become even more difficult when the prosecutor requires the defendant to accept or reject the offer on the spot, leaving no time for substantial consultation with counsel or investigation of possible defenses. Some defendants feel compelled to accept the offer because the prospect of a certain and lengthy prison term is too frightening.

The prosecutor's charging power and control over the plea bargaining process define her role as a law enforcement officer in the executive branch of government. However, she also serves a quasi-judicial role in that her primary duty is to see that justice is done. Various professional codes and standards and the United States Supreme Court have noted that the prosecutor's duty is to seek justice, not merely convictions.[18] However, the vagueness of this standard and the prosecutor's unfettered discretion permit her to define justice as she sees fit, and many equate justice with convictions and incarceration, regardless of the circumstances of the case.

In sum, the move toward certain and much lengthier prison terms has inflated drastically the role, and consequently the power, of the prosecutor. This inflation of prosecutorial power is an unintended consequence of the overincarceration phenomenon that has significantly damaged the adversarial process. Draconian sentencing laws have automatically increased the significance of prosecutorial decisions and have impaired an already broken system by radically tilting the delicate balance of the adversarial system toward the prosecutor. As the balance of power has shifted toward the prosecutor, the roles of the defense attorney and judge have weakened.

MINIMIZATION OF THE DEFENSE FUNCTION

The defense attorney's role is, and should be, fundamentally different from that of the prosecutor. An advocate always fights for her client's best interests, and in the criminal justice system the client's primary interest is to avoid a criminal conviction and/or punishment, especially punishment that involves the loss of liberty. Where the prosecutor's responsibility is to seek justice through the enforcement and execution of the laws, the defense attorney's duty is to present the best defense possible with the goal of achieving either an acquittal or a dismissal of the charges.

Even if a defendant tells his attorney that he committed the crime and wants to plead guilty, the defense attorney has a responsibility to explain the defendant's constitutional right to a trial and his right to present a defense at trial. She should further explain that at a trial, the government is required to prove guilt beyond a reasonable doubt before a person can be convicted and incarcerated. The defense attorney should explain that the defendant has the right to remain silent and force the government to go forward with evidence of his guilt, and if the government can't meet the heavy burden of proof beyond a reasonable doubt, he has the right to be free.

The defense attorney has the responsibility of investigating the case to determine whether there is a defense to the charges. Investigation involves getting all of the police reports and other relevant documents, interviewing the government's witnesses, and interviewing any witnesses that may support a valid defense to the charges. The defense attorney should file appropriate motions, visit the location of the allegations against the client, hire appropriate experts, and take any other steps necessary to explore and present the best defense possible for his client. Throughout this process, she should maintain contact with her client, consulting with him and informing him of the results of her investigation and preparation of the case.

It is only after the defense attorney has thoroughly investigated the case and explored all possible defenses that she is in a position to provide competent advice to her client. The most critical advice that the defendant seeks is whether to exercise his right to trial or to plead guilty. This decision can only be made intelligently if the defendant has all of the relevant information, including knowledge of the evidence against him, whether he has a legal and viable defense, and whether the government has made a plea offer. The defense attorney should have in-depth discussions with her client about all of these issues and be in a position to competently advise him of the strengths and weaknesses of the government's case, the risks of going to trial, and the advantages and disadvantages of accepting the plea offer. Frequently, it is in the client's best interest to accept the government's plea offer, and the attorney who advises the client to reject the offer and go to trial under these circumstances is not representing her client well. However, when an attorney advises a client to plead guilty, that advice should be based on investigation, research, and a thorough evaluation of the case.

Most criminal defendants are indigent and represented by public defenders or other court-appointed attorneys who have crushing caseloads and woefully inadequate resources.[19] Most of these attorneys are unable to provide the thorough pretrial preparation, investigation, and counsel necessary to provide the best defense possible for each of their clients. Neither poor people charged with crimes nor their families have the political influence and power to effectively lobby for adequate funding of indigent defense programs. Thus, the representation they receive is rarely adequate.

Of course, there are many public defenders who are aggressive advocates for their clients despite the constraints they face.[20] However, it is difficult to provide zealous advocacy without adequate resources. Examples of overworked and underfunded defenders abound. The public defender office in New Orleans is one such example: It represented 418 defendants, entered 130 guilty pleas at arraignment, and had at least one serious case set for trial on every single trial date during the first seven months of 1991.[21] The office had no investigative support for most cases because the three investigators on staff were responsible for more than 7,000 cases per year. There were also no funds available for expert witnesses.

Inferior representation for poor people in the criminal justice system has always been a problem, but the problem has intensified since the implementation of mandatory minimum sentencing laws and the corresponding increased importance of plea bargaining. Although insufficient resources for indigent defense have always prevented court-appointed attorneys from adequately investigating their cases before advising clients about plea offers, the specter of certain and lengthy incarceration has intensified this problem. Many attorneys take the position that clients should never take the risk of going to trial when they are facing such extreme sentences. Many believe that regardless of the strength of the defense, there is always some chance a jury will convict, so trials are never worth the risk. This might be a rational position to take, but defense attorneys who routinely advise clients to accept plea offers solely because of the potential sentence are not competently representing their clients.

The prosecutor knows that criminal defendants fear the possibility of certain and lengthy incarceration, and may take advantage of this fact. In addition to the phenomenon of overcharging, the prosecutor may make a plea offer soon after the defendant is charged and require a response within twenty-four hours or less. She knows the defense attorney cannot possibly investigate the case, acquire the relevant police reports, explore possible defenses, and adequately advise the client in such a short period of time. In fact, she may fail to advise the defense attorney of weaknesses in her case, even though she is required to inform the defense of all exculpatory information.[22] The defense attorney is then in the position of presenting a plea offer to the client and advising him without the benefit of essential information. As one prosecutor puts it:

> Only the U.S. attorney knows the strengths and weaknesses of his case but you don't have to show that hand. . . . I don't know how many cases I've had where a defendant pleaded guilty when he saw how we'd charged him and where I thought I'm lucky they didn't know how weak my case was if I'd had to take it to trial.[23]

In essence, many defense attorneys have become little more than a conduit for information—conveying the prosecutor's plea offer and calculating the possible sentence after trial and after a plea. This is not zealous representation, and it is certainly not the way the adversarial system is supposed to work. Unfortunately, even good defense attorneys who want to represent their clients zealously are forced to handle their cases this way when their clients are facing lengthy, mandatory prison sentences. An attorney would be remiss if she failed to convey a plea offer to a client before it expired or rejected an offer without consulting with the client. However, if the attorney has not investigated the case, she is in no position to advise the client to either accept or reject the offer. Her role is minimized, and she becomes little more than a facilitator of the plea process.

This minimization of the defense function can be a dangerous threat to the fair administration of justice. If the defense attorney is not given the opportunity to question and test the government's evidence, the adversarial system malfunctions and doesn't come close to achieving justice. This is as true when a defendant pleads guilty as when he chooses to go to trial. When a prosecutor makes a plea offer, she will give the defense attorney a summary of the evidence that the government would present if the case proceeds to trial. Generally this summary is very cursory and does not include weaknesses in the government's case. If the plea offer expires before the defense attorney has the time to investigate the case, she will not have the opportunity to discover the identity of the government's witnesses, interview them, or assess their credibility. The government's witnesses may be convicted perjurers or their identifications of the defendant as the perpetrator of the crime may be very weak. A witness may be a codefendant who has pled guilty to a minor offense in exchange for his testimony. Or perhaps the witness has been coerced to testify against the defendant to avoid prosecution himself. All of these scenarios are common occurrences in the criminal justice system, and any of them may be sufficient to raise a reasonable doubt in the mind of one or more jurors.

A defendant may choose to plead guilty even if he is aware of weaknesses in the government's case. He may decide that despite these weaknesses, there is a good chance he may be convicted of all charges. If so, his decision may be prudent. But if the decision is made without the sound and helpful advice of his attorney, there is no assurance that the case has been resolved fairly.

Another overarching result of the mass incarceration movement is the possibility that more defendants are pleading guilty even when they've been fully advised that they have an excellent defense. Some people may see this result as positive if the defendant is actually guilty and wants to accept responsibility for his crime. On the other hand, there is the possibility that defendants who are not guilty may plead guilty to a minor offense nonetheless for fear of a lengthy prison sentence. Such a result is the height of unfairness and should never be a desired result in a criminal case.

Thus, one of the most devastating collateral consequences of the mass incarceration movement has been the waning model of the zealous defense attorney battling the prosecutor and protecting the client's liberty. Even the most conscientious defense attorney with the time and resources to represent her client zealously finds herself in a catch-22 situation. Whether she advises the client of a plea offer without adequately investigating the case or fails to advise the client of the offer, she is not fulfilling her responsibility to her client. Although the model defense attorney should serve as a shield to protect her client from the power of the government, tough, mandatory sentencing laws often compel her to do little more than facilitate her client's incarceration, even if for a shorter period of time than he would otherwise face.

THE DECLINE OF JUDICIAL DISCRETION

Judges are the most powerful, respected, and revered officials in the criminal justice system. They enjoy prominent stature and are afforded special respect in and out of the courtroom. No other criminal justice official wears special attire, sits in an elevated position in the courtroom, and expects to have the audience rise whenever she enters and leaves the courtroom. The judge is even afforded "ownership" of the courtroom— as in "Judge Smith's courtroom." All of these ceremonial traditions demonstrate the esteem with which the judge is held in the criminal justice system.

Judges have, in many ways, maintained their preeminent role in the criminal justice system since its dramatic shift toward incarceration. Judges are still afforded the same respect in and out of the courtroom and maintain the prestige and stature of their positions. They still control their courtrooms and make many important decisions that affect criminal cases. The judge schedules hearings and decides the outcome of procedural and substantive motions filed by either the defense or the prosecution. Many of these decisions determine the outcome of a case. In addition to deciding dispositive motions, the judge controls the substance and procedure of a criminal trial, and thus frequently influences the outcome of the trial.

Although the judge wields considerable power over cases that are resolved through trial and pretrial litigation, her power wanes significantly in cases where the defendant enters a guilty plea. Since guilty pleas resolve over 90 percent of all criminal cases, and the judge's role in the plea process is limited, her sphere of power is fairly restricted. This is especially true since the increased use of mandatory minimum sentencing laws. The judge's ability to influence the outcome of a criminal case is limited to the small percentage of cases that go to trial or involve pretrial litigation of substantive legal motions. The same issues that minimize the defense function apply to the judicial function—mandatory minimum sentencing laws and guidelines have increased the importance of guilty pleas, and the prosecutor controls the plea bargaining process.

Although judges participate in the plea bargaining process in some jurisdictions,[24] most judges' participation is limited to presiding over the guilty plea in the courtroom after the prosecutor and defense attorney have negotiated the final terms of the plea. Most guilty pleas are very perfunctory. The prosecutor sets forth the agreement and reads a brief summary of the evidence (sometimes merely a paragraph). The judge asks a few questions to assure that the defendant is competent and is entering the plea voluntarily, asks the defendant if he is, in fact, guilty of the offense, and schedules the case for sentencing. This process is so perfunctory that in some jurisdictions, judges accept numerous pleas at one time in an assembly line fashion, with all of the defendants standing before the judge at once. Judges have the obligation of assuring that there is a factual basis for the plea and that it is a legal and fair disposition of the case, but most simply rubber-stamp the process.[25]

As with defense attorneys, judges often find themselves in a catch-22 situation. Most judges want to encourage guilty pleas for a variety of reasons. If a defendant has committed a criminal offense, his acknowledgement of guilt and acceptance of responsibility appears to be a fair resolution of a criminal case for all involved. When the stakes are high due to severe, inflexible sentencing laws, the judge should not interfere with an agreement that allows more lenient treatment in appropriate cases. In addition, judges are always concerned about judicial efficiency. The ever-growing number of criminal cases fosters the expeditious resolution of as many cases as possible. However, judges should not encourage guilty pleas when to do so would create an injustice. If a defendant is not factually guilty or if the government's proffer of evidence is suspect, it is the judge's role to prevent the guilty plea. Unfortunately, many judges engage in blind willfulness by not making thorough inquiries during the implementation of the guilty plea.

Although judges make the ultimate and most important decision at sentencing hearings involving the exercise of judicial discretion, they have no power at all if the charge requires a mandatory minimum sentence or the application of mandatory sentencing guidelines. Mandatory minimum sentencing laws require the judge to sentence a defendant to a minimum term of years for certain criminal offenses. The judge is not afforded the discretion to take into account the circumstances of the case or the individual characteristics of the defendant. The federal sentencing guidelines and similar state guidelines require judges to sentence according to a preset formula that adds prison time for certain aggravating factors and substracts for certain mitigating factors, none of which include the personal characteristics or circumstances of the defendant. In essence, judges don't make judgments when these laws apply; they simply perform mathematical calculations, often imposing sentences that they don't believe to be fair or appropriate in particular cases.

Some judges have refused to follow mandatory sentencing laws when they require the imposition of sentences these judges consider to be patently unfair or inappropriate.[26] Judge Harold Greene of the U.S. District Court of the District of Columbia was one such judge. Sharon Ortega was convicted of distributing crack cocaine after an undercover law enforcement agent testified that he had urged Ms. Ortega to convert powder cocaine to crack cocaine before selling it to him. He admitted that he did so because he knew that the penalty for selling crack was substantially stiffer, by a one-hundred-to-one drug quantity ratio. Judge Greene was so outraged by the agent's behavior that he refused to sentence Ms. Ortega to the mandatory minimum sentence of fifteen years to life. He found that the agent had violated Ms. Ortega's due process rights, and sentenced her to ten years instead.[27] Judge Louis Oberdorfer of the U.S. District Court of the District of Columbia and U.S. District

Judge Clyde Cahill of St. Louis also have noted the unfairness of the federal sentencing guidelines and have refused to apply them in particular cases. However, both judges were overturned on appeal.[28] Despite these examples, judges who have disregarded mandatory sentencing laws remain a very small minority.

Hence judges, like defense attorneys, have lost considerable power and influence in the criminal justice process since the increase in mandatory minimum laws and sentencing guidelines. Like defense attorneys, judges are severely hampered in the performance of their primary duties—presiding over cases, making decisions after a fair and complete presentation by the prosecutor and defense attorney, and serving as the ultimate arbiters of justice. This reduction in judicial discretion and power has damaged the adversary process and the criminal justice system as a whole.

There is a public perception of unfairness and ineffectiveness in the criminal justice system that unfortunately is based on fact. The harsh realities of race and class disparities at every step of the process for victims and defendants, the underfunding of many criminal justice functions, and the intractable socioeconomic factors that influence case outcomes are all problems that have plagued the system for some time. The mass incarceration movement has intensified other problems that impact the fundamental structure and functioning of the criminal justice system. Assembly-line justice facilitated by powerful prosecutors, helpless defense attorneys, and increasingly powerless judges now characterizes the system that determines whether a person will lose his liberty or even his life. Fairness and justice for defendants, victims, and society will never be achieved unless there is major reform of the laws and policies that have disturbed the delicate balance of power and decision making in the criminal justice system.

5

Imprisoning Women: The Unintended Victims of Mass Imprisonment

*Meda Chesney-Lind**

When the United States embarked on a policy that might well be described as mass incarceration, few considered the impact that this correctional course change would have on women. Women offenders have been largely invisible or "forgotten" by a criminology that emerged to complement, explain, and occasionally critique state efforts to control and discipline unruly and dangerous men. In the classic texts on crime, women literally "disappeared" from data sets, from discussions of crime patterns, and, most important for this discussion, from plans regarding the structure of jails and prisons. Very often, little or no thought was given to the possibility of a female prisoner until she appeared at the door of the institution.[1] It was as though crime and punishment existed in a world in which gender equaled male, and women were correctional afterthoughts, at best.

Some of this intellectual and institutional neglect was understandable. In the early seventies, about half the states and territories did not even have separate institutions for women inmates,[2] and there were so few women in prison that the system was for all intents and purposes male (97 percent male in 1970).[3]

The long-standing correctional pattern of ignoring women, however, laid the foundation for a policy and programmatic crisis, as the number of women sentenced to jail and prison began to increase dramatically in the last two decades of the twentieth century. As this chapter will show, most of this startling increase was simply an unintended consequence of the nation's move to mass incarceration as a result of a "war on drugs" and a host of other "get tough" sentencing policies. Rather than any substantial increase in women's involvement in serious crime, the growth of women's incarceration has been a reflection of public policy decisions that have often ignored any consideration of women's needs and behaviors.

In the case of women's incarceration, dramatic and gendered consequences also began to emerge. In a system long used to ignoring women and assuming that all those in prison were male, just treatment of women emerged as a real challenge. How do you handle women in a world built to house presumably violent men? Often a response emerged that "fairness" meant treating women as if they were men; this pattern of what might be called "vengeful equity" emerged alongside other unanticipated problems clearly related to undeniable gender difference (including sexual abuse scandals and severe problems with women's health service delivery).[4] Almost overnight, the "forgotten" offender was very much on everyone's mind as states scrambled to address an emerging and continuing gender crisis in corrections.

TRENDS IN WOMEN'S IMPRISONMENT IN THE UNITED STATES

For most of the last century, the United States imprisoned about 5,000 to 10,000 women, only reaching the level of 12,000 by 1980.[5] By 1999, this figure had climbed to more than 90,000. Thus, in two decades, the number of women being held in the nation's prisons increased more than sixfold, and the women's imprisonment boom was born. While men's imprisonment was also rising during this period, the increase in women's imprisonment was not simply a mirror image of the male numbers but in fact represented the cumulative impact of a number of policy changes with unique consequences for women.

In recent decades the scale of women's imprisonment has risen even more dramatically than the unprecedented increase for men. At the turn of the twentieth century, women comprised 4 percent of those imprisoned; by 1970, this had dropped to 3 percent, and women accounted for only 3.9 percent of those in prison in 1980. By 1999, though, women represented 6.7 percent of prison inmates.[6] In the 1990s alone the number of women in prison more than doubled (110 percent), compared with a 77 percent rise in the male prison population.[7] Similar patterns can be seen in adult jails: Women constituted 7 percent of the population in the mid-1980s, but today account for 11.4 percent of the total.[8]

Nationally, the rate of women's imprisonment is at a historic high, having risen from a low of six sentenced female inmates per 100,000 women in the United States in 1925 to sixty-six per 100,000 in 2000. In 2000, Texas led the nation with 12,714 women in prison, followed by California, with 11,432; Florida, with 4,019, and New York, with 3,423.[9]

As a result of these increases, the number of women incarcerated in prisons and jails in the United States is now about ten times greater than the number of women incarcerated in all of Western Europe. This is despite the fact that Western Europe and the United States are roughly equivalent in terms of population.[10]

What has caused this shift in the way that we respond to women's crime? What unique challenges have these remarkable numbers of women inmates produced, and what could we do better or differently, as we struggle to create a woman-centered response to the current state of affairs?

BUILDING CELLS: INVENTING WOMEN'S CORRECTIONS

The number of women's prisons has always been quite small. Ignored because of their small numbers, female inmates tended to complain, not riot, making it even easier for institutions to overlook their unique needs. By the mid-1970s, only about half the states and territories had separate prisons for women, and many jurisdictions housed women inmates in male facilities or in women's facilities in other states.[11]

The correctional establishment was taken by almost complete surprise when the numbers of women sentenced to prison began to expand in the 1980s. Initially, women inmates were housed virtually anywhere (remodeled hospitals, abandoned training schools, and converted motels) as jurisdictions struggled to cope with the soaring increase in women's imprisonment. More recently, though, states have turned to opening new prisons. Between 1930 and 1950, the United States opened only about two to three facilities for women per decade, but over thirty-four were opened in the eighties alone.[12] By 1990, the nation had seventy-one female-only facilities; five years later, the number had jumped to 104—an increase of 46.5 percent.[13]

This remarkable increase should not be seen simply as a reflection of trends in male incarceration; in many states there was simply *no* system at all for women when the numbers began to rise. For this reason and for good or ill, the United States also embarked on the invention of, or more precisely, the reinvention of, women's corrections in America. The last such experiment had occurred during the Progressive Era, when women reformers, many affected by the first wave of feminism, began to enter the previously male field and create women's reformatories. A natural outgrowth of earlier involvement of feminists in prison reform, the reformatory movement enthusiastically embraced female imprisonment in institutions that were designed to "save" fallen girls and women.[14]

The current revolution in women's corrections has been thrust upon correctional administrators, including many gifted women who happened to be working in the mostly male environment of modern corrections. This group of women might be fairly cast in the role of "reluctant" incarcerators, since many of them believe that most of the women in U.S. prisons today do not necessarily need to be there.[15] Like their earlier counterparts in the reformatory movement, these women also have a strong belief in the value of gender-specific or gender-responsive programming. As Bona Miller, then warden of the Pocatello Women's Correctional Center, wrote in 1999, "Working effectively with women offenders requires an in-depth understanding of their specific characteristics and needs, as well as a broader comprehension of the major social and economic challenges facing women today."[16]

How, then, do we craft a system (not simply prisons) that responds to the issues presented by women offenders? And, how do we avoid responses to women's crimes that, in the name of equality, treat female offenders as though they were males? To explore these two issues briefly, we will examine shifts in women's offending as well as detail issues that have surfaced around their treatment in the criminal justice system, with a special focus on their treatment in prison.

COLLATERAL DAMAGE: ADULT FEMALE OFFENDERS AND THE U.S. IMPRISONMENT MANIA

Setting aside the legal aspects of this dispute, will treating women offenders as if they were men result in effective responses to their behavior? Research on women's pathways into crime clearly disputes this and suggests that gender plays a major role in the forces that propel women into criminal behavior. For this reason, gender must be taken into account in the crafting of effective responses to their problems.

Hints about this come from a national survey of imprisoned women. Justice Department surveys have found that women in prison experience far higher rates of physical and sexual abuse than their male counterparts. Well over half (57.2 percent) of the women serving time in state prisons reported they had been either sexually or physically abused at least once before their current admission to prison; the comparable figure for men was 16.1 percent.[17]

For about one-third of all women in prison (36.7 percent), the abuse started when they were girls, but it continued as they became adults. A key gender difference emerges here. A number of young men in prison (14.4 percent) also report abuse as boys, but this victimization does not continue to adulthood. One in five women reported that their abuse started as adults compared with less than 2 percent of male offenders. Fully 46.5 percent of the women surveyed reported physical abuse, and 39 percent had been sexually abused either as girls or young women compared with a relatively small percentage of men (5.8 percent).[18] The report notes that "men who reported abuse generally had been age 17 or younger when they suffered the abuse. . . . Women, however, were abused as both juveniles and adults."[19] Such victimization patterns are significant because research on girl's and women's crime often exposes significant links between these traumatic experiences and behavior that later involves them in the criminal justice system.

As an example, girls are much more likely than boys to be the victims of child sexual abuse, with some experts estimating that roughly 70 percent of victims are girls.[20] Other evidence also suggests a link between this problem and girls' delinquency—in particular, running away from home.[21] Because studies of adult women in prison clearly indicate the role that girlhood victimization has played in their lives, these studies suggest that society's failure to address girls' serious problems (and in fact the criminalization of girls' survival strategies, such as running away from home) may be inextricably linked not only to girls' delinquency but also to later criminal behavior in adult women.

WOMEN'S LIVES AND WOMEN'S CRIME

A look at the offenses for which women are incarcerated further puts to rest the notion of hyperviolent, nontraditional women criminals. Today, 60 percent of all women in the nation's prisons are serving time either for drug offenses or property offenses, compared with 41 percent of men in prison.[22] Further, nearly half of women inmates have never been convicted of a violent offense.[23]

Even when women commit violent offenses, gender plays an important role. Research indicates, for example, that of women convicted of murder or manslaughter, many had killed husbands or boyfriends who repeatedly and violently had abused them. In New York, for example, of the women committed to the state's prisons for homicide in 1986, 49 percent had been the victims of abuse at some point in their lives, and 59 percent of the women who killed someone close to them were being abused at the time of the offense. For half of the women committed for homicide, it was their first and only offense.[24] An earlier, but more specific, study of intimate partner violence[25] found that of the thirty women incarcerated in a California prison for killing their mates, twenty-nine had been abused by them, and twenty indicated that the homicide had resulted in their attempt to protect either themselves or their children from further harm.[26]

But what of the less dramatic, and far more common, offenses among women? Kim English approached the issue of women's crime by analyzing detailed self-report surveys she administered to a sample of 128 female and 872 male inmates in Colorado.[27] Her research provides clear information on the ways in which women's place in male society colors and shapes their crimes.

English found, for example, that women were far more likely than men to be involved in "forgery." Follow-up research on a subsample of "high crime rate" female respondents revealed that many had worked in retail establishments and, therefore, "knew how much time they had" between stealing the checks or credit cards and having them reported. The women said that they would target "strip malls" where credit cards and bank checks could be stolen easily and used in nearby retail establishments. The women reported that their high-frequency theft was motivated by a "big haul," which meant a purse with several hundred dollars in it as well as cards and checks.[28] English concludes that "women's over-representation in low-paying, low status jobs" like working in retail may actually increase their involvement in certain property crimes, much like women's employment in bar and entertainment outlets often increases women's likelihood of getting involved in prostitution and drug abuse.[29]

English's findings with reference to two other offenses, where gender differences did not appear in participation rates, are worth exploring here. She found no difference in the "participation rates" of women and men in drug sales and assault. However, when examining frequency data, English found that women in prison reported significantly more drug sales than men, but not because they were engaged in big-time drug selling. Instead, the high number of drug sales was a product of the fact that women's drug sales were "concentrated in the small trades (i.e., transactions of less than $10)." English found that because they made so little money, 20 percent of the active women dealers reported twenty or more drug deals per day.[30] A reverse of this pattern was found when she examined women's participation in assault. Here, slightly more (27.8 percent) women than men (23.4 percent) reported committing an assault in the past year. However, most of the women reported only one assault during the study period (65.4 percent) compared with only about one-third of the men (37.5 percent).

In sum, English found that both women's and men's crime reflected the role played by "economic disadvantage" in their criminal careers. Beyond this, though, gender played an important role in shaping women's and men's response to poverty. Specifically, women's criminal careers reflected "gender differences in legitimate and illegitimate opportunity structures, in personal networks, and in family obligations."[31]

Finally, careful research on the role of the worsening economic situation facing women on the economic margins is necessary to understand what forces, if any, are propelling changes in women's crime. Women, and particularly women of color who increasingly are heads of households, have certainly not participated in the boom economy of the latter part of the last century in meaningful ways.

Indeed, in a very careful assessment of the role of economic marginalization in women's crime, Karen Heimer argues that what narrowing has occurred in the gender gap (the gap between male and female participation in crime) in the last few decades is likely caused by the confluence of three disparate trends: "dramatic changes in the composition of the family," "persistent wage inequality across gender," and finally, "increasing inequality or dispersion in income among women and men."[32] Heimer links women's deteriorating economic conditions to an increase in women's participation in property crimes (including both traditionally female crimes like larceny and embezzlement as well as some relatively nontraditional offenses such as motor vehicle theft, burglary, and stolen property) and some crimes of violence (particularly assault) but notably, not murder. To this list, one might be tempted to add drug arrests, since increases in women's arrests for these offenses have also increased while other women's arrests—particularly women's arrests for violent crimes—decreased in recent years.[33]

Since crime has been declining rapidly in the United States by almost any measure (arrests or victimization data), most careful researchers would suggest that much of the run-up in women's imprisonment is not due to a change in women's crime so much as a change in how the society handles drug offenses (a point that will be discussed in detail in the next section). However, Heimer's argument still merits further exploration. She marshals powerful evidence that some women's economic circumstances, particularly those of women who are single heads of households, have deteriorated considerably over the past few decades (particularly in communities of color). Such trends must be systematically examined when attempting to theorize women's crime. Beyond this, she correctly notes that recent mean-spirited changes in welfare policies (and one might add draconian laws prohibiting those found guilty of drug offenses from accessing welfare, public housing, and many other federal programs), may well encourage economically marginalized girls and women (particularly those who have already been convicted of crimes) to seek to survive through crime in much the same fashion that their male counterparts have long done.

WAR ON DRUGS AS A WAR ON WOMEN

In contrast to media images of the 1980s that portrayed women's crime as a problem spiraling out of control, research on the backgrounds of those in prison gives little indication of this, nor do studies of the pathways of contemporary women offenders. These continue to reflect a history of victimization and participation in crimes of economic marginalization, not serious, nontraditional offenses.[34] In addition, arrest data do not suggest major changes in women's criminal behavior. As an example, the total number of arrests of adult women, which might be seen as a measure of women's criminal activity, increased by only 14.5 percent between 1990 and 1999, while the number of women in prison increased by 105.8 percent.[35] And, despite media images of hyperviolent women offenders, the proportion of women doing time in state prisons for violent offenses has been declining steadily from about half (48.9 percent in 1979 to just over a quarter (28.5 percent) in 1998.[36]

What, then, explains the rise in the women's prison population? A recent study by the Bureau of Justice Statistics indicates that growth in the number of violent offenders was the major factor for male prison growth in the 1990s, but for the female prison population it was drug offenses. One explanation, then, is that the "war on drugs" has become a largely unannounced war on women. Two decades ago (1979), one in ten women in U.S. prisons was doing time for drugs. By 1998, it was one in three (33.9 percent).[37] Finally, while the intent of "get tough" drug policies was presumably to rid society of drug dealers and so-called kingpins, many of the women swept up in the war on drugs are minor offenders. An analysis by Human Rights Watch of women incarcerated under New York's draconian Rockefeller drug laws, for example, documented that nearly half (44 percent) had never been in prison before, and 17 percent had never been arrested before.[38]

POLICIES THAT INCREASE WOMEN'S IMPRISONMENT

It is now increasingly clear that the huge increases seen in women's imprisonment are due to an array of policy changes within the criminal justice system rather than a change in the seriousness of women's crime. Often, these policy changes were implemented with absolutely no thought to their impact on women's lives—particularly the most vulnerable of women living on society's economic margins.

Certainly, as the data on the characteristics of women in prison indicate, the passage of increased penalties (mandatory sentences) for drug offenses has been a major factor. Also important has been the implementation of a variety of other sentencing "reform" initiatives.

Nowhere is this pattern clearer than in the federal system. Here, the passage of harsh mandatory minimums for federal crimes, coupled with new sentencing guidelines intended to "reduce race, class and other unwarranted disparities in sentencing males,"[39] have operated in ways that distinctly disadvantage women. Specifically, they discourage judges from considering gender-based factors that result in a woman's prison sentence being far harsher than that of her male counterpart. For example, many women in prison face a "double punishment for their crimes: a prison sentence and the threat of termination of their parental rights," since so many more women are the sole custodial parent.[40] In fact, appellate courts have expressed "distaste" for judges seeking exceptions to the federal sentencing guidelines based on extreme family hardship.[41] Beyond this, the guidelines offer no possible departure for histories of physical and sexual abuse—conditions that might well mitigate women's sentences.

As a result of these various policies, more women are being sentenced to prison and for longer periods of time. Twenty years ago, nearly two-thirds of women convicted of federal felonies were granted probation. But after the implementation of sentencing guidelines in 1987, along with mandatory minimums, these proportions changed considerably. By 1991, only 28 percent of women were given straight probation.[42] Further, the mean time to be served by women drug offenders increased from twenty-seven months in July 1984, to a startling sixty-seven months in June 1990.[43]

Similar trends can be observed in many state prison systems, since all states now have mandatory sentences for drug offenses in at least some form. Estimates are that these policies increased the likelihood of being imprisoned for a drug offense by 447 percent between 1980 and 1992.[44]

On the surface, mandatory sentences appear to be gender blind, but in practice they result in a considerable disadvantage for women in plea negotiations. Essentially, one of the few ways that mandatory sentences can be altered is if the defendant can provide authorities with information that might be useful in the prosecution of other drug offenders. Because women tend to be working at the lowest levels of the drug hierarchy, they are often unable to negotiate plea reductions successfully. Added to this is the ironic fact that it is not uncommon for women arrested for drug crimes to be reluctant to testify against their boyfriends or husbands. Such was the case in one of the most high-profile of these cases, that of Kemba Smith, who was sentenced to twenty-four years in a federal penitentiary for her role in aiding her kingpin boyfriend's drug deals. Even though Smith had never handled or sold drugs, she received the mandatory sentence for the entire amount of cocaine distributed in the operation (255 kilograms), largely because of her initial reluctance to testify against her lover (who was found murdered prior to her trial); she was later pardoned by President Clinton.[45]

Other less obvious, but related, policy changes have also played a role in increasing women's imprisonment. Consider the role of new technologies for determining drug use (e.g., urinalysis). Many women are being returned to prison not for new offenses but for technical parole violations because they fail to pass random drug tests. Of the 6,000 women incarcerated in California in 1993, approximately one-third (32 percent) were imprisoned due to parole violations. In Hawaii, 55 percent of the new admissions to the women's prison during a two-month period in 1991 were being returned to prison for violations (largely drug violations).

In Oregon, during a one-year period (October 1992 to September 1993), only 26 percent of female admissions to prison were for new convictions; the rest were probation and parole violators. By contrast, 48 percent of male admissions were for new offenses.[46] More recent Hawaii data amplify this point: of individuals released from prison during fiscal year 1998 and tracked for two years postrelease, nearly half (43 percent) were returned to prison. The reasons for return, though, show a gender difference. Although fully 73 percent of the women were returned to prison solely for technical violations of parole conditions (as opposed to new crimes), this was true for a smaller, though still significant, proportion of male parolees (64 percent).[47] Some of this pattern is no doubt explained by the less serious criminal histories of many women being released from prison, but other factors may be in play as well. Recall that the earliest era of women's imprisonment was fueled by the impulse to use imprisonment to "save" and "reform" "fallen" women.[48] It may be that the historic correctional pattern of monitoring the moral as well as the criminal behavior of women is now spilling over into women receiving a longer list of probation and parole conditions (including a focus on parenting and drug treatment), which in turn set women up for failure.[49]

The impact of gender-blind sentencing, then, coupled with what might be seen as an increased policing of women's behavior while on probation or parole, have both played major, though largely hidden, roles in the growth of women's imprisonment.

EMERGENCE OF VENGEFUL EQUITY

An additional theme is also emerging in the modern correctional response to women inmates: vengeful equity. This is the dark side of the equity or parity model of justice—one that emphasizes treating women offenders as though they were men, particularly when the outcome is punitive, in the name of equal justice.

Perhaps the starkest expression of this impulse has been the creation of chain gangs for women. Whereas these have surfaced in several states, the most publicized example comes from Arizona. Here, a sheriff pronounced himself an "equal opportunity incarcerator" and encouraged women "now locked up with three or four others in dank, cramped disciplinary cells" to "volunteer" for a fifteen-woman chain gang. Defending his controversial move, he commented, "If women can fight for their country, and bless them for that, if they can walk a beat, if they can protect the people and arrest violators of the law, then they should have no problem with picking up trash in 120 degrees." Other examples of vengeful equity can be found in the creation of women's boot camps and the argument that women should be subjected to capital punishment at the same rate as men.

While these examples might be seen as extreme, legal readings by correctional administrators and others that define any attention to legitimate gender differences as "illegal" have produced troubling outcomes. It is clearly misguided to treat women as if they were men with reference to cross-gender supervision, strip searches, and other correctional regimes while ignoring the ways in which women's imprisonment has unique features (such as pregnancy and vulnerability to sexual assault). Recently, this approach has been correctly identified by Human Rights Watch as a major contributing factor to the sexual abuse of women inmates.[50]

Instead of vengeful equity we must craft a women-centered correctional system—a system that is conservative, and careful to be sure, but one that derives its modes of supervision at all stages of the correctional process directly from the problems and needs of girl and women offenders. And, given what we know about women offenders—that they are largely minor offenders, that they have unique needs, and that most can be safely returned to the communities where they lived—this system can clearly attempt programming that the male system cannot.

This suggests that emerging women's corrections can and should rely, probably to a far greater extent than is currently the case, on community or alternative sentencing programs instead of on conventional prison settings. These programs, though, should be crafted (or re-crafted) with gender in mind. Many traditional forms of community sentences, as an example, involve home detention—clearly unworkable for women with abusive boyfriends or husbands, but also problematic for women who are drug dependent and/or unemployed. Restitution is also not a viable choice for women offenders, for many of the same reasons.

Women's programs must also give participants strategies to deal with their profound substance abuse problems. Estimates are that "up to 80 percent of women offenders in some state prison systems have severe, long-standing substance abuse problems,"[51] and while substance abuse plays a role in men's crime as well, the relationship appears to be stronger in the case of women's crime. Specifically, women who have used illicit drugs are six times more likely than women who have not to be arrested in the year prior to their arrest; for males, the differential was half that, or three times greater.[52] Drug treatment programs must also be gender sensitive. They need to understand that the traumatic history of many female offenders means that they may be taking drugs as a form of self-medication rather than for adventure or challenge, as men do.[53] They must be sensitive to women's unique circumstances (by providing such services as child care and transportation). Community programs must also deal with women's immediate need for safe housing and stable employment, an undertaking made more difficult by the passage of the felony drug provision of the 1996 Welfare Reform Act, which prohibits women with drug convictions from receiving welfare benefits *for life* unless a state opts out of the ban. Clearly, any national strategy for dealing with the problems of women in prison must include a call for repeal of this initiative, as well as advocating for the creation of women-centered programs to accompany any efforts to shift women from prison back to their communities.

The United States, without any public discussion or debate, has embarked on the construction of an extensive new women's prison system. Women's imprisonment soared not as a response to a female crime problem out of control but rather as an unexamined consequence of a gender-blind drug war that swept up many women and a considerable number of men into prison. This chapter and others in this book (see Richie) have argued that most of the women now in U.S. prisons could be safely housed and treated in the community rather than behind bars (as they were in past decades).

It is now time to count the cost of the new women's prison policy: open the cell doors and see the faces of the women we've chosen to mindlessly incarcerate—perhaps on a day when their children try to visit them. The experiment in women's corrections was an inadvertent outcome of a misguided notion that "getting tough" on drugs and other crimes would make us safe. Not only has women's incarceration failed to deliver on that promise, it has created further havoc in families and communities that had already been ravaged by poverty and racism.

CONCLUSION

All good feminist research is challenged to both investigate aspects of women's oppression while "seeking at the same time to be part of the struggle against it."[54] Clearly, this mandate is much needed in the area of women's crime and imprisonment. Women in conflict with the law have become the hidden victims of our nation's imprisonment binge, and as a consequence women's share of the nation's prison population, measured in either absolute or relative terms, has never been higher. All of this has occurred without serious planning, consideration, or debate. Even more alarming, it appears that the incarceration binge is beginning to spread to the juvenile justice system as well, where stark increases in girls' detention have been observed.

With reference to girls' and women's crime, we face a clear choice: we can continue to spend tax dollars on the costly incarceration of women guilty of petty drug and property crimes, or we can seek other solutions to the problems of economically marginalized, abused, and often drug-dependent women. Given the characteristics of the women in prison, it is clear that the decarceration of large numbers of women in prison would not jeopardize public safety. Further, the money saved could be reinvested in programs designed to meet women's needs, which would enrich not only their lives but the lives of many other women who are at risk for criminal involvement.

Perhaps, in this new millennium, we could as a nation choose to chart a course far different from the one that closed out the waning decades of the last. We could begin seriously to reconsider incarceration as a first-choice response to crime—a costly, mean-spirited, and destructive course that most of the rest of the civilized world has critiqued for some time. It is important to remember, as this chapter has noted, that as a nation we once did precisely that with women offenders—all states arrested women, but only about half had prisons during the middle of the twentieth century. We need to find the courage to open the cell doors and welcome these women back into our society. Moreover, we should consider extending the lessons we will learn from the decarceration of women to the many nonviolent men we currently imprison. In that sense, the decarceration of women can begin the much-needed national conversation of how to develop criminal justice policies that heal and treat rather than solely punish.

6
Entrepreneurial Corrections: Incarceration As a Business Opportunity

Judith A. Greene *

The $2 billion private prison industry was launched in the mid-1980s after a decade of "get tough" sentencing reforms had swelled prison overcrowding to crisis proportions in the United States. The extraordinary rise in incarceration created significant opportunities for privatization. As soon as a few fledgling private prison companies were able to get a foothold in the burgeoning prison system, they began to spend millions to promote its growth. Claims that the private sector could deliver better prison services at a cheaper price sounded appealing to a public that was cynical about government and eager to buy quick-fix solutions. For many politicians, privatization was good politics, offering an opportunity to look tough on crime and look fiscally conservative at the same time.

Private financing offered prison construction on the installment plan—avoiding bond measures that might require approval by voters, and making end runs around public debt limits. Private construction could cut the red tape entailed in the public procurement process and speed the time to completion. These arguments for privatization were bolstered with generous campaign contributions and political emoluments delivered by squadrons of well-heeled lobbyists.

From 1991 to 1998 the annual growth in private adult prison beds averaged 36 percent per year. The number of private prison beds in the United States as of 2001 was reported to be in the neighborhood of 119,000, but not all of these were in use.[1] The U.S. Bureau of Justice Statistics (BJS) reports that in December 2000 there were 87,369 state and federal prisoners in private prison beds. About 6,200 of the 37,000 detainees held by the U.S. Marshals Service (USMS) were housed in private facilities, as were about 3,000 of the approximately 20,000 immigrants detained by the Immigration and Naturalization Service (INS). BJS data show that at the end of June 1999, there were 13,814 inmates in forty-seven privately operated jails, but that number includes some portion of the INS and USMS detainees along with local prisoners.

EARLY DEVELOPMENT: THE PRIVATE PRISON BOOM

The economic downturn in the late 1970s provided an opportunity for ideologues at conservative think tanks such as the Heritage Foundation in Washington, D.C., and the Reason Foundation in California to push for privatization of government services. A handful of small facilities for juveniles began operation on a private, for-profit basis in the late 1970s. But incarceration of adults in private prisons was not attempted until after the Reagan administration's broad privatization initiative was launched.

When Ronald Reagan was elected president in 1980, proponents of prison privatization gained the leverage necessary to bring their ideas to fruition. The Reagan administration quickly identified 11,000 governmental activities that could be privatized. Administration officials encouraged both the USMS and the INS to contract for privately operated detention beds. Behavioral Systems won a contract to house INS detainees in 1983. The Corrections Corporation of America (CCA) commenced operation of its first contract facility in 1984, opening a 350-bed INS detention center in Houston, Texas.

The first contract to operate a state prison for adult prisoners was won in 1985 by U.S. Corrections Corporation. The firm opened a minimum-security two-hundred-bed facility in St. Mary, Kentucky. By 1988, some twenty-eight states were said to allow private operation of nonsecure or minimum-security correctional facilities—from halfway houses and juvenile group homes to detention centers for undocumented immigrants and prisons.

Hailed by Wall Street brokerage houses like Donaldson, Lufkin and

Jenrette as an exciting new industrial prospect, prison privatization's warm reception in financial circles was spurred by the already booming business of prison expansion—the private construction firms that were raking in hundreds of millions—and fueled by the investment bankers who were underwriting prison bond sales and the investors who were making a fortune in tax-free bond yields.

From the beginning, private prisons were sold as a prison reform panacea. The antiquated U.S. prison system was plagued from coast to coast with overcrowding and substandard conditions. The start-up companies were barely inaugurated when their executives began making flamboyant claims and igniting a glowing response from the national media. The *Wall Street Journal* enthused about how private prisons could take the toughest "high-risk" prisoners off the hands of beleaguered public prison managers. They envisioned the industry specializing in handling high-cost populations such as prisoners suffering with AIDS.

Ted Nissen, the founder of Behavioral Systems, claimed that innovative programming would allow maximum-security prisoners to be housed in less expensive medium-security facilities. The former San Quentin guard and self-styled prison reformer invited contracts that would require dramatic reductions in recidivism. Before he secured a single correctional contract, Wackenhut Corrections' CEO, George Zoley, pledged that his company would *never* tolerate inordinate turnover, improper treatment of prisoners, or bad food.[2]

CCA enjoyed strong financial backing from top Wall Street investment houses from the start. In 1985 the fledgling corporation held just a handful of small contracts—none for prison operations—when the company's founders made an audacious bid to take over and run the entire Tennessee state prison system. Top executives made an offer of $100 million in cash and notes in exchange for a ninety-nine-year lease of the prison facilities. When CCA President Tom Beasley sat down with Governor Lamar Alexander and the state's legislative leadership to present "the best corrections plan ever written," he brought along a Merrill Lynch official to explain how the money—along with another $150 million for capital improvements—would be financed with help from Merrill Lynch Capital Markets and Prudential-Bache.[3]

Beasley promised that CCA management would provide improvements across the board. Prisons would be built faster and cheaper. Prison management would cost less. Prison guards would earn higher pay. Prisoners would get better living conditions and improved program services, and all who were "able-bodied" would work or study forty hours a week. With the private financing CCA would bring to the table, legislators could avoid voting a tax increase. Within five years, CCA would be realizing a comfortable profit margin, and Tennessee's prisons would be the best in the nation.[4]

CCA's bid to take over the entire state prison system won support from the governor (whose wife had been a stockholder at the firm's start-up), but the scheme sparked immediate criticism in other quarters. Tennessee attorney general Michael Cody expressed misgivings about delegating such a wide span of state authority to a private contractor, pointing out that the state would lack leverage in bargaining with the company because it would lose the capacity to take the system back under public management if privatization failed to work as promised. Most legislators were not prepared to turn over the state's annual prison operating budget of $170 million to a private company without a substantial track record. CCA had to wait another six years before they finally secured a contract to run a single state prison in Tennessee.

But privatization of prisons caught on fast elsewhere. A 1988 "guide to privatization" issued by the Heritage Foundation claimed that private management had already produced evidence of "frequent" cost savings. Hailing the advent of joint venture agreements between local firms and corporate giants, the author of the *Heritage Foundation Backgrounder* expected that the involvement of huge corporations would play a significant role in advancing prison privatization. Bechtel, the multinational construction firm, was reported to be building a medium-security prison in Colorado with financing by South Korea's Daewoo International Corporation and bond underwriting by Shearson Lehman Brothers.[5]

The industry's founders promised to introduce the latest develop-

ments in business administration and technology in order to revolution-
ize the management of prisons. But from the very beginning, the key
management positions in private prisons were filled with public corrections veterans who more or less followed the familiar public model for
prison operations. Some of these left their public prison systems under
fire. David Myers resigned his post as warden of a Texas prison in 1985
to take up employment with CCA after he was accused by federal court
monitors in the landmark Texas prison case *Ruiz v. Estelle* of urging
guards to beat up inmates who had been involved in a prison disturbance. Myers rose through the management ranks at CCA to serve as
president of CCA.[6]

Myers is not the only example of a private prison executive whose exit
from the public sector came after serious accusations about prison management issues. Lane McCotter, director of business development for
the Management Training Corporation, resigned as corrections director
in Utah amid controversy after the death of a mentally ill prisoner who
had been strapped for sixteen hours in a prison restraint chair. McCotter
was already under fire for his handling of problems with medical and
mental health care when it came to light that the psychiatrist who authorized the use of restraints had been hired after he was put "on probation" by state licensing authorities for a variety of fraudulent and
questionable practices.[7]

From the beginning, prisoners placed in private correctional facilities
voiced complaints that private management did *not* provide improved
services. According to prisoners at Eclectic Communications' minimum-security facility at La Honda, California—one of the first for-profit
facilities for youthful offenders—educational and vocational training
programs there were skimpy, and Eclectic's guards were inexperienced
and unprepared to handle volatile situations.[8]

But prisoners' voices were not heeded in state legislatures or on Wall
Street. Through the next decade the industry prospered. CCA in particular became the darling of growth investors. The value of its shares
soared from $50 million when it went public in 1986 to more than $3.5
billion at its peak in 1997. CCA was ranked among the five top perform-

ing companies on the New York Stock Exchange (NYSE) from 1995 through 1997, when CCA stock traded at a high of $45 per share.

THE INDUSTRY MATURES: TROUBLES MULTIPLY

In July 1998, disaster struck CCA. When six prisoners escaped from the Northeast Ohio Correctional Center, CCA suddenly found itself in the glare of a national media spotlight. This fourteen-month-old prison had been a complete failure from the day it had opened for business. CCA managers had hired an almost completely inexperienced staff, and then they had knowingly imported hundreds of the most unmanageable prisoners from the District of Columbia's Lorton prison complex. The prison was soon awash with crudely made weapons. Twenty prisoners were stabbed, and two of them died.[9]

CCA is not the only private prison company that has been plagued with management disasters and abuse of inmates. Wackenhut prisons in New Mexico have repeatedly erupted in violence and disturbances. The death toll of five in less than a year culminated in the murder of a guard during a riot in August 1999 in the Guadalupe County Correctional Facility. Most people think that kind of violence is the norm in America's prisons, but in reality prisoner homicides are rare events. In 1998, the U.S. prison system held 1.3 million prisoners, yet there were just 59 inmate-on-inmate homicides, a rate of one murder for every 22,000 prisoners. The prisoner homicide rate in Wackenhut's New Mexico prisons from December 1998 to August 1999 was one for every 400 prisoners—not counting the death of Ralph Garcia, the Wackenhut guard.[10]

Physical abuse of youngsters by Wackenhut guards at the Jena Juvenile Justice Facility in Louisiana led to a shutdown of the institution in April 2000. A juvenile court judge in New Orleans held that the youths confined in the facility had been treated no better than animals.[11]

After these vivid lessons, one might expect that the leading companies in the private prison industry would have gotten the message that their operational practices needed a fine-tuning, but consider the chain of events over the next fifteen months in CCA's private prisons.

In August 2000, two prisoners escaped from a CCA prison in Bartlett, Texas. State investigators found serious security deficiencies. Doors had been left unlocked. No one was watching the closed-circuit TV surveillance monitors. When the prisoners cut their way through the prison's perimeter fence, a security alarm sounded, but staff in the prison's control center turned it off and did nothing.[12]

On September 12, a riot erupted in CCA's Florence Correctional Center in Arizona, a "spec" prison that holds prisoners under contracts with both the State of Hawaii and the INS. Hawaii's security experts speculated that rival prison gangs were vying for power in the facility.[13]

In October, two guards at a CCA prison in Walsenburg, Colorado, pleaded guilty in federal court to repeatedly beating a prisoner who was handcuffed, shackled, and unable to resist.[14]

In November, the Bartlett facility erupted in a disturbance that left five prisoners injured.[15] Two days later, five guards were stabbed and three others were injured when prisoners at a CCA prison in Estancia, New Mexico, took them hostage.[16]

Then, on December 14, a jury in Columbia, South Carolina, delivered a verdict that CCA guards had abused the youths confined in their juvenile prison with use of force so malicious, evil, callous or reckless, and so "repugnant to the conscience of mankind" that they determined that CCA had to pay a $3 million punitive damage award.[17]

CCA's prison operations were relatively quiet for the next few months, but in April 2001 a series of disturbing events unfolded at CCA's Florence Correctional Center. First, a Hawaiian prisoner's jaw was broken in a fight on April 6. Then, on April 11, a riot erupted in the prison yard; twenty-three prisoners were involved, of whom three were hospitalized. A prison guard received a serious injury requiring six stitches.[18]

Two prisoners turned up dead at the prison during the month. It was reported that one suffered a heart attack on April 16 after swallowing several packets of drugs in an effort to conceal them. A second prisoner died on April 25, also reportedly of a heart attack. In addition to the riot and the deaths, prison records show that six prisoners had been assaulted during the month, some of whom had been severely beaten.[19]

When prison auditors flew in from Hawaii to scrutinize the prison, they found "a prison in turmoil," with an atmosphere so hostile that most areas of the prison were deemed too dangerous to be inspected. They determined that a prison gang had taken control and was running the prison. Gang members were said to be attacking other prisoners and staff, dealing drugs, and having sex with women housed at the prison under a contract with the INS. Some staff were said to be "working" for the prison gang. One guard admitted providing drugs for prisoners in exchange for protection.[20]

Meanwhile, on the evening of April 23, 2001, prison guards at CCA's Cibola County Correctional Center in New Mexico teargassed almost seven hundred prisoners who had staged a daylong nonviolent protest of conditions at the facility.[21]

On April 24, the addiction treatment manager at CCA's Tulsa County Jail resigned, charging that she had been asked by the warden to make a "sales pitch" to local judges about sentencing offenders to a treatment program in the jail that had virtually been closed down in order to cut operating expenses.[22] Three prisoners were mistakenly released from this same facility in May.[23]

At the end of May, ten guards at CCA's District of Columbia Treatment Facility were indicted on federal bribery charges. It is alleged they had accepted money from an undercover FBI agent in exchange for smuggling two-way pagers and cash into the facility.[24]

In June, back at the Tulsa County Jail, a CCA guard resigned his post after ten Valium tablets were reportedly found hidden in his sock during an employee shakedown.[25]

On July 5, four hundred prisoners imported from Indiana to a CCA prison in Wheelwright, Kentucky, touched off their own kind of fireworks in the prison recreation area. Before they were through, they spread the disturbance to four housing units, lighting fires and tossing televisions and commodes through the windows.[26] Although the cause of the uprising had not yet been fully explained, two weeks later, CCA fired the warden and his top assistant, citing "policy violations."[27]

Industry executives will tell you that the prison management disasters catalogued here are just isolated events, confined to a handful of "underperforming" facilities. But evidence is mounting that a number of key structural deficiencies—high staff turnover, defective classification and security procedures, inadequate program services—are found in many private prisons. Although the nation's public prisons are far from problem-free, there is a growing body of evidence indicating that the private prison industry is fraught with a higher level of serious operational deficiencies than the public prison system.

A research project directed by this writer compared the quality of correctional services in a private prison run by CCA with public prisons in Minnesota. There were much higher levels of operational problems in the CCA prison: program deficiencies, unreliable classification methods, and high rates of staff turnover resulting in inadequate levels of experienced, well-trained personnel.[28] These types of operational deficiencies link directly to higher rates of problems with prison security and safety. The most troubled private facilities have shown an extremely high incidence of problems such as these.

The disparity in staff turnover rates found in Minnesota are mirrored in national data indicating that correctional officer turnover is 41 percent for the private prison industry, compared with 15 percent for public prisons.[29] Because wages and benefit costs are substantially lower in the private sector and the labor market is tight, this problem is both predictable and preventable—but the profit motive seems to bar effective action.

A private prison industry survey by James Austin, a researcher at George Washington University, compared major incidents in medium and minimum private facilities with national data from similar public facilities. There were 49 percent more assaults on staff and 65 percent more inmate-on-inmate assaults in private facilities.[30] A comparison of serious incidents in public and private prisons in Oklahoma found a far more shocking disparity. Oklahoma Department of Corrections data indicate there were 190 percent more serious incidents in private prisons in that state.[31]

Reports of escapes from secure private facilities indicate that the public safety record is also poor. There were at least thirty-seven escapes of adult prisoners from secure private prison facilities in 1999 (not counting escapes of private prisoners and detainees from juvenile facilities, transportation vans, or escorted hospital visits). The escape record of New York's state prisons—a large system of seventy facilities that hold approximately 70,000 prisoners—has been much lower. Since 1995 there have been only eight escapes from secure facilities—a rate of less than two per year.

These examples clearly show that the private prison system as a whole is falling behind the public prison system in maintaining the basic human rights of prisoners to a safe and humane correctional environment, as well as in protecting the safety of the prison staff and the public.

By 2000, the private prison industry was in bad financial shape—overleveraged and undercapitalized—because of dissatisfaction with poor industry performance on Wall Street and a growing reluctance on the part of state governments to contract for the services they offered. Between them, CCA and Wackenhut commanded 75 percent of the industry's market share. The track record of problems amassed by these two industry leaders had thrown the industry into a downward financial spiral.

It should come as no surprise that the financial viability of this industry is affected by operational disasters. From 1994 until 1999, Wackenhut's profits grew at an annual rate of 58 percent, but the impact of Wackenhut's problems in New Mexico and Louisiana severely constricted corporate earnings. And Wackenhut's stock price slid 28 percent in just two days after the guard was murdered in August 1999.

CCA was hardest hit. Mismanagement in its prisons and poor business judgment at its headquarters produced a financial meltdown. Having built new prisons "on speculation" that contracts to fill them would follow, the company found itself with a huge occupancy shortfall. With more than 9,000 prison beds standing empty, CCA stock lost 93 percent of its value during 2000. The day after the South Carolina jury hit the company with a huge punitive damage award, CCA stock hit an all-time low of nineteen cents a share. At the end of the year the company reported a fourth-quarter loss of more than a third of a billion dollars.

As operational problems sent the industry leaders into a financial slump, new contracts to house state prisoners were hard to come by. Pressure mounted against privatization from human rights advocates, public prison correctional officers, prison activists, and student leaders. The media spotlight was relentless, and public officials in many states responded by increasing their scrutiny of the private prison industry, intensifying contract compliance monitoring, "fining" vendors when services were found to be deficient, and ending contracts when problems spiraled out of control.

Colorado corrections officials stopped sending prisoners to CCA's prison in Burlington, Colorado, after security and staffing problems involving alleged guard-inmate sex scandals and lawsuits drew an intense media spotlight.[32] Texas state officials levied $625,000 in fines against Wackenhut for chronic staff shortages before reports of alleged criminal activity at the Travis County State Jail led to termination in 1999 of a contract with the operating company, and indictments of a dozen guards for alleged sexual abuse of prisoners.[33]

In North Carolina, the Department of Corrections fined CCA more than $1 million for chronic failure by the company to meet contract requirements before the management contracts at two CCA prisons were terminated in the fall of 2000.[34] Two prisons Wackenhut had operated since 1998 in Arkansas were taken over for state operation in June 2001. After the company was criticized for unsanitary conditions and prisoner idleness, Wackenhut decided not to seek renewed contracts for the two prisons, citing a tight local labor market and high medical costs.[35]

Given the recent record of serious problems, it is not surprising that demand for new private prisons at the state level had all but disappeared by 2000. Yet while most state correctional managers were taking a hard look at the private prison industry, the federal government began to fill the breach with an unprecedented level of new contract solicitations for private prison beds.

The Federal Bureau of Prisons (FBOP) faced unprecedented growth in its inmate population at the end of the 1990s. Between 1995 and 1999, the incarceration rate in the United States grew by 16 percent for the nation as a whole, but by 31 percent for the federal prison system. The FBOP population grew by 7.5 percent in 2000, while the aggregate state prison population increase was only 1.3 percent.

As the industry's troubles escalated, Congress required the FBOP to contract for more private beds, insisting on private prisons for at least half the prisoners at the District of Columbia's prison complex at Lorton, Virginia, which was scheduled to shut down.

In 1999, the FBOP began to lay the groundwork for a second massive privatization initiative, soliciting private prison beds for so-called "criminal alien" prisoners—noncitizens convicted of federal offenses who face deportation when their prison terms are completed. Proposals for more than 9,000 "contractor-owned, contractor-operated" beds were requested in less than two years.

CCA was selected in June 2000 for two new FBOP contracts—one for 2,304 beds at their long-empty "spec" prison at California City, and the second for 1,012 beds at their Cibola facility in Milan, New Mexico. These contracts were worth $760 million over the next ten years. Although a service contract is not a loan, these two contracts provided a virtual "bail-out" of an extremely troubled company that was teetering on the brink of bankruptcy.

By 2001, private prison executives were claiming that the federal contracting windfall might grow to provide as many as 20,000 beds. If true, the federal government would shower this failing industry with billions of dollars in service contracts. But while the federal government was offering a lifeline for companies that were struggling to survive, the state-level market for private prison beds remained stalled. And while CCA scoured the country for prisoners to fill more than 9,000 empty prison beds, company managers found themselves facing vigorous competition from an unexpected quarter.

CROSS-FERTILIZATION: ENTREPRENEURIAL CORRECTIONS

Proponents of privatization have long argued that competition between public and private sector corrections would breathe new, innovative vigor into the public sector. Spurred by market discipline, inspired by private-sector innovation, public managers with their sights focused on performance measures would strive for increased efficiency and enhanced performance. "Cross-fertilization" would result in improvements across the entire correctional system. Yet a review of the current state of correctional practice reveals scant evidence of innovation in private corrections. And too often the impact of competition on public correctional costs has looked less like increased efficiency and more like a race to the bottom line.

Nevertheless, the competitive spirit has spawned at least one unexpected and ironic result in the realm of public corrections. The decline of the state-level market for new *private* prison contracts has been marked by the emergence of *public* competition. Over the decade of the 1990s the private prison industry created a highly profitable national "interstate commerce" in prisoners by offering private beds in states that allowed them to build prisons "on speculation" to house prisoners shipped from other states' overcrowded prisons. By the end of the decade, between 10,000 and 15,000 prisoners were being held in prison beds in jurisdictions other than the one where they were convicted and sentenced.

In 1998, a bold new entrepreneur entered this market. Public prison managers in the state of Virginia found themselves with an excess stock of prison beds. Following the lead of the private prison industry, they opened them for business. This unprecedented development can be traced back to the national drive for "get tough" sentencing reforms that consumed the United States in the mid-1990s.

In 1994, the "tough on crime" movement hit Virginia with a vengeance. Governor George Allen had been swept into office on a campaign promise to lock up a rising tide of "violent, career offenders." During his first year in office the rate of parole release in Virginia dropped to just 6 percent, down from 40 percent under Governor Douglas Wilder. Allen's Commission on Parole Abolition and Sentencing Reform held a series of town meetings across the state, taking emotion-charged testimony from victims of violent crime. He quickly moved a legislative package that abolished parole release and introduced "truth in sentencing" guidelines that he promised would at least double the length of prison terms for violent offenders.

Allen estimated that abolition of parole would require a massive prison building program. On the eve of the 1995 legislative session he said his reforms would require building 8,100 prison beds. He proposed a $408.6 million mix of general obligation and lease-revenue bonds to finance the needed construction. Democrats countered that the governor's forecast wildly inflated the necessary number of prison beds.

Legislative critics notwithstanding, Virginia's correctional officials built six new prisons between 1995 and 2000, adding a total of 8,000 additional cells. While most crime occurs in Virginia's populous eastern cities, rural countries in the western region bear the state's highest rates of unemployment. Local officials in these areas lobbied hard for a prison. Some facilities were sited near rural towns so tiny that prisoners outnumber the local citizen population.

Four of the six prisons were designed to hold a maximum security prisoner population. In 1995, ground was broken for two "super-maximum" prisons in southwest Virginia's Wise County—the Red Onion and the Wallens Ridge state prisons. Wallens Ridge was built in an area of the state where the Westmoreland Coal Company ceased operations that had supported 750 jobs. The Wallens Ridge facility was financed by lease-revenue bonds issued by the Big Stone Gap Housing and Redevelopment Authority. The state is buying the prison facility through a twenty-year lease-purchase contract. Land for Red Onion was donated by the Pittston Coal Company. Two more maximum security prisons, Sussex I and Sussex II, were built side by side in tiny Waverly, Virginia. The $71 million Sussex I prison began receiving prisoners in 1998.

Virginia's prison construction program was further augmented when the Corrections Corporation of America opened the Lawrenceville Correctional Center, a medium-security 1,500-bed private prison, in 1998. Private construction of the prison was financed through bonds issued by the Brunswick County Industrial Development Corporation.

Despite elimination of parole and other "get tough" measures, Virginia's prison population growth slowed in 1997. With the huge prison expansion program well underway, state budget analysts realized that Virginia would have a surplus of 4,000 prison beds by 2000.[36] Governor Allen suggested that the beds could be used to reduce double-celling in the state's prison system, or to replace some of the state's older prison facilities. He proposed that the St. Brides Correctional Center in Chesapeake be closed down. But local Chesapeake politicians opposed the plan, citing the loss of jobs and local business revenues provided by the prison.

Ron Angelone, Allen's corrections director, had other ideas about how to put the projected prison bed surplus to use. Angelone decided to make as many as 3,290 prison beds available to other states for lease in order to reduce the costs of incarcerating the state's own prisoners. Even before the opening of Red Onion and Sussex II, contracts were under negotiation with Delaware, Vermont, Michigan, and the District of Columbia to import prisoners.[37]

In 1999, Sussex II opened and was housing prisoners from Washington, D.C. By the end of the year, Virginia's prisons were holding more than 3,000 prisoners imported from other states, and had negotiated a contract to import almost 500 prisoners from Connecticut to the troubled Wallens Ridge super-maximum prison. Legislative analysts began to worry that the system had become dependent on the outside cash flow, but Department of Corrections managers said they were confident they could manage to keep the beds filled.

The construction boom kicked off by Governor Allen in 1995 was completed in 2000. It had produced a surplus of 4,500 beds. By the end of the year, the state's prisons held prisoners imported from six states. At the beginning of 2001, about 1,000 state prisoners were backlogged in local jails, and 3,419 prisoners from other jurisdictions filled more than 10 percent of the state's prison beds.

Since the state placed prison beds on the national market in 1998, prisoners from Connecticut, Delaware, Hawaii, Iowa, Michigan, New Mexico, Vermont, and Washington, D.C., have been among those housed in Virginia's surplus prison beds. The revenues for housing prisoners from other jurisdictions in Virginia's public prisons provides the state with $78 million a year. This provides a significant margin of "profit." Sending jurisdictions pay $60 to $64 per prisoner per day to house their prisoners in Virginia, while the average per diem estimate for housing the state's own prisoners is just $51.14 a day. After retaining $56.7 million for operating expenses, the Department of Corrections sends $21.3 million to the state's general fund. State officials claim the excess revenue helps pay for the cost of building prisons. In January 2001, Director Angelone pushed for permission from the legislature to import another 686 prisoners, arguing that this would generate another $13.9 million for the state's general fund.[38]

The spirit of entrepreneurial corrections has taken hold in every part of the state, with more than a third of the state's local and regional jails jumping into the action. The federal government will pay from $40 to $75 per day for housing its detainees, while operational costs for local jail beds average $52.25. Thirty Virginia jails harvested a total of more than $22 million from per diem fees collected from the U.S. Marshals Service and the INS in fiscal year 2000. Fourteen of these jails derived more than 10 percent of their operating budgets from this outside income stream. The state gets its cut of this bounty, too. Virginia's Federal Overhead Recovery Fund siphoned off almost $3 million that year.[39]

While serving as a pioneer in public prison profitability, Virginia's new economic enterprise also serves to demonstrate that the private sector has no corner on operational problems. While hosting prisoners from other jurisdictions has proven to be lucrative for Virginia's state treasury, staff at some of the high-security prisons that are underwritten by the per diem fees have been charged with responsibility for a series of serious human rights violations. Critics have charged that corrections officers at Virginia's super-maximum prisons have made excessive and punitive use of electric shock stun devices, which are fired on prisoners without serious cause, and subjected them to racist remarks and harassment.[40] After a prisoner died at Wallens Ridge following repeated shocks administered with an "Ultron II" device, the American Civil Liberties Union filed a class-action lawsuit charging that use of excessive force was endemic at the prison.[41]

Despite the many claims of prisoner abuse raised against Virginia's Wallens Ridge super-max, other jurisdictions continue to send prisoners to this facility. At the end of May 2001, the Wyoming Department of Corrections transferred seventy-two ill-behaved prisoners to the facility after the U.S. Department of Justice declared that conditions in the housing unit where they had been confined at the Wyoming State Penitentiary constituted a fire hazard.[42] Two months later, the attorney general of the U.S. Virgin Islands announced a "crack down on malcontents." Prisoners who do not adjust to life in the Virgin Islands prisons would be sent to maximum-security confinement in Virginia.[43] Apparently Virginia's overbuilt prison system has found its "niche" as the convenient solution to management problems that exceed the capacity of other states' correctional managers to solve.

CONCLUSION

The private prison industry has ridden the crest of the unprecedented expansion in the scale of imprisonment in the United States. Its advent has also marked a fundamental shift in the perceived function of the correctional system. Prior to the decade of the 1980s, prisons were seen by most Americans as essential social institutions, but not ones to be welcomed "in my backyard." But then the collapse of rural economies and a lack of jobs paying a living wage set the stage for public officials and pri-

vate entrepreneurs alike to begin pushing prison construction and operation as a leading rural growth industry—and as a prime financial opportunity for investors in stocks and bonds.

"If we build it, they will come" became the watchword—particularly
at CCA—where prison development on speculation that contracts to
house prisoners would follow became a principal route to revenue
growth.[44] Construction of "spec" prisons in turn created a vast national
market in prison beds (both private *and* public) where prisoners are
bartered as commodities to be confined by the lowest bidder. Thousands of prisoners have been shuttled from prison to prison, held for
years at great distances from their families and from the communities to
which most will eventually return.

The added spur of private prisons as economic development in the
context of our "tough on crime" political atmosphere has had a corrosive effect on criminal justice policy making. Through political campaign contributions and deployment of the best lobbyists money can
buy, the industry has spared no expense to promote the idea that prison
privatization is the easy solution to the problem of overcrowded, dilapi-
dated public prisons. In state after state the availability of private prison
beds—especially those built "on spec"—has short-circuited important
public policy debates about the appropriate balance between prevention
and punishment, rehabilitation and incapacitation.

Many early critics of prison privatization predicted that industry executives would lobby for tougher sentencing laws, directly influencing
the decisions about who goes to prison and for how long. Indeed, CCA
has wielded influence on these issues through a key leadership role
within the American Legislative Exchange Council's criminal justice
task force—a powerful body that brings state legislators together with
corporate executives to draft and promote a conservative "get tough"
crime-control agenda, as well as to promote the privatization of prisons.

Putting the profit motive ahead of the public interest undercuts
sound correctional practice. A corporation's fundamental obligation is
to increase its stockholders' profits, not to increase public safety, to improve prison conditions, or to rehabilitate prisoners. Low wages pro-

duce a less qualified, less experienced correctional workforce. And skimping on food, medical services, and prison programs is not only likely to increase prison management problems in the short run; it undermines the long-term goal of preparing prisoners for release back to the community.

In the summer of 2001, still haunted by high-profile operational debacles, the two major private prison companies were struggling to revamp the image of the industry. CCA and Wackenhut joined forces with other private prison firms and service groups to launch a trade association, the Association of Private Correctional and Treatment Organizations. Attempting to recast themselves as caregivers—purveyors of drug treatment and rehabilitation services—they began trying to shift gears to meet new market realities.

Wackenhut executives stated they were turning their sights toward mental health and substance abuse clinics. The company took on operation of a 350-bed psychiatric hospital in south Florida. And they bid for a chance to construct and operate a 600-bed secure treatment facility for Florida's sex offenders who face civil confinement at the end of their prison sentences. Wackenhut's CEO George Zoley expected that 20 to 30 percent of the company's revenues would be derived from mental health and drug treatment correctional facilities in the future.

The declining crime rate, slower growth in state prison populations, and the budget squeeze brought on by a cooling national economy have combined with negative media coverage of private prison escapes, riots, and bad management to stall the market for new private prison beds—at least at the state level. CCA's speculative construction binge has left the company under tremendous pressure to fill thousands of empty prison beds while reducing its huge debt load. Ironically, stiff competition from Virginia's profit-seeking public prison system is giving the company a hard run for the money.

PART III

Fractured Families

7
Families and Incarceration

Donald Braman *

INTRODUCTION

On any given day in our nation's capital, over 10 percent of African-American men between the ages of eighteen and thirty-five are in prison, and over half are under some form of correctional supervision.[1] Inmate records also show that approximately 7 percent of the adult black male population in the District of Columbia return to the community from jail or prison over the course of a given year.[2] Estimates of the lifetime likelihood of incarceration in the District are similarly striking: Under current conditions, well over 75 percent of African-American men in the District can expect to be incarcerated at some time in their lives.[3] Finally, it is worth noting that the incarceration rate in the District is similar to the rates of other cities, suggesting that this is not a local phenomenon.[4]

While these statistics are striking in and of themselves, it is not entirely clear what they represent in terms of the lived experience of real people. What are the consequences of our extensive reliance on incarceration? What does it mean for families that live in neighborhoods that these statistics represent? Are they better off now that we have adopted "tough" sentencing practices? These are questions that can be framed using statistical data, but which, without fine-grained ethnographic data, we can't hope to answer. This chapter describes findings of a three-year ethnographic study of male incarceration in the District of Columbia designed to shed light on these questions.[5] The central finding of the study is that the dramatic increase in the use of incarceration over the last two decades has in many ways missed its mark, injuring the families of prisoners often as much as and sometimes more than criminal offenders themselves.

The impact of incarceration on families ranges from lost income and help with child care to diminished relationships and social isolation. While these impacts are felt within the families of individual prisoners, the broader social impact of mass incarceration reverberates through communities and our society as a whole. When most families in a neighborhood lose fathers to prison, the distortion of family structure affects relationship norms between men and women as well as between parents and children, reshaping family and community across generations. And, while families in poor neighborhoods have traditionally been able to employ extended networks of kin and friends to weather hard times, incarceration strains these sustaining relationships, diminishing people's ability to survive material and emotional difficulties. As a result, incarceration is producing deep social transformations in the families and communities of prisoners—families and communities, it should be noted, that are disproportionately poor, urban, and African-American.

I. COSTS OF INCARCERATION

Incarceration has immediate and direct effects on families. They lose income, assistance with child care, and bear expenses related to supporting and maintaining contact with incarcerated family members. Incarceration also has immediate effects that are less tangible, such as the added stress of knowing that one's son, husband, or father has lost his freedom and is kept in what is often a hostile and dangerous environment. The stress related to the incarceration of a family member takes a toll not only on relationships with the prisoner, but on relationships between other family members who disagree about the need to maintain family ties.

A. Lilly and Anthony

Lilly has four children. Like many prisoners, Lilly's oldest son, Anthony, relies on his family for support in many ways, including financial assistance and care for his three children. Anthony has been incarcerated for ten years, since the age of eighteen, for his involvement in a fight over a girlfriend. He was given additional time for an assault while in prison, which he claims was in self-defense, and he has another four years to serve in a privately run facility in Youngstown, Ohio, before he is likely to be considered for release.

Anthony's mother, Lilly, is fifty-one. She was married with three children by the age of nineteen when her husband left her. A single parent without a high school education and functionally illiterate, she has worked as a beautician, a construction worker, a cook, a day care provider, and at a host of other odd jobs to support her family. She is Anthony's closest family connection and provides the most emotional support and monetary assistance to him. His brother, Billy, also helps to care for Anthony's children, and sends money when he can.

B. Prison Worries

Anthony's incarceration has taken an emotional toll on Lilly, who often refers to her "prison worries." When asked what she worries about, she describes the various problems her son has had while inside:

> He was beaten over the head with a pipe, and when he protected himself, they gave him more time. And then there's the guards. He's got a skin condition and needs medical showers. Well, the guard wouldn't bring him, so he lit some paper on fire outside his cell, as protest. The guard turned the extinguisher on him. All those chemicals made him sick for weeks with breathing problems. Then they dragged him to the shower and put a fan on him to dry him. This is in winter. They [are] trying to kill him. That's my worries.

Lilly then produces affidavits from other inmates and guards describing these events in detail, and a letter promising an investigation. After she tells me about the various injustices he suffers on a daily basis, from hidden beatings to segregation and denial of visitation, she begins to cry, saying she is afraid to say or do anything because she fears her son will be mistreated as a result. Although issues regarding her son's treatment while incarcerated may be more complicated than Lilly knows or describes, her experience of her anxiety is real and persistent. To her, it is devastating and unjustified, and she feels powerless to help.

Lilly's efforts to bring her family to visit her son have also been frustrating, something she blames on the correctional system's poor handling of visitors. Indeed, most family members can rattle off a list of what they consider to be needless indignities suffered during visitation, the most common of which is flat refusal of entry on any number of grounds but which often extend to cavity searches and the offhand insult.

> The grandmother went to see him, and they wouldn't let her in because she had on a sweatshirt that was the wrong color. Can you believe, a sixty-three-year-old woman, and they wouldn't let her in. And she didn't want to go in the first place. So there I am, that's what I have to deal with, a family that doesn't want to go see their own in prison, and who would? But I got to try to bring them because he needs them, and the kids need him. And that's what I got to deal with.

C. Family Economics

Reviewing Lilly's various expenses related to her son's incarceration, it is clear that her worries about money are also fairly directly related to Anthony's imprisonment. She lives on a fixed income of $530 a month, a good portion of which is spent on Anthony. "Lord, just look at my phone bill. You know the only people this helps is the corporations."[6] One of the more unpleasant surprises to many families is the high cost of phone calls from prison. Inmates can only call collect, and additional charges for monitoring and recording by the prison phone company add up quickly—indeed, many families have their phones disconnected within two months of an incarceration.

Rather than risk another disconnection and a subsequent hefty reconnection fee, many families block calls from the prison because they cannot bring themselves to say no to the collect call. In an arrangement that is not unusual, Lilly is the main conduit for all her son's calls; because no one else will accept collect calls from prison, she patches him through to whomever he needs to talk to.

> That's the main thing I have to make sure I keep going. It's for him and his kids to keep the contact. That's why it's so hard for me. I have to pay for a three-way on the telephone so I can hook him up with the kids, hook him up with the lawyer. That's what I'm always doing, hooking him up.

Lilly's most recent bill is just over $130, over a hundred of which is for prison calls—about average for her since Anthony was transferred out-of-state five years ago; in effect, prison-related phone costs have taken up 20 percent of her total income.

Lilly also spends money on regular visits to Ohio, bringing her daughter and Anthony's children. She visits every month now; when she was younger and in better health and her son was in the District or Virginia, she would visit every week. For each visit to Ohio, the extended family pools resources for car rental, food, and a motel for a two-day trip, usually spending between $150 and $200. There are also the regular postal money orders and the twice yearly care packages allowed at the prison sent by Lilly, and Anthony's sister, grandmother, and great-aunt. But getting family to help her out is increasingly difficult.

As incarceration places additional demands on the extended networks of kinship that sustain people while outside prison, it can result in heightened tensions as well. For example, Anthony's incarceration has created problems between his mother and other family members. Lilly has lost respect for many of her kin, who she feels ought to do more to help Anthony. When asked if her relationship with the rest of her family had changed since Anthony's incarceration, Lilly says that her siblings avoid talking to her because she reminds them of what they are not doing and questions their religious "righteousness." "If you got family members that don't participate like you do, it will be a conflict, and that's what it is for me. I just tell them the way I feel. 'You running to church and you got your own people that need you.' "

In addition to phone, travel, and child care costs, there are a number of additional expenses that are difficult to quantify, such as stress-related medical expenses, Anthony's lost income (he was employed full-time prior to his incarceration), or what now amounts to years of effort by a host of friends and family members to aid him in his legal battles. Lilly makes do by getting groceries from the local food pantries, keeping her lights off, and not using the air conditioner in the summer. Given her limited income, any additional sacrifice is a significant one.

The costs of incarceration to families like Lilly's have been largely absent from discussions about incarceration. Unfortunately, these costs bear down disproportionately on families that are least able to absorb them. The effects of incarceration are particularly devastating to these families because they generally have the highest marginal costs—that is, their above-subsistence resources are already severely taxed, so any additional expenses or burdens are more keenly felt. So, when states collect tens of millions of dollars in kickbacks from collect phone calls to prisoners' families, they disproportionately burden poor and minority families that are struggling not only to keep their families together but also simply to make ends meet. And, when these families lose a family member's income or the child care that the incarcerated family member provided, the loss is significantly more acute.

II. INCARCERATION AND FAMILY ORGANIZATION

In addition to the practical and financial strain that incarceration places on relationships are its more subtle effects on family organization. Most male inmates are fathers, and most incarcerated fathers are in monthly contact with their children.[7] Added to the immediate costs described above are a host of other difficulties that, over the longer term and across generations, serve to undermine family formation and promote family dissolution. Though rarely mentioned in discussions about family integrity or family values, there is a growing body of evidence that over the last twenty years incarceration has been pulling apart the most vulnerable families in our society.[8] Interviews with families of prisoners strongly support these findings.

In addition to the clear material and emotional strain that incarceration places on relationships are more subtle effects on gender norms and behavior. As men are removed from their neighborhoods, gender ratios are skewed. Men and women in neighborhoods where incarceration rates are high described this as both encouraging men to enter into relationships with multiple women, and encouraging women to enter into relationships with men who are already attached. Further, men feel they can commit to less and ask for more from women in their relationships.

The material and emotional stresses that incarceration places on premarital and marital relationships, combined with the effect of incarceration on gender relations, produces an environment in which men and women are more likely to have children by multiple partners and children are less likely to live in households with their fathers present. Both of these consequences are strongly related to a host of negative consequences, including diminished parental investment, increased risk of sexual and physical abuse for children, and increased risk of children's own involvement in the criminal justice system. While these consequences describe many of the common stereotypes of poor, black, inner-city families, the stereotypes obscure the ways in which incarceration is intricately involved in the dissolution of the families negatively characterized by the stereotypes.

A. Davida and Charles

Davida's father, David, is in his early thirties, and he has been using and selling heroin, crack cocaine, and other drugs since he was in high school.[9] When Davida was born, her father was seventeen and serving his first adult sentence. He has been in and out of prison for her entire life, but for all the anger and disappointment that come with having a father who is addicted to and sells drugs, she still loves him. Her first

memory of her father's return home from prison is a happy one. Her father was waiting by the gate at her grandmother's when she came home
from school. "I just looked, and I was, like, 'Daddy!' And I just ran."

"At that time," she says crossing her fingers, "we was like this, you
know?" For the few months that he was out of prison, he did what he
thought a father should: prepared her breakfast, drove her to school,
bought her new clothes, and took her out to the movies. "I mean, it was
just so much that me and my father did, and it's like I missed that when
he got locked back up."

For Davida, her father's subsequent arrest remains a vivid memory:

> I remember the night the police came. They chased him in the house, and I was sitting
> there screaming "Daddy! Daddy!" . . . They came and pulled my father from under
> the car and started beating him. And I was standing there looking at them beating my
> father with nightsticks, and they dragged him through the alley and put him in the
> paddy wagon.

For Davida, though she was only twelve at the time, the arrest began a
difficult period for her. "I was *upset* by that. I started hanging out more,
started drinking. I wasn't going to school. I was, like, 'Forget school.' In
sixth grade I dropped out of school completely, I didn't want to go no
more."

Davida's reaction is not an uncommon one; other families have described the negative affect of the incarceration on the attitude and school
work of children in strong terms.[10] In Davida's case, however, her father
and her grandmother, Dolores, convinced her to return to school, telling
her that if she didn't, her grandmother would be cited for neglect and
would lose custody of her. Like many children of prisoners, Davida had
been raised largely by her grandmother. Her grandmother was not only
a surrogate-mother figure for Davida, but by accepting David's collect
phone calls and by bringing Davida to visit the prison, she was Davida's
point of contact with her father.

Davida completed the sixth grade the next year, and her father was released just before the end of the school year, surprising her at gradua-
tion. For Davida, it was one of the best days of her life: "I was just so

happy that whole day. . . . It was just me and my father, it wasn't nobody else, just me and my father." The next year, though, just after she started junior high, her father was incarcerated again. She and her grandmother had moved into her father's house, but without his income they couldn't make the payments.

> They took the house and we moved to Morse Road in Southeast. I was supposed to go to Douglass [Junior High]. I enrolled, but I never went. I never went to school. I started hanging out more now I was in Southeast; I knew a lot of boys out there, so I was hanging out with the boys, leaving home like for weeks at a time. So finally, I got locked up for truancy. Then send me down to Spruce Cottage [a juvenile facility for girls].

Davida eventually returned to live with her grandmother, but when her grandmother was hospitalized with a stroke, Davida was left alone in their apartment. She would visit her grandmother every day, and her grandmother would tell her how to take care of the house, giving her money to buy groceries and instructions on how to pay the bills. When it became clear that her grandmother would need extended care, though, Davida was packed off to stay with her mother.

Davida had a poor relationship with her mother, and she knew she would have to tread lightly in her mother's household, a fifth wheel to her mother, her mother's boyfriend, and their two sons. Davida started back to school, but as soon as she felt like she was settling into a routine, her mother's boyfriend sexually assaulted her.

> I was, like, "What am I gonna do? If I tell my mother, she not gonna believe me. 'Cause she already tell me if it come down to it, she choosing him over me anyway." So it was, like, "I could hurt myself and tell my mother and get put out on the street, or I could just . . . don't say nothing." I decided not to say nothing. I didn't want to hurt my mother.

When her grandmother had recovered sufficiently to move into an apartment of her own, Davida moved back in with her. But her grandmother's fixed income couldn't cover the rent, groceries, and other bills. Davida tried to hold down a job to help out her grandmother, but at sixteen, trying to attend school to avoid more truancy charges, it wasn't working out. Davida's grandmother couldn't keep up with the rent, and they were evicted. In Davida's mind, her father's incarceration was a significant contributing factor to her predicament. As she told me on the day of the eviction:

> My father is very important to me and grandmother, because by me not being old enough to get a regular job that maintain a stable place for us to stay, and my grandmother's retired, she only gets one check a month, we don't have much money to do this, or, you know, food or whatever. She's not with Section 8 yet, public housing, food stamps, so it's, like, my father needs to be here. . . . I'm going through a hell of a life while he's not home.

Davida's half brother, Charles, hasn't fared much better in his father's absence. Charles is thirteen, but has already been arrested three times for auto theft. His mother, Charlene, took him to a psychiatrist when he stole his first car at age six. "[The psychiatrist] told me that badness was inherited. She didn't say it in front of Charles. She said Charles has the trait of a bad child, but it was inherited from his father." At first Charlene did not believe the psychiatrist, but over time she has become convinced that she was right, and that her child is a bad seed. "Because in my heart [I think] he really do act like him, and I don't want him to act like him, because David been incarcerated from the age of twelve. And his son moving in the same footsteps, just that Charles started off six years earlier."

At the same time, she sees that Charles acts up every time that his father is reincarcerated. "If his father was here he wouldn't be acting like that. Because when Charles is on the street, he don't act like that because he know that you could page David, and David going to be right here." Charles's father, David, agrees. "A lot of things he get into, it's probably only because I'm not there."

B. Losing Families

A significant effect of incarceration is that marriage and coparenting are far less common and single female–headed households are far more

Incarceration and Father Absence in the District of Columbia

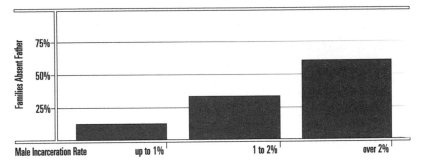

common in areas where incarceration rates are high. In the District, for example, in neighborhoods where the male incarceration rate exceeds 2 percent, fathers are absent from over half of the families.[11]

And, if we look at the 10 percent of District families living in the areas with the highest incarceration rates, we find that fewer than one in four of these families has a father present.[12]

The relationship between incarceration and father absence is, of course, a two-way street. Children like Davida and Charles, made fatherless by incarceration, are not only more likely to be abused, live in poverty, and burden their extended family, but are also more likely to be involved in the criminal justice system themselves,[13] contributing to a cycle of abuse and neglect across generations.

C. "The Ratio"

David has been married twice, but his daughter Davida and his son Charles were born outside of those marriages. Although father absence and out-of-wedlock births are not uncommon in American society in general, they are particularly common among families of prisoners. Residents of areas where incarceration rates are high relate the phenomenon to the transformation of gender ratios resulting from incarceration. As the ex-girlfriend of one prisoner told me, her options were limited because "it's just less men out here for the women."

Putting numbers to the perceived disparity, we can see that perceptions reflect a real gender imbalance in the District—particularly in areas where incarceration rates are the highest. For about one-half of the women in the District—those living in areas with relatively low incarceration rates—the gender ratio is about ninety-four men per hundred women. The other half of the women in the District—those living in areas with relatively high incarceration rates—live in areas where the gender ratio is under eighty men per hundred women. And, within this population, as the incarceration rate increases, so, too, does the imbalance. One-quarter of all women in the District live in areas where the incarceration rate exceeds 6 percent, and where there are approximately seventy-five men per every hundred women. And for the 10 percent of District women who live in areas where the male incarceration rate is the highest—about 12 percent of adult men in these areas are incarcerated—there are fewer than sixty-two men per every hundred women.[14]

The fact that men and women both perceive a significant shortage of eligible men shapes the way they approach relationships in troubling ways.[15] David, for example, found the perception of the "male shortage" widespread and influential:

> Oh, yeah, everybody is aware of it. . . . And the fact that [men] know the ratio, and they feel that the ratio allows them to take advantage of just that statistic. "Well, this woman I don't want to deal with, really because there are six to seven women to every man."[16]

As one prisoner's ex-wife lamented, women often had to lower their standards to find a man to date or marry, something that she found common and disturbing:

> Women will settle for whatever it is that their man [wants], even though you know that man probably has about two or three women. Just to be wanted, or just to be held, or just to go out and have a date makes her feel good, so she's willing to accept. I think now women accept a lot of things—the fact that he might have another woman or the fact that they can't clearly get as much time as they want to. The person doesn't spend as much as time as you would [like] him to spend. The little bit of time that you get you cherish.

III. SOCIAL SILENCE

Because incarceration places significant burdens on families of prisoners, and because these families constitute a sizable majority in the District, one might expect a fair degree of social solidarity around and public opposition to incarceration. Yet there is little public resistance to any part of the criminal justice system, and little public outcry over the level of incarceration. More striking still, most family members rarely discuss their relative's incarceration at all outside the immediate family, even in neighborhoods where incarceration rates are high. The explanation most family members gave for their silence related to concerns about the stigma associated with incarceration.

A. Louisa and Robert

Louisa and Robert are in their midthirties, and are married with one son, Jimmy. Their small, close-knit family, like many working-poor families in the District, is deeply religious. Their family is not something they take for granted, but rather something they have worked hard to achieve. Ten years ago, Robert became addicted to crack and left Louisa and three-year-old son Jimmy. After being incarcerated and completing a drug treatment program, he sought out his family and, after a period of reconciliation, they were reunited. For the next three years they attended a local church and, in Louisa's words, "kept on the straight-and-narrow," both of them working full-time at entry-level jobs, trying to save up enough money to make the down payment on a house.

Louisa looked beyond Robert's earlier abandonment and criminal activity, focusing on his return and recovery: "You know, unfortunately, we were separated. That happened. And when we reunited, he had to pay the penalty. I accepted his wrongdoing, because I just wanted our family to rejoin and reunite." Robert's criminal history cast a permanent shadow, however, as they both knew he was still wanted for a robbery he had committed during his addiction.

He was telling me, "It's inevitable," because he did do it. He said, "Well, I've got a bench warrant out on me and the inevitable might come." But he was running because he knew what it was like [in prison]. He didn't want to go back. And he wanted his life. So he got a job. We remained being a family. But he was always conscious. "Okay, we can't go that way. Too many police." Always being conscious. Trying to avoid going back.

Robert cleaned himself up and stayed off drugs for two years, got a job, started attending church and—of great significance to Louisa— praying with the family. Then, one afternoon he was pulled over for a traffic violation and it was over.

Robert's arrest and reincarceration has been particularly hard in light of the changes Louisa saw in her husband prior to his arrest, and the aspirations they had developed. They had the enthusiasm of converts for family life, and had come to think of and present themselves as morally upstanding citizens and family members. As a result, Louisa felt the stigma of her husband's most recent incarceration all the more intensely. She began to avoid friends and family, not wanting to talk about Robert's incarceration, and lying to them when she did.

You isolate yourself because, you know, even though the other person don't know what you going through, you really don't want to open up and talk to them about it. You don't want them knowing about your business. Or it's a certain amount of respect you want them to have. I just don't like the idea of people knowing that he's incarcerated. . . . You know. So I live a lie.

While Louisa is able to distinguish between her husband's past actions and who he is now as a person (as she put it, "He did commit a crime, but he is not a criminal"), she feels others are unlikely to make the same distinction. As a result of her withdrawal, her old friendships have suffered, and she has held back from making new friends.

Louisa has a number of reasons to remain guarded. Concerned for her husband's reputation when he returns, she said, she hides his incarceration so that "when they look at him, they won't slap all these labels on him and have to be afraid of him." She also feels the possibility of people judging her and her son. When asked to explain what that feeling was like, she said, "It's how people look at you. The respect you want and they don't respect you because your husband is incarcerated."

Louisa is very wary of discussing the matter not only with her coworkers and fellow church members but with other family members as well. She has told her family that he is in on a serious traffic violation instead of an armed robbery charge. It is a story that was, at least at first, believable given that a serious traffic violation would violate the terms of his parole. As she said:

> I don't talk to them. I evade the subject. They evade the subject. They, like, pleases me not to say anything about it. They pleases me not to question me about it. Every now and then my oldest sister asks. "Well when is he coming home?" And I'll just evade the question—"He'll be home soon." She said, "Oh, well didn't you say he had a traffic violation or something? Well, why are they keeping him so long for such small thing?" And I'll go and say, "Well did you go shopping and get the pink or purple blouse?" And they'll pick up. "Oh, she don't want to talk about that."

Many spouses and parents of prisoners that I have spoken with will not tell the extended family about the incarceration of a loved one, or will lie about the type of crime committed. Unfortunately, Louisa's withdrawal from friends and family has had an indirect effect on her ability to cope with her increased parenting duties, as she does not want to open herself up to discussions about her husband.

Low-income families often rely on extended networks of family and friends to cope with poverty and hardship.[7] The fluid households and expansive exchange networks that these families maintain are, while not necessarily their own ideal image of family, adaptive necessities for making ends meet in the long run. Perhaps the most significant consequence of stigma among families of prisoners, then, is the distortion, diminution, and even severance of these social ties. Stigma related to incarceration is powerful, in part, because the families know that the very same relationships on which they have come to depend can be turned against them, as social networks that provide resources are transformed into social networks of approbation. It is little wonder, then, that many family members carefully guard information about incarceration.

As a result, some family members are forced on a daily basis to choose between sacrificing the honesty of their relationships or the relationships themselves. The result can be draining and painful. For Louisa, in addition to her concern about potential labeling by the people she knows, she feels the pull of her evasion and deception at her own conscience. As Louisa describes herself lying, her voice quivers with disappointment in herself and she begins to cry. Although she does not want her husband to be branded a criminal, she does feel guilty about her lying. "[I feel] terrible because I'm living a lie. I'm living a lie. I'm not normal. I'm abnormal. Being a God-fearing woman, I have to repent and ask forgiveness from the creator, from God."

While Louisa describes crying often, depression, and a growing sense of isolation from family and friends, Robert's reaction to his incarceration is strikingly different. As is the case with many of the incarcerated men in this study, Robert is coping far better with his incarceration than is his wife. While occasionally depressed, he more frequently feels angry at the criminal justice system that has incarcerated him, and his anger and indignation are voiced in political terms that help him cope. His ability to articulate this anger in terms of the race and class bias of the criminal justice system and the supportive network of offenders around him are both tools that enable him to reframe his punishment in terms that are less stigmatizing than they might otherwise be. In fact, he often receives sympathy and encouragement from other prisoners, who sympathize with his bad break and recognize him as a basically good and decent person.

Robert's ability to cope well is in part due to his perspective on the social and political context in which his incarceration takes place. In a letter, he laid out what he thought was behind his own incarceration and that of many other black men in prison:

> Even though an annual study at the University of Michigan confirms that the overwhelming majority of drug users, abusers and sellers in America are white, even though the 1992 National Household Survey on Drug Abuse revealed that 8.7 million whites used drugs in one month versus 1.6 million blacks, the drug problem, which is an American problem, has been conveniently depicted as a black problem. The war on drugs essentially is a war on black men, America's favorite bogeyman.

Although Robert makes greater use of statistics about the criminal justice system than most of the prisoners I interviewed, his general argument was a refrain that ran through my interviews with many inmates. Robert, like many offenders, feels that he is being treated unjustly, and his ability to develop an explanation for his incarceration that extends beyond his own moral culpability is one of the things that has helped him cope with his isolation from family and community.

B. Missing the Mark

Why is Louisa bearing the brunt of the social burden for Robert's incarceration? The literature on stigma and shame indicate some of the reasons for the different reactions. First, stigma is, in many respects, "contagious"—associated not only with those who offend a social norm, but also with those associated with them.[18] As the sociologist Erving Goffman has noted, stigma travels through relationships, tainting those associated with the stigmatized.[19] The implications for families of prisoners is clear: The stigma of criminality associated with incarceration marks them as well as the person incarcerated. One family member described what he considered to be the biggest misconception about families of prisoners: "[B]asically . . . that if there's one criminal, there's another, and another . . . a consistency within every family."

Second, stigma and shame are experienced in relation to the judgment or perceived judgment of a social group.[20] So, whereas Robert lives among other offenders, Louisa remains in the community and is subject to the attendant social pressures that apply there. While many offenders may experience stigma related to their incarceration, unless their offense is considered particularly disgraceful by their co-offenders (as in cases of child sexual assault), their experience will be mitigated by the tacit acceptance of their peers, at least while they are incarcerated. Family members, on the other hand, live and work outside the prison setting, and are exposed to the judgment and condemnation of their neighbors, churchgoers, coworkers, supervisors, employers, and other community members.

Third, female relatives of prisoners also bear a significant burden as a result of gender differences in their reactions to stigma and shame. While men and women can experience shame in many ways, and gender differences do not hold true in every case, there are gender patterns that are well documented in the clinical literature. Generally speaking, women are more likely to "attribute their success to others and to blame themselves for failure" and, when they do blame themselves for failure, "are more likely to make global attributions of failure than males,"[21] and, as such, they are more likely to experience shame than males.[22] When women do experience shame, the most common sequelae are depression and withdrawal;[23] when males experience shame, on the other hand, they are more likely to respond by deflecting blame.[24] As a result, women relatives of prisoners, like Louisa, often feel the brunt of the expressive function of punishment.

Female members of nearly every family that I have spoken with have felt some stigma related to the incarceration of a loved one. Those who felt less ashamed had positive experiences of acceptance and sympathy after disclosing the status of their loved one to a close friend or family member. Significantly, however, even these family members still attempted to manage who knew and who did not, and none had "come out" completely to their extended families and at church and work.

Indeed, most of the participants in this study told no one outside of the immediate family about their relative's incarceration, and many were hiding the incarceration from extended family members. Accounts of nervous covering, public humiliation, and deeply felt stigma were common. Far from being unconcerned about criminality, familial integrity, or honesty, families of prisoners wrestle with each of these issues every day in an environment that they often perceive as hostile and unforgiving.[25] They are not shameless but, rather, deeply stigmatized and often significantly injured. While lawmakers may consider shame and injury appropriate sanctions for criminal offenders, the stigma related to incarceration is often borne by the nonoffending relatives of prisoners, something we do not see or hear about because it is in the family's interest to hide it.

IV. CONCLUSION

By employing incarceration—the bluntest of social instruments—as the primary response to social disorder, policy makers have significantly missed the mark. The overuse of incarceration harms the families of prisoners as much as, if not more than, the prisoners themselves. It does so not only through direct costs that families bear, but by restructuring families and by distorting and diminishing the relationships between family and friends. In this sense, the incarceration of an offender is not simply the sanctioning of an individual, but part of a broader corrosion of social bonds—bonds that sustain people, particularly people in difficult circumstances. And as these bonds are strained, the resources available to members of the family, both material and emotional, are also diminished. As a result, not only individual families suffer from the overuse of incarceration, but the extended networks of kinship and friendship that make up a community suffer as well.

That our public policies injure the most vulnerable families and communities in our nation is perhaps an inadvertent by-product of our determination to punish criminality, but it cannot remain inadvertent for long. Though debates about criminal justice and family have yet to converge to any significant degree, eventually they must if they are to produce any significant measure of success. Where can we start? We can begin by attending to the lives of those most directly involved. Their stories tell us that the difficult task that lies ahead is bringing offenders further into the social fold of family and community rather than removing them ever further from it.

8

The Social Impact of
Mass Incarceration on Women

Beth E. Richie

INTRODUCTION

Women in general, and women of color from low-income communities in particular, occupy a set of uniquely vulnerable positions when we consider the social impact of mass incarceration. Women's vulnerability within the prison industrial complex mirrors other settings—including traditional nuclear families, conservative community and cultural groups, occupational hierarchies, and other hegemonic social institutions—in which gender arrangements serve to marginalize some women by limiting access to social resources and undermining women's participation and our power. In the case of incarceration, these issues are further complicated by a racialized justice system designed almost exclusively by and for men. The nature of interaction within this system leaves women directly vulnerable to harsh criminal justice practices that have caused skyrocketing incarceration rates and sets in place a tightly organized system of injustices, disenfranchisement, and social stigmas that leave women the indirect victims of some of the most pernicious effects of the prison industrial complex.

The complex intersection of issues relating to race and gender is seen in a variety of social institutions. In an era of mass incarceration, these effects are magnified, both directly through increased social control and indirectly through their impact on other relationships. Thus, we can now see the interplay among processes that include the divestment of health and human services from low-income neighborhoods, increasingly rigid public policy restrictions that disproportionately affect women, and the expanding penal industry.

To explore these dynamics I will focus on several related areas of concern that suggest that the collateral consequences of mass imprisonment have had a particularly pernicious impact on women both within the criminal justice system and in the broader community. These areas are: the dramatic rise of women's imprisonment growing out of mass incarceration; the effect of mass imprisonment on women's parenting relationships while incarcerated; the effects of these trends on public responses to women's victimization; and, the changing roles of women as community caregivers. A final area, where women's roles have been enhanced as a consequence of mass imprisonment, relates to the growing leadership presence of women as antiprison activists.

INCREASING NUMBER OF WOMEN DETAINED
BY THE CRIMINAL JUSTICE SYSTEM

Although designed with a largely male image of the "criminal" in mind, the development of mass imprisonment has taken a particularly heavy toll on women. Each year 3.2 million women are arrested by the police, charged with a crime, removed from their communities, and taken to jail to await a trial or other disposition of their case.[1] Even though some women who are arrested are released within a short time period, approximately 156,000 women are held prior to trial or as sentenced prisoners, representing more than a tripling of the female inmate population since 1985.[2] While the actual numbers are much smaller than their male counterpart, the rate of increase was nearly double that for men in the period 1980 to 1997, 573 percent to 294 percent. This precipitous increase can be attributed to enhanced law enforcement strategies, formal changes in arrest protocols, rigid sentencing policies, as well as actual changes in patterns of crime.[3] Attention to the impact of mass incarceration requires that we look beyond the debates about causation, however, and consider the profile of women detained by the criminal justice system and the community conditions that they face.

Incarcerated women have a history of unmet social, educational, health and economic needs in addition to a history of victimization.[4] Typically, prior to being arrested they live in neighborhoods where they experience many of the difficulties that have come to be associated with contemporary urban poverty. Less than 40 percent of women in state prisons report they have been employed full-time prior to arrest, and about 35 percent had incomes less than $600 each month. Only 39 percent had a high school diploma or a GED. They come from communities where rates of homelessness have increased substantially, reaching 40 percent in some studies of women detained in U.S. jails.[5]

Not surprisingly, these low-income neighborhoods are often communities of color. Consequently, the racial/ethnic profile of women in jails and prisons represents one of the most vivid examples of racial disparity in our society; by far, the majority of women who are incarcerated in this country are women of color. Nearly two-thirds of those confined in jails or in state and federal prisons are black, Hispanic, or of other (nonwhite) ethnic groups.

Given the dramatic rise in the incarceration of women, we know that over the course of a lifetime, 11 out of 1,000 women will be incarcerated. Here, too, the racial/ethnic dynamics are dramatic. Five out of 1,000 white women can expect to go to prison, compared with 36 of 1,000 black women and 15 of 1,000 Hispanic women.[6]

The majority of incarcerated women have been convicted of nonviolent, economically motivated drug-related offenses that account for the largest source of the total growth among female inmates in the 1990s (35 percent nationally). In some states, these dynamics have been particularly dramatic. In New York State, for example, the number of women arrested for drug offenses increased by 98 percent between 1986 and 1995, convictions increased by 256 percent, and prison sentences by 487 percent.[7] Some scholars have argued that this pattern of illegal behavior is decidedly gendered; that drug sales and other nonviolent crimes are "survival crimes" committed by women to earn money, to feed a drug-dependent life, and to escape both terrifying intimate relationships and brutal social conditions.[8]

The profile of women detained in the criminal justice system suggests that the increased incarceration of disadvantaged women of color with a history of traumatic experiences for drug-related offenses is senseless and cruel. Being lured into the illegal drug economy in an attempt to earn a living or support an addiction, being threatened or coerced into property crime by fear of abuse, or being denied services because of a felony conviction is evidence of the collateral damage women experience as a result of the growth in the penal state. There is very little that is "just" about incarcerating women who are in conflict with the law because of their social and economic circumstances, and incarceration merely exacerbates the diversion of resources from needed community-based services.

WOMEN PRISONERS AS PARENTS

One of the most significant consequences of mass incarceration for women is the almost irreparable damage done to their role as mothers and their status as parents when they are removed from their communities and detained in correctional facilities. Conservative estimates suggest that 75 percent of women in prison are mothers, and two-thirds have children under the age of eighteen. Currently, 1.5 million children under age eighteen have parents in prison[9]; of these, 125,000 have a mother in prison. These figures actually underrepresent the full scope of the problem in that they do not count women who are nonbiological caretakers of dependent children, women who are arrested while raising their younger siblings, nieces, and nephews, or children in their extended social network.

Conditions of confinement in most correctional facilities pose serious obstacles to parenting. First, there is the obvious: sudden and unexpected forced separation of mothers and children. Then, most state and federal facilities are located long distances from the urban neighborhoods where children of incarcerated women live, making visiting logistically and economically difficult if not impossible. The lack of accessible public transportation, obscure visiting hours, and long waits present serious barriers to children's visits. In the case of jail visits, the policy trend is to limit contact with visitors, to prohibit children from entering jails altogether, or to otherwise create regulations that interfere with maintaining family bonds. With a few notable exceptions, correctional facilities do little to support mothers in their parenting role despite evidence that suggests that parenting may hold a central place in women's rehabilitation and future success.

Perhaps one of the most blatant examples of the disregard held toward mothering can be found by exploring the treatment of pregnant women who are incarcerated. Between 6 percent and 10 percent of all women entering correctional facilities are pregnant, most with high-risk prenatal conditions. Recognizing that health access in general is shaped by economic status, it may not be surprising that comprehensive reproductive health care is not a priority in most correctional facilities. However, the overt contempt for pregnant women is deeply troubling. In some states until recently, women were forced to deliver babies while in shackles. Most departments of corrections deny regular access to contraception and HIV prevention strategies, and women are almost unilaterally denied abortion services. The serious long-term medical and psychological consequences of neglectful and hostile treatment during pregnancy must be counted as collateral damage associated with mass incarceration.

There are other important aspects of this crisis that warrant attention, including the concrete impact on family systems when women lose custody of their children, the more subtle impact on low-income women of color when motherhood is delegitimized, and, of course, the direct impact of mass incarceration on children.* Those women who are most

---

* It is important to consider the paradoxical ways that any consideration of mothering, while important to the overall argument in this paper, potentially serves to reinscribe the traditional gender roles that have not always served women well. That is, while barriers to low-income women's mothering is an important aspect of an assessment of collateral damage, focusing on women only as mothers or caretakers of children can be used to erase women's other social roles. Here the attempt is to place a full analysis of women's lives at the center of the discussion of the social consequences of mass incarceration and to discuss mothering as only one aspect of this.

vulnerable to the dimensions of the penal state are also most vulnerable to "child welfare" policies and practices. Thus, for example, a woman of color in a low-income neighborhood may have an open case or a history of child protective involvement with her family. Once she is arrested and detained, she is vulnerable to losing custody of her children. Because women are often the primary caretakers, the result is often placement of their children in a chaotic foster care system.

It should be emphasized that many women in conflict with the law understand their limitations as parents and therefore seek assistance from the system that may result in voluntary termination of parental rights. For the purposes of this discussion, I am distinguishing those situations, where women have initiated termination voluntarily or truly cannot care for their children, from the automatic or coerced termination of parental rights that often accompanies women's arrest and incarceration. A recent ruling by the Illinois Supreme Court illustrates this point, declaring that parents could lose custody of their children based on past jail time. Thus, a woman who went to prison and then, years later, became a parent could have her rights terminated if she ever went to prison again.

The second area of impact on parenting is the more subtle effect that comes when a whole sector of society is robbed of one of its most fundamental social and emotional roles, that of mothering. The combined impact of the rate at which low-income women of color are losing custody of their children and the erosion of citizenship rights resulting from involvement with the criminal justice system has had a devastating impact. This crisis of legitimacy and the serious stigma and shame it causes is one of the most profound aspects of imprisonment today.

This discussion would be incomplete without an examination of the serious impact that delegitimizing the mothering function has on children themselves. Children of incarcerated women are among society's most vulnerable citizens and are the hidden victims of the expansion of the penal state. Their lives are destabilized when they are passed from household to household and when their material needs go unmet as financial resources are absorbed by the costs associated with a family member's incarceration. If they are placed in the foster care system, there is often little monitoring of the quality of their environment, and there may be a series of disincentives for their foster parents to maintain a relationship with the incarcerated parent. Shame, guilt, anger, and resentment are typical reactions of children to the loss of a parent through incarceration, and the lack of acknowledgment, support, and services may result in long-term consequences for them.

THE VICTIMIZATION OF WOMEN

Ironically, while mass imprisonment is premised on a goal of crime control, low-income women of color who are victims of violence may in fact suffer directly as a result of these policies. This is true for several related reasons. First, because of the devastating incarceration rates for men of color, within these communities concerns for women's safety is often placed in a competitive position for attention. Second, as a result of often-eroding trust between low-income communities and law enforcement agencies, women may be more reluctant to seek help from the justice system. Finally, the punitive orientation of mass imprisonment policies has in many ways blinded us to more comprehensive approaches to the problem of women's victimization.

Mass incarceration not only diverts attention from more constructive approaches to the problem of violence against women, but it also fuels the division between potential allies by constructing false dichotomies that serve to undermine a truly progressive movement for social change. Progress toward that goal, however, cannot be made without sensitivity to the ways that some women of color are victimized by men in their families and neighborhoods and how, in most cases, the perpetrators are not held accountable for their abuse.

The scope of the problem of violence against women has been clearly established as a significant and persistent social issue with serious consequences for individuals, families, and for society as a whole.[10] In the case of domestic or intimate violence, a million women experience violence from a male partner (husband, ex-husband, boyfriend, or former boyfriend) each year. Although most research has focused on physical abuse, evidence suggests that emotional abuse also has serious psychological consequences for female victims of domestic violence.[11]

A review of the literature on sexual assault reveals a problem of similar proportions. According to the Crime Victims Research and Treatment Center of the National Victim Center, close to 700,000 women are raped every year in the United States, the highest rate of any industrialized nation.[12] The 1998 Violence Against Women Survey found that 17 percent of all women aged eighteen years and older had been raped.[13] Although less well documented, sexual harassment, stalking, and exploitative involvement in the sex industry are also understood to be serious, common, and threatening experiences for women who carry significant physical, emotional, and social consequences.[14]

Women of all races and ethnic backgrounds experience domestic and sexual violence. While less well documented, there is also solid evidence to suggest that the incidence and types of domestic violence in same-sex relationships are comparable to that in heterosexual relationships.[15] However, while the overall rates may be similar, emerging research suggests that variables such as socioeconomic status, cultural background, sexual orientation, and age may influence the impact of domestic violence on different groups of women.[16] Factors such as the limited availability of crisis intervention programs, differential use of weapons during an assault, fear of exposing one's sexuality, and lack of trust of law enforcement agencies may heighten some women's vulnerability to intimate violence.[17]

Beyond a general concern about women's safety and the particular dynamics that complicate seeking help by some women lies the urgent need for a new analysis of violence against women whose experiences fall outside the paradigms that have informed the mainstream literature reviewed above.[18] For, while there is ample evidence to suggest that violence against women is a shared problem across different sectors of society, the particular experiences of some women are not at all represented in the prevailing body of research or the advocacy response to it.

One such population that has not been studied is women of color from low-income neighborhoods, where the impact of mass incarceration is being most keenly felt. In these communities, a collateral consequence of mass imprisonment may be that relations between law enforcement and the community have become so strained that women have lost faith and confidence in the very societal institutions that should be addressing their needs. For example, women who are abused may be particularly reluctant to call the police, to use mainstream social services, or to report incidence of abuse to agencies because of their marginalized social position, their precarious legal status, or their loyalty to their vulnerable (albeit abusive) partners. If they themselves are involved with illegal activities, then these issues become even more complex; the standard law enforcement response to violence against women simply does not work. Research on workplace violence, for example, does not include places where illegal drug transactions are taking place. Similarly, women involved in prostitution or otherwise working in the sex industry are less likely to report having been raped by a customer or stalked by a pimp. Young women who are truant do not appear in data collected at school regarding sexual harassment, and if a woman is hurt by her crime partner during a robbery or sexually harassed in a place where stolen goods are collected, there is little likelihood that she will call the police.

The Bureau of Justice Statistics has confirmed the work of scholars such as Angela Browne that indicate the need for research on violence against women who are involved in illegal activities.[19] Their research indicates that half of all women in jails and prisons reported having been physically or sexually abused before their imprisonment, a much higher rate than for the overall population. The National Clearinghouse for the Defense of Battered Women reports that more than half of all women in detention have been battered or raped.[20] Higher rates of physical and sexual abuse of women in communities from which the prison population is drawn is important in and of itself; however, when considered within the context of mass incarceration, other important issues emerge.

It has been tempting—given the deadly consequences of violence against women—for some advocates to call for increased law enforcement responses when cases of serial assailants emerge. But, in fact, mass incarceration and the buildup of the prison industrial complex has done little to protect women from abuse, to increase the likelihood of safety in their neighborhoods, or to hold men who batter, rape, stalk, and harass them accountable. Their particular vulnerability is not considered by advocates of mandatory arrest approaches or pro-prosecution efforts that are theoretically designed to decrease the rate of violence against women. In effect, perpetrators of violence against women in low-income communities who may have a substance abuse history, who may be involved in the illegal sex industry, or who may be homeless are typically not held accountable. Law enforcement agencies, neighborhood organizations, and community leaders do not take the issue of violence against these women seriously, in great part because the women, themselves, are not valued. Real safety for women, especially economically marginalized women, will only come through a broad-based approach that recognizes that a criminal justice response is only one of several components to an effective strategy. The additional necessary elements include addressing the economic circumstances of low-income women's lives that constrain their options, providing culturally sensitive social services, particularly housing and employment assistance, and initiating a community dialogue that gives prominence to a search for constructive and empowering responses.

WOMEN AS FAMILY MEMBERS
AND COMMUNITY CAREGIVERS

Critics of the prison industrial complex have argued that one of the most significant social consequences of mass incarceration is the destabilization of communities. This impact has typically been considered from the perspective of men being removed and reentering the community and the effect of structural adjustment and labor market shifts on social and human capital in low-income neighborhoods. Few of these discussions focus specifically on women in these communities, except to describe what happens to them when there aren't men available for the establishment of traditional families. As in the case of responding to the problem of violence against women, framing the argument so narrowly in male-centered terms ignores particular gender relationships and important community dynamics.

In addition to the social, cultural, and economic impact of mass incarceration on mothering and other functions of the nuclear family, high rates of incarceration have altered other aspects of life that have particular effects on women who reside in the communities from which most of the incarcerated population are drawn. Life has become more difficult for the women "at home" (just as it is increasingly difficult for incarcerated women) in a society where criminal/legal systems are viewed as the primary method of resolving health, social, and economic problems. The already overburdened role of caretaker in low-income families is further complicated by the constant threat women face of possible arrest and detention of a family member, chaotic trials, long prison sentences, expensive visits and phone calls from correctional facilities, confusing parole hearings, probation requirements that may involve making a change in household arrangements if more than one family member has a felony conviction, and the ever-present risk of rearrest. Women are busy attempting to shelter their children from dangerous environments, trying to protect them from aggressive law enforcement practices, and keeping themselves out of the state's child protection apparatus.

Thus, in the era of mass incarceration, women must assume new burdens as community caregivers. Some women describe this as the constant work that they are required to do to keep their family members from the long reaches of the criminal justice system. Divestment of community-based services has meant that there are few supports for these gender-specific efforts and, typically, women pick up the slack and must deal with the long-term social and emotional consequences to their communities.

We can see this clearly in the many ways in which women need to cope with the problem of drug abuse. By and large, it isn't agencies but women who are dealing with the consequences of addiction in families and households: women struggling to manage budgets consumed by addictions; women trying to hold families together when ties are weakened by prolonged absence; women attempting to manage the shame and stigma of incarceration; and women trying to prevent children from becoming casualties of the war on drugs.

Not only are these caretaking activities being performed within the context of seriously disadvantaged neighborhoods, but family unions are also seriously weakened by mass incarceration; fewer and fewer adults are available to assume these tasks or to offer emotional or material support for them. Women's contributions are invisible, undervalued, misinterpreted and, in some instances, even criminalized, as in the case of women charged with conspiracy for not cooperating with law enforcement's investigations of their family members.

Women's caretaking roles have historically been undervalued in most sectors of society. Against the backdrop of divestment of basic services in low-income neighborhoods and mass incarceration, women of color are now burdened in ways that have untold costs and consequences.

WOMEN AS ANTIPRISON ACTIVISTS

Along with the impact of mass incarceration on women's victimization, parenting, and the stress and stigma associated with community caretaking, other areas of women's lives have been affected as well. One such effect has been a growing leadership presence of women involved as resisters and activists on issues of penal reform. While low-income women of color occupy an extreme position of structural disadvantage, their struggles, strategies, pain, and triumphs over despair offer key lessons for organizing policy reform.

In the realm of issues related to incarceration, women have assumed key leadership positions, advocating for critical resistance to the prison-industrial complex, sentencing reform, a moratorium on the death penalty, and the development of alternative sanctions. Many of these campaigns, while they include women's issues, are not specifically focused on gender inequality or disenfranchisement of women of color in low-income neighborhoods. This is also true when looking at the work being done by activists on high profile cases of unjust treatment, false accusations, or other miscarriages of justice. That women have assumed key national leadership roles in various campaigns to interrupt the process of mass incarceration—despite the fact that the kind of gender-specific collateral damage presented in this paper has not always made its way into the discussions of the social consequences of mass incarceration—is noteworthy.

A similar pattern is emerging at another level, where women are active workers in grassroots mobilization efforts to resist the growth of the prison industrial complex. In some places these efforts take the form of protesting local ordinances, challenging budget allocations, passing protective legislation and working on cross-issue collaboration on issues such as prisoner reentry. An essential part of this work has been engagement with those progressive elements of the feminist-based antiviolence movement to provide support for women of color who have been victimized by domestic and sexual violence, challenging patriarchal institutions in communities of color while at the same time demanding respectful attention to the impact of institutional racism on survivors' experience of abuse. This has not been an easy agenda; however, women have been key activists at these crossroads.

The last area of activism and resistance work that is important to note is what I call the daily work of building community. Here I include the work of women who visit jails and prisons as family members or volunteers, accepting responsibility for nonbiological children, and standing with people being released back to their community. I also include here the ways that women who are incarcerated support one another and build community on the inside despite harsh conditions of confinement. This work is not routine, but courageous and exhausting, involving daily efforts to develop trust and support within an ever-expanding penal system.

CONCLUSION

These long-term investments—on a grand national scale and in local or private spaces—offer those attempting to understand the impact of mass incarceration an important glimpse of hope. For against the backdrop of sometimes-extreme victimization, aggressive hostility, rigid public policy, and devaluing of key contributions, women are resisting. The story of collateral damage is seriously incomplete without understanding the particular ways that women are affected by mass incarceration and the ways we are engaged in the process of change.

9

Children, Cops, and Citizenship: Why Conservatives Should Oppose Racial Profiling

James Forman, Jr. *

"How can you tell us we can be anything if they treat us like we're nothing?"
Sophomore, Maya Angelou Public Charter School, Washington, D.C., 2001

T he Maya Angelou Public Charter School in Washington, D.C., is the kind of institution conservatives support—a place that offers opportunity but demands responsibility. Students are in school ten and a half hours a day, year-round, mostly studying core subjects such as reading, writing, math, and history. When not in class, they work in student-run businesses, where they earn money and learn job skills. Students who achieve academically are held in esteem not only by their teachers but by their peers. Those who violate the school rules are subject to punishment, including expulsion, as determined by a panel of students.

The school delivers a profoundly traditional message to kids: work hard and play by the rules, contribute to your community, and no matter what your background, society will give you a chance. As for race, the message is that our nation's history of racial oppression should be a motivation, not an impediment, to higher achievement.

The results have been impressive. The Maya Angelou student body is 98 percent African-American; over 95 percent of our students qualify for free or reduced lunch. Most Maya Angelou students have had academic difficulty at their previous schools. More than one-half had stopped attending school on a regular basis, and more than one-third had been in the juvenile justice system. Yet more than 90 percent of graduates go on to college, compared with a citywide rate of just 50 percent. This success stems in part from the school's small classes, innovative curriculum, and dedicated staff. But it is also in part due to the school's conservative ethos: if you work hard and don't make excuses, society will give you a chance, no matter what your background is. Though Maya Angelou is the school I know best, I also know there are other adults, both in this city and in others, who are struggling hard to teach similar skills and values.

But what does it mean to preach these virtues if the government's most visible representatives in your community violate those rules routinely, and at your expense? Police officers are the principal arm of the state that inner-city kids see. With the exception of teachers, whom adolescents do not see as public officials, police officers are the government representatives with whom they have the most contact. This places an awesome responsibility on officers of the law, because how they treat young people, particularly in inner-city neighborhoods that tend to be heavily policed, will have a profound impact on how kids begin to see the state, society, and themselves.

Unfortunately, the news is not good. Since the early 1970s this country has increasingly turned to the criminal justice system as a solution to urban problems. The most striking result has been the huge growth in the nation's overall prison population between 1972 and today.[1] The costs of our increased commitment to incarceration are disproportionately borne by the African-American community. Increasingly, the same impulses that have led the nation toward accepting higher and higher incarceration rates have also fueled support for increasingly punitive approaches to policing. Here, too, communities of color are most directly impacted.

Most of the nation is now aware of the phenomenon of racial profiling. In state after state, statistical studies are showing that being black substantially raises the prospect of a person's being stopped and searched by the police.[2] Responsible law and order conservatives concede what is happening on the street to people of color.[3] These studies confirm what black people (and, frankly, many police officers)[4] have long known. As Henry Louis Gates has pointed out, stories of being singled out by the police are shared regularly within the black community.

> Blacks—in particular, black men—swap their experiences of police encounters like war stories, and there are few who don't have more than one story to tell. Erroll McDonald [Pantheon Books' executive director] tells of renting a Jaguar in New Orleans and being stopped by the police—simply "to show cause why I shouldn't be deemed a problematic Negro in a possibly stolen car." Wynton Marsalis says, "Shit, the police slapped me upside the head when I was in high school. I wasn't Wynton Marsalis then. I was just another nigger standing out somewhere on the street whose head could be slapped and did get slapped." The crime novelist Walter Mosley recalls: "When I was in Los Angeles, they used to stop me all the time, beat on me, follow me around, tell me that I was stealing things." Nor does William Julius Wilson—who has a son-in-law on the Chicago police force—wonder why he was stopped near a small New England town by a policeman who wanted to know what he was doing in those parts.[5]

Some incidents take an almost comical twist, such as when the police targeted Paul Butler, an African-American law professor at George Washington University. Butler was walking home to his house in Washington, D.C., while carrying a copy of *Race, Crime and the Law*, by Randall Kennedy, perhaps the nation's most well-known African-American law professor. During the impasse between Butler and the officers, Butler asked for the opportunity to read from a section of Kennedy's book that discusses racial profiling. The officers listened, but they nonetheless refused to leave Butler's presence until his neighbor identified him as a resident.[6]

These well-publicized cases, however, threaten to obscure an important reality. Celebrities and law professors can tell their stories and file lawsuits. But for the everyday black kid in the neighborhood struggling just to survive, being targeted by the police is not only more routine, it is more disempowering. There doesn't appear any way to fight back. These kids face officers who, as one admitted, "are willing to toss anyone who's walking with his hands in his pockets. . . . We frisk 20, maybe 30 people a day. Are they all by the book? Of course not; it's safer and easier to just toss people."[7]

The "tossing" of kids happens with alarming regularity to Maya Angelou students. Here is a sampling of stories, each of which occurred on the corner of 9th and T Streets, NW, in front of our school, during the spring of 2001:

—On numerous occasions, officers have arrived at the corner in front of our school, thrown our students against the wall, and searched them. These searches are not polite encounters. They are an aggressive show of force in which children are required to "assume the position" (legs spread, face against the wall or squad car, hands behind the head). They are then searched by officers, who feel every area of their body. Our students have committed no crime other than stand outside of a school that is unfortunately in a high-drug neighborhood. At no point during these frequent searches have officers recovered any drugs, and none of our students has ever been found in violation of the law as a result of these stops.

—A few weeks after we began complaining about these incidents, another police officer chased one of our male students into the school, wrestled him to the ground, and then pulled out a gun. According to the officer, this was because the officer "knew this kid" from the past and believed he was a bad kid, likely carrying drugs. No drugs were found.

—Two weeks later, after one of our students refused to leave the corner in front of our school (the student was in compliance with school rules and D.C. law, taking a short break between classes), an officer grabbed the student and began to arrest him and place him into a police van. Only after a staff person came outside did the officer let the student go.

Liberals generally decry such incidents; conservatives generally deny that they take place. "The racial profiling we're all supposed to be outraged about doesn't actually happen very much," explained Jonah Goldberg in the *National Review*. "The idea that legions of law-abiding black folks are pulled over just for 'Driving While Black' is wildly over-hyped." And even those conservatives who admit the practice's frequency still insist it does more good than harm. "The evidence suggests," William Tucker wrote in the *Weekly Standard*, "that racial profiling is an effective

law enforcement tool, though it undeniably visits indignity on the innocent."

But conservatives who deny the reality of racial profiling or dismiss its
importance are missing the fact that racial profiling profoundly violates
core conservative principles. Conservatives, after all, are who remind us
that government policy doesn't affect only resources; it affects values,
which in turn affect people's behavior. This argument was at the heart of
the conservative critique of welfare policy. For years, conservatives argued that welfare policies—such as subsidizing unmarried, unemployed
women with children—fostered a culture of dependency.[8]

If sending out welfare checks with no strings attached sends the
wrong message, so does racial profiling. For the conservative ethos about
work and responsibility to resonate, black citizens must believe they are
treated the same way as white citizens—that with equal responsibilities
go equal rewards. In *The Dream and the Nightmare*, which President
Bush cites as one of the most influential books he has ever read,[9] the
conservative theorist Myron Magnet writes, "What underclass kids need
most is an authoritative link to traditional values of work, study and self-
improvement, and the assurance that these values can permit them to
claim full membership in the larger community.[10] Magnet quotes Eugene
Lang, a businessman who promised scholarships to inner-city kids who
graduated from high school: "It's important that [inner-city kids] grow
up to recognize that they are not perpetuating a life of a pariah, but that
the resources of the community are legitimately theirs to take advantage
of and contribute to and be a part of."[11]

Magnet is right. But random and degrading searches do exactly the
opposite. They tell kids that they are pariahs, that no matter how hard
they study, they will remain potential suspects. As one Maya Angelou
student explained: "We can be perfect, perfect, doing everything right,
and they still treat us like dogs. No, worse than dogs, because criminals
are treated worse than dogs." Or, as another student asked me in pointing out the contradiction between the message delivered by the school
and that offered by the police: "How can you tell us we can be anything
if they treat us like we're nothing?" The stigma from this mistreatment

makes it all the more difficult for striving kids to achieve Magnet's laud-
able goal of "claiming full membership in the larger community." Not
only do they not have full membership in the community, they do not
have the most basic right to stand in front of their school or walk down
the street without being searched.

These searches make those of us who are telling kids to do right look
like dupes. Kids of color in inner-cities are pulled in opposite directions.
On the one hand, there are teachers, counselors, youth workers, and
other responsible community members who push, pull, cajole, beg, and
otherwise do everything possible to keep kids on the right path. This
group is doing just what conservatives welcome—we are addressing
what conservative criminologist James Q. Wilson calls "the intangible
problems, the problems of values," the problems that sometimes make
"blacks less likely to take advantage of opportunities."[12] Against this
group is arrayed a variety of forces pressuring kids to choose crime and
other irresponsible options. By treating kids who are trying to do the
right thing as if they are hoodlums and thugs, police harassment rein-
forces the notion that the good guys are deluded, thereby undermining
our legitimacy as role models. Why should kids believe anything we say
if we are regularly proven wrong about something so fundamental? The
police instead reinforce the legitimacy of those who teach young people
that since the state will forever treat you as an outlaw, you might as well
act like one.

Racial profiling also runs contrary to another conservative tenet:
Everyone must follow the rules. If there is anything we preach at Maya
Angelou, it is that rules matter. We say that students have to live by and
be governed by a set of rules because as citizens in society we live by
rules. Order and security depend on a community's commitment to
abide by these rules. But these teachings are undermined whenever police stop and search innocent children. Teenagers have a general sense of
how the police are supposed to treat them. While only some can name
the specific constitutional command (the Fourth Amendment's protection against unreasonable searches and seizures), all are aware that the
government does not have the unfettered right to search you when you

have done nothing wrong. These young people know it is wrong when the police shove and search them for no reason; they know it is wrong when an officer chases them into their school simply because the officer "knows" them from the neighborhood; they know it is wrong when the police arrest them because they have not heeded an unlawful directive to move from outside their own school. Yet police misconduct teaches them that the government violates these rules every day and that they have no recourse. If their government does not follow the rules, reason the students, why should they?

And then there is the question of color blindness. If there is a single fundamental tenet of conservative philosophy on race, it is that historic governmental discrimination against minorities has been eliminated (and that private discrimination has radically diminished).[13] Conservatives argue that given that racial discrimination is on the wane, continuing to focus on race is counterproductive. Against the backdrop of historic discrimination, it is essential, say conservatives like Abigail and Stephen Thernstrom, that we fight the "politics of racial grievance" and counter the "suspicion that nothing fundamental ha[s] changed."[14] Failure to do so will consign poor people of color to another generation of missed opportunity, says Magnet, because "when you believe that the government or the whole white race is waging genocidal biological warfare against you, how can you possibly see that opportunity is open to you? If you believe that the government is forcing blacks into such self-destructive acts as taking drugs and sharing dirty needles, how can you possibly think that you have the power or the responsibility to forge your own fate?" Seizing the day for the underclass means overcoming the victim mentality, understanding that there is a core fairness to the system that did not exist two generations ago, and acting accordingly. According to Magnet, society "needs to tell [blacks] that they *can* do it—not that, because of past victimization, they cannot."[15]

We will not convince young people of color that race is no longer an obstacle, however, when the government through the police teaches that it is. Students such as those at Maya Angelou are acutely aware that when they are searched and seized illegally, race has played a factor. They know that police are not treating young people the same way across town at Sidwell Friends and St. Albans, schools for Washington's elite. They don't need Ron Hampton, executive director of the National Black Police Association, to tell them that "the way you police in an affluent white community is not the way you police in a poor black community."[16] That the police are the ones doing the harassing is all the more demoralizing for those who seek to move beyond the color line. For African Americans, mistreatment at the hands of the police is a historical fact with great resonance. By turning Magnet's "past victimization" into present victimization, the police undo efforts to move beyond race.

Conservatives should also be able to understand (and understand more quickly than liberals, who have trouble with this point) that police harassment of kids of color is a problem regardless of the race of the officer. For a host of reasons, including the fact that many police forces are only recently overcoming their segregated past, many mistakenly assume that racism is only an issue when the officers are white. The uncomfortable truth is that police harassment comes in all colors. As Ta-Nehisi Coates says in the *Washington Monthly*, "In more and more communities, the police doing the brutalizing are African-Americans, supervised by African-American police chiefs, and answerable to African-American mayors and city councils. In the case of [Washington, D.C., suburb] Prince George's County, the brutality is cast against the backdrop of black America's power base, the largest concentration of the black middle class in the country."[17] That's why the typical remedy of hiring more police officers will not by itself change practices. As Jill Nelson points out, more officers of color will not "somehow create a kinder, gentler police force, when evidence shows that, as often as not, the blue uniform trumps black or brown skin."[18] Changing the complexion of the officers won't make a difference, says Ron Hampton, "Not if we are going to send [black officers] through the same training academy that [white officers] have been going through. The policies and practices change when the philosophy changes. Why do we think that if we hire more blacks and women, that if we send them to the same institutions, that things will change?"[19] In the meantime, black faces on officers doesn't change the equation on 9th and T Streets. As one Maya Angelou student responded when asked whether black and white officers treated kids differently, "No, black or white, none of them know us, they don't know who we really are or what we're trying to do with our lives, they just see us and think trouble. You think they would try that stuff with white kids? Never."

In response to the random stops and searches the Maya Angelou students experienced this past spring, students organized a meeting with the local police officers. After students explained their perspective, the officers present responded by suggesting that students who wanted to be exempted from random seizures should wear large "Maya Angelou Public Charter School" identification cards in a prominent place on the outside of their clothing. Throughout the antebellum South, of course, any unsupervised black person was suspect, and in North Carolina, to make it easier for law enforcement, blacks who were not slaves had to wear shoulder patches with the word "free."[20] It would trivialize slavery to equate those laws to the officers' suggestion of I.D. cards for students. Still, given our nation's racial history, it cannot be denied that a child's sense of victimization will not be quickly overcome as long as the government suggests that I.D. cards are necessary for black children to avoid being searched by the police.

So, what is the downside to changing how police treat minority children? Will taking a stand against police targeting of inner-city kids jeopardize law and order? No. Let me be clear: this is not a call for an end to policing, or for a relaxation of crime control. Nor do I suggest we abandon the many law-abiding minority community members who seek relief from neighborhood drug dealers and gang-bangers. Maya Angelou students also want to be protected from crime. But there is nothing inconsistent between wanting order and seeking a new approach to policing. We want the police in our communities *and* we want them to treat us equally and fairly.

Indeed, changing the way police do business may be the only way to achieve lasting crime control. Current police practices have created a level of hostility between police and communities of color that undermines community support for crime fighting. Imagine that you are seventeen, standing outside of your school during a break from class, talking to friends, laughing, playing, and just relaxing. Imagine that, for no reason, squad cars pull up, officers come out shouting, guns drawn, and you are thrown up against the wall, elbowed in the back, legs kicked apart, and violently searched. Your books are strewn on the ground. You ask what's going on, and you are told to "shut the fuck up" or you will be taken downtown. When it finally ends, the officers leave, no apology, no explanation, and you are left to fix your clothes, pick up your books, and gather your pride. Imagine that this is not the first time this has happened to you, that it has happened, in one form or another, routinely throughout your adolescence. Now imagine that the day after this latest random search, there is a crime in your neighborhood, about which you have heard a rumor. You hear that the police are looking for information, and you see one of the officers who searched you yesterday (or indeed any officer) talking to other people about the recent crime. What are you likely to think as you decide whether to talk to the officer? What are the chances you will cooperate with the police in their investigation?

Research indicates that if the same officers had gone about their business differently, they would get better results. As criminal justice professor Stephen Mastrofski points out, citizens care most that police officers are fair. Fair procedure is so critical that those who are treated fairly reported a stronger inclination to obey the law in the future. Indeed, procedural fairness is so important to people that it had a more powerful impact even than the outcome of the process. People also care about simple things like manners, and bad manners are among the most frequent complaints that citizens have about their contacts with the police. How police treat citizens with whom they interact is so important that citizens are more likely to be law abiding in the future when those who enforce the law do so respectfully.[21]

The costs imposed on law enforcement by hostile policing are increasingly evident. Why did crime-plagued New York City public housing residents cheer accused murderer Larry Davis after a seventeen-day manhunt finally resulted in his arrest? Not because public housing residents support crime. They cheered because they resent the actions of the police. It is the principle of "the enemy of my enemy is my friend" taken to unfortunate lengths. As Randall Kennedy explains,

> The communities most in need of police protection are also those in which many residents view police with the most ambivalence, much of which stems from a recognition that color counts as a mark of suspicion relied upon as a predicate for action—stopping, questioning, patting down, arresting, beatings, and so forth. This causes people who might otherwise be of assistance to police to avoid them, to decline to cooperate with police investigations, to assume bad faith or dishonesty on the part of police officers, and to teach others that such reactions are prudent lessons of survival on the streets.[22]

The impact that racially based policing has on citizen involvement is tellingly told by Paul Butler, the African-American law professor who was followed by the police in his neighborhood. Butler reports that after his encounter, once the police determined that he resided in the neighborhood, the officers invited him to an upcoming neighborhood crime prevention meeting. Of course, Butler, himself a former federal prosecutor, is exactly the sort of person who would benefit his neighborhood by becoming involved in community action, including crime control. Conservatives know that community involvement from responsible citizens is the most important way to reduce crime. "The best defense against crime is not a thin, blue line, but a community of individuals respectful of others."[23] This is because, as urban anthropologist Jane Jacobs explained over thirty years ago: "The first thing to understand is that public space—the sidewalk and street peace—of cities is not kept primarily by the police, necessary as police are. Rather, it is kept by an intricate, almost unconscious, network of voluntary controls and standards established and enforced by people themselves."[24]

Unwarranted racial harassment further hurts law enforcement by reducing the stigma that concerned neighborhood residents attach to seeing a person being detained by the police. The notion that a community together fights crime by keeping an eye out for those who are up to no good turns in part on an accurate assessment of who is potential trouble.

Historically, part of that assessment comes from watching whom the police are themselves eyeing, stopping, and searching. Random police searches undermine that calculus, for many black people now report that when they see the police pulling over a car with a black driver, or searching a black kid on the street, they no longer ask: "What did that guy do?" but instead wonder, "Why is that cop harassing that guy?"

Fortunately, while the problems with how we police inner-city communities are entrenched, there is reason to be hopeful. Empirical evidence suggests that when high-crime communities respect the police, crime goes down at least as much as it does when police bust heads. Look at San Diego. During the 1990s, San Diego police divided the city into small residential boundaries (according to a local captain: "We basically threw out the original beat boundaries. We went to the community and said, 'Where do you think your neighborhood boundaries really begin and end?' "). They assigned officers to those specific beats, engaged community leaders in an ongoing dialogue about how to solve various problems, and developed a corps of over 1,200 citizen volunteers who became the eyes and ears for the police.

Compare this with New York, which (particularly after Commissioner William Bratton, architect of the city's original police reform program, left) pursued an ultra–hard-line policy of "zero tolerance." That policy, as practiced by the city's now-notorious Street Crimes Unit, quickly became an invitation to hyperaggressive abuse. The Street Crimes Unit adopted "We Own the Night" as its motto, and some of its officers wore T-shirts reading, "Certainly there is no hunting like the hunting of man, and those who have hunted armed men long enough and like it, never really care for anything else thereafter." [25] It was a deliberately antagonistic posture, one that contributed to the attack on Abner Louima and the killings of Amadou Diallo and Patrick Dorismond. And it has left many black New Yorkers profoundly alienated from the policemen and women who are meant to protect and serve them. In a 1998 Justice Department survey of citizen satisfaction with police in twelve American cities, San Diego was the second highest rated force; New York finished next to last.

But the important point for conservatives is that for all the ill will they sowed, the New York police were no better at stopping crime than their San Diego counterparts. In fact, they were slightly worse. While homicide in New York fell 71 percent between 1991 and 1998, San Diego's results were even more impressive: a reduction of 76 percent—the best in the country. The same for robbery: it fell 60 percent in New York, but 63 percent in San Diego.[26] As Professor David Harris concluded after evaluating these numbers: "Making the streets safer does not require the sacrifice of the civil liberties of those in areas with crime problems." And because they enjoyed more help from average citizens, the San Diego police got those results with a much smaller force: the city has just 1.7 officers per 1,000, while New York has 5.[27] In other words, it has smaller government—something else conservatives care quite a bit about.

And the San Diego experience is not unique. As Heritage Foundation fellow Eli Lehrer has shown, cities that have instituted genuine community oriented approaches to policing have seen crime decline while simultaneously developing stronger relationships with citizens. According to Lehrer, the most successful forces do not rely on iron-fisted special units like New York's, but rather invest in neighborhood patrols. When I brought up Lehrer's thesis to several Maya Angelou students, they thought it self-evident. "What do you expect?" asked one. "We know who is doing right and who is doing wrong, and if they talked to us instead of jumping us they might find out too." Such words could be music to conservative ears—but only if they are willing to listen.

PART IV

Communities in Crisis

Black Economic Progress in the Era of Mass Imprisonment

Bruce Western, Becky Pettit, and Josh Guetzkow*

The 1990s was a decade of extraordinary prosperity. After nearly twenty years of slow growth and periodically high unemployment, the U.S. economy expanded rapidly, gathering speed as the decade unfolded. By most accounts, the labor market performed impressively, sharing the spotlight only with the stock market in the extraordinary story of the 1990s economic expansion. As unemployment fell across the labor force as a whole, black workers registered strong gains according to standard measures of employment. By the end of the decade it appeared that wages for young black men were growing faster than for any other group. More than any jobs program or hiring policy, it seemed that sustained economic growth had brought prosperity to the most disadvantaged workers.

While the renewal of the American economy is relatively recent, the expansion of the penal system dates from the early 1970s. After fifty years of relative stability in the proportion of people incarcerated, the prison population doubled in size between 1970 and 1982. Between 1982 and 1999, the prison population increased threefold. These broad trends conceal substantial inequality. Prison incarceration rates are about eight times higher for blacks than whites, and high school dropouts are more than twice as likely to be in prison than high school graduates. Consequently, much of the growth in imprisonment in the three decades after 1970 was concentrated among young minority men with little education. By the late 1990s, about two-thirds of all state prison inmates were black or Hispanic, and about half of all minority inmates had less than twelve years of schooling.

The growth of the penal system has profoundly affected both our understanding of actual employment rates as well as the economic situation of the young low-skill African-American men whose incarceration rates are highest. In measuring employment or wages, the predominantly low-skill and minority men locked up in prisons and jails are not included in the standard labor force. Thus imprisonment effectively conceals economic inequality by excluding large numbers of poor men from official accounts of the labor market. As we will see, when we adjust employment and wage figures to take account of imprisoned populations, the economic progress of young black men has been substantially overstated. The penal system also fuels inequality by weakening the economic opportunities of prison and jail inmates after they are released. In this way, the growing incarceration rates offset many of the economic gains reported for black men during the decade of the 1990s, widening the earnings and employment gap between young black and white men.

The growth of the penal system puts the economic boom of the 1990s in a different light. Although most sections of the labor force were not dramatically affected by mass incarceration, young black men—particularly those with little schooling—routinely faced the risk of imprisonment. They thus obtained few of the benefits of economic growth and low unemployment that buoyed the labor market as a whole. We begin this story by documenting the concentration of incarceration among young low-skill men. We then detail the effects of incarceration on conventional employment and earnings statistics. Finally, we examine how the experience of time in prison or jail affects the life chances of ex-convicts after release.

INEQUALITY IN INCARCERATION

To examine the distortion created by omitting prison and jail populations from economic calculations, it is useful to look at incarceration rates broken down by age, educational background, and race. Combined data from correctional and labor force surveys, as shown in Figure 1, indicates that incarceration rates broadly increased for all groups of black

Figure 1
Prison and jail incarceration rates for black and white men by age and education

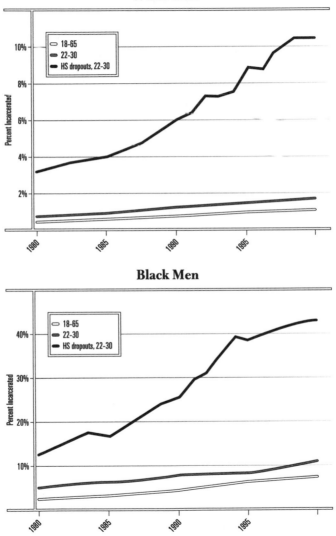

and white men in the two decades after 1980. Among whites, incarceration rates are about 50 percent higher for young men in their twenties than for the working-age male population as a whole. Among young high school dropouts, incarceration rates are higher still. By the end of the 1990s, one out of ten young white men with little schooling was in prison or jail.

The lower panel of Figure 1 shows a similar pattern for African Americans. The absolute level of incarceration rates for black men (indicated by the scale on the vertical axis) is much higher than for whites. Among all working-age black men, 7.5 percent were incarcerated on an average day in 1999, compared with 11.7 percent of black men in their twenties. The incarceration rates for young black unskilled men are dramatically higher. In the early stages of the prison boom, in 1980, 14 percent of young black male dropouts were behind bars. By 1999, the incarceration rate had climbed to 41.2 percent.

Table 1 shows that the rate of growth in incarceration was slightly faster for whites than blacks. Thus racial disparity in imprisonment, measured by the black-white ratio in incarceration rates, declined slightly from 1980 to 1999. Even so, black men between the ages of eighteen and sixty-five were nearly eight times as likely as whites to be in prison or jail in 1999. Despite small declines in racial disparity, the largest absolute gains in incarceration were recorded by black men. Racial disparity in incarceration is partly explained by the relatively low level of schooling of young black men compared with that of young whites. If we look just at high school dropouts, the black-white ratio in incarceration rates is just half as large as for the population as a whole. Even among dropouts, however, blacks remain four times more likely to be in prison or jail than whites.

Although black-white disparity in incarceration rates declined between 1980 and 1999, the ratio of minority to white incarceration increased due to the growing imprisonment of Hispanics, the vast majority of whom are categorized for racial purposes as white. Hispanics accounted for only a few percentage points of the prison and jail population in 1980, but around 15 percent of all inmates by the end of

Table 1. Prison and Jail Incarceration Rates for Black and White Men by Age and Education, 1980, 1999

	All (Ages 18–65)	Young Adults (Ages 22–30)	Young Adult H.S. Dropouts
White Men			
1980	0.4	0.7	3.1
1999	1.0	1.6	10.3
Change from 1980–1999	0.6	0.9	7.2
Black Men			
1980	3.1	5.5	14.0
1999	7.5	11.7	41.2
Change from 1980–1999	4.4	6.2	27.2
Black-White Ratio 1980	7.8	7.9	4.5
Black-White Ratio 1999	7.5	7.3	4.0

the 1990s. In contrast, the share of whites in prison shrunk from 42 to 33 percent. In 1980, the combined prison incarceration rate of blacks and Hispanics outnumbered that of whites by 5.9 to 1; by 1996, that ratio was 6.2 to 1.[1]

Incarceration rates indicate high levels of imprisonment, but because the rates record imprisonment at a single point in time, they understate the frequency of prison admission over the life course. An alternative measure of incarceration records the fraction of the population that has ever served time in prison. We estimated the proportion of men who had ever served time in prison by age thirty to thirty-four (Table 2). In 1999, more than one in five black men aged thirty to thirty-four had been to prison. The high concentration of incarceration among poorly educated men is also reflected in these figures. At the end of the 1990s, more than half of all black male dropouts in their early thirties had served time in prison. Cumulative risks of incarceration are also extremely high even among men with high school diplomas. By 1999, nearly one-quarter of black men with twelve years of schooling had been to prison. Unlike in-

Table 2. Percentage of Men Born 1965–69 with Prison Records by 1999, By Race and Education

	All	Education		
		High School Dropouts	H.S./GED	Some College
White Men	3.2	12.6	4.3	1.1
Black Men	22.3	52.1	23.5	8.6
Black-White Ratio	7.0	4.1	5.5	7.8

carceration rates, racial disparity in the cumulative risk of incarceration over the life course clearly increased through the 1990s. By the end of the decade, African-American men were about seven times more likely to have a prison record than white men. In short, serving time in prison is now extremely common for young black men, and has become a modal experience among young African-American men with little schooling.[2]

These disaggregated incarceration statistics suggest that the experience of prison or jail is common for young black men, and virtually pervasive for young, unskilled black men in recent birth cohorts. Because incarceration is so highly concentrated among the most disadvantaged in the labor market, the effects of the penal system on this group are large.

INCARCERATION AND INVISIBLE INEQUALITY

By excluding prison and jail inmates from the population count, standard labor force figures overstate the rate of employment. In the early 1970s, before the growth of the penal system, the inequality-concealing effect of incarceration was negligible. By the 1990s, however, the invisible inequality generated by the penal system accounted for large portions of the black-white difference in employment and earnings among young men.

Some might object that many in the penal system are working in prison industries and are thus employed in some sense. By counting prison and jail inmates among the jobless, we follow the definition of employment used by the U.S. Bureau of the Census. The Census expressly excludes those employed in correctional facilities from the employment count. The Census employment concept recognizes that a paying job on the open labor market confers a degree of economic independence, including rights to a minimum wage and to union membership. Employment in prison work programs carries few of these benefits.

Table 3 contrasts the usual employment-population ratio with an adjusted employment statistic that includes prison and jail inmates among the jobless. For white men, adjusting for the size of the penal population makes little difference to the employment rates of those aged eighteen to sixty-five, or twenty-two to thirty. Among young white male dropouts, however, counting the incarcerated population lowers conventional employment about 2 percentage points in 1980 and 9 percentage points in 1999. Thus, while conventional statistics suggest that employment increased slightly for young white dropouts from 1980 to 1999, correcting for the size of the penal population shows that employment actually declined.

The discrepancy is much larger for black men. Among working-age black men, conventional figures overstate employment by about 5 percentage points in 1999. Among young black men, excluding prison and jail inmates from the population leads us to overestimate employment by 9 percentage points. And, not surprisingly, the adjustment to employment rates is most dramatic for young black high school dropouts, where conventional rates overstated employment by 9 percentage points in 1980 and 21 percentage points by 1999. Conventional statistics indicate that about half of young black male dropouts had jobs, in contrast to the true employment rate of only 29.9 percent.

More detail about the employment rates for young unskilled men is provided in Figure 2, which plots the unadjusted and adjusted employment series for black and white male high school dropouts. Although the

Table 3. Percentage of the Population Employed, Black and White Men by Age and Education, 1980, 1999

	1980		1999	
	Unadjusted	Adjusted	Unadjusted	Adjusted
White Men				
Ages 18–65	84.2	83.9	84.8	83.9
Ages 22–30	86.5	85.9	88.6	87.2
H.S. dropouts, 22–30	77.1	74.7	81.3	72.9
Black Men				
Ages 18–65	70.1	68.0	72.1	66.7
Ages 22–30	73.9	69.8	76.4	67.4
H.S. dropouts, 22–30	64.5	55.5	50.9	29.9

Note: Unadjusted employment rates are calculated as a percentage of the noninstitutional population; adjusted employment rates are calculated as a fraction of the noninstitutional and incarcerated population.

gap between standard employment rates and those adjusted for incarceration widened for whites, both employment statistics show similar trends. Employment among young white male dropouts increased through the 1980s, and then again from 1995 to 1999. Adjusting employment rates for the penal population results in a much larger correction for young black dropouts. Conventional statistics suggest that employment among young black unskilled men declined in the decade after 1984, but increased through the second half of the 1990s. Counting prison and jail inmates in the population shows that the decline in employment through the 1980s and early 1990s was steeper than standard measures suggest. Furthermore, there was no recovery in employment through the 1990s for black male dropouts in their twenties.

The relatively large correction for incarceration in the employment rate of blacks also affects measures of black-white inequality in employment. According to standard employment rates, young white dropouts were about 1.5 times more likely to have a job than young black dropouts throughout the 1990s. Correcting for incarceration, our calculations

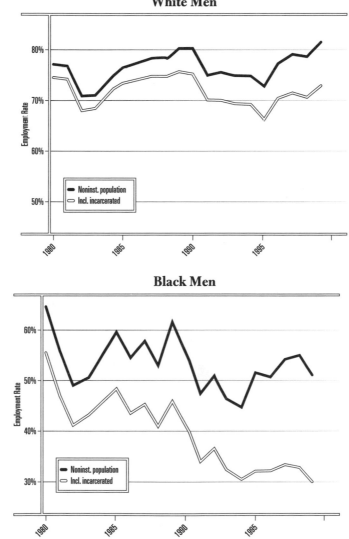

Figure 2

Adjusted and unadjusted employment-population ratios for black and white male high school dropouts, ages 22–30

Figure 3

Black-white inequality in employment. Top panel: white-black employment ratios measured by adjusted and unadjusted employment-population ratios for black and white male high school dropouts, ages 22–30. Bottom panel: the percent difference in black-white ratios by adjusted and unadjusted employment series.

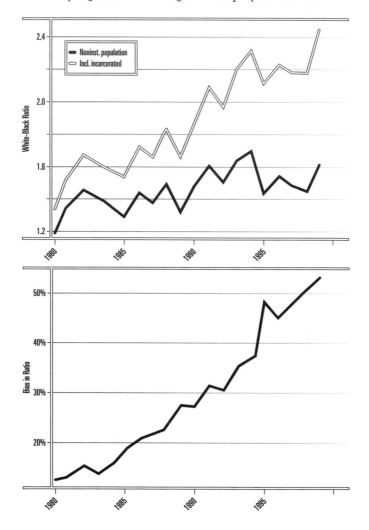

show that young white male dropouts were in fact 2.4 times more likely to be employed than their black counterparts by 1999. Thus standard employment rates understated racial inequality in employment among unskilled men by about 50 percent.

Inequality in wages is also affected by the invisible disadvantaged in prisons and jails. The penal system raises average wages by removing low-wage workers from the labor force. The rise in average wages doesn't represent a real improvement in living standards, but rather is an artifact of incarceration that is concentrated among low earners. By looking at the wages of workers at the same ages and levels of education as inmates, we estimate that the wage gap in 1999 between young black and white men would be 20 percent higher if all those not working, including those in prison and jail, were fully employed.[3] Whereas labor force surveys show that the wage gap between black and white young men has narrowed over the last fifteen years, about half the decline in inequality can be attributed to falling employment among black men due to imprisonment and more conventional joblessness.

DOES INCARCERATION INCREASE BLACK-WHITE INEQUALITY?

While black-white inequality is obscured by employment figures that ignore high incarceration rates, the penal system itself also increases inequality by reducing the employment and earnings of ex-inmates after release. Labor market researchers explain the low earnings and irregular employment of ex-convicts in three main ways. First, criminal conviction carries social stigma. Employers view job candidates with criminal records as untrustworthy. Surveys show that employers would rather hire welfare recipients or inexperienced applicants than ex-convicts. The stigma of conviction also has legal significance. Commonly, a felony record can temporarily disqualify employment in licensed or professional occupations. These prohibitions typically extend beyond the professions to include jobs in health care and skilled trades.[4]

Second, incarceration erodes job skills. At a minimum, time in prison or jail limits the acquisition of work experience that would be obtained on the open labor market. In addition, behaviors that are adaptive for survival in prison are likely to be inconsistent with work routines outside of prison. Incarceration may also exacerbate preexisting mental or physical illnesses. These effects may be especially large in the recent period as support declines for job training, drug treatment, and health care.

Third, incarceration undermines social connections to good job opportunities. Criminologists find that juvenile delinquency embeds young offenders in social contexts with weak connections to stable employment. There is also evidence that in adult facilities, particularly those with significant gang activity, inmates build social connections to those promoting opportunities for further criminal activity after release. Social ties to legitimate employment are weakened as a result.[5]

Although social stigma and skill and network erosion help explain how incarceration undermines employment, it is difficult to calculate precisely the economic effect of imprisonment. The young, unskilled minority men who are most likely to go to jail have poor job opportunities, even in the absence of incarceration. Statistical studies try to compare the wages and employment of men who are similar in all respects except for their criminal records. Many of these studies estimate that the ex-convicts earn between 10 and 30 percent less than similarly situated workers who have not been to prison or jail. Still, when very stringent comparisons are employed, several studies find no loss of earnings among ex-convicts. This research implies that men at high risk of incarceration have such poor job prospects, prison time confers no additional economic penalty.[6]

Much of the statistical research is based on a very simple model in which incarceration generates a one-time decline in earnings or employment among ex-convicts. However, the economic effects of incarceration on poor and minority communities may be more complicated. One alternative approach places the effects of incarceration in the context of the life course of young men as they try to make the transition from school to stable employment. Another approach examines the impact of incarceration not just on individuals, but on the communities from which individuals are drawn.

The life course perspective argues that the experience of incarceration is a punctuating event that can interrupt a young man's transition into stable employment. While many young men leave school and ultimately find steady jobs that provide regular growth in earnings, men with criminal records experience virtually no growth in earnings at all. This suggests that ex-convicts have few job opportunities outside of day labor or other kinds of precarious employment.[7] Ethnographers paint a similar picture. Mercer Sullivan's vivid account of young ex-convicts in New York City describes a cycle of disadvantage resulting from entanglement with law enforcement and correctional authorities: "Participation in income-producing crime and the resulting involvement in the criminal justice system in turn kept the [research subjects] out of school and forced them to abandon their occupational goals. . . . By the end of their teens most of these youths had found and lost several jobs. . . . Wages, though irregular, replaced theft as their major source of income. . . . They were still frequently unemployed and generally made low wages when they did work."[8] From the life course perspective there is not a single earnings gap between nonconvicts and ex-convicts. Instead, the earnings of ex-convicts diverges from the earnings of nonconvicts as men get older. Nonconvicts by their late twenties have settled into a stable path of earnings growth, while ex-convicts follow an unstable trajectory of irregular employment.

Although most research on the economic effects of incarceration focuses on the earnings or employment loss of individuals, the penal system may also have large aggregate-level effects. In a very simple sense, incarceration widens the earnings gap between black and white men because incarceration lowers earnings and blacks are more likely to be incarcerated than whites. A rough estimate of the impact of incarceration on the black-white earnings gap can be obtained from figures on the lifetime risk of incarceration and average earnings. Our estimates suggests that 22.3 percent of black men have prison records by ages thirty to thirty-four, in contrast to 3.2 percent of white men. The earnings gap between black and white men under age thirty is around 18 percent. Following the statistical studies, we can assume that prison or jail time lowers earnings by around one-tenth. Some simple calculations show that the black-white gap in earnings would be reduced from 18 to 12 percent if blacks and whites were incarcerated at the same rate.

Beyond statistical aggregation, incarceration may have spillover effects for entire demographic groups or communities. Highly concentrated incarceration may create discrimination. For example, employers often report avoiding job candidates from high-crime neighborhoods. In these cases, an individual's employment opportunities are limited by coming from a particular neighborhood rather than by having a criminal history. Similar effects may follow the contours of demography. About a third of black men born since the late 1960s with only a high school education have been sentenced to time in prison. Under these conditions, incarceration may be collectively, rather than individually, stigmatizing. Employers may assume that all young, low-skill black men are ex-convicts. This would help explain the finding in some studies that the employment penalty of incarceration is smaller for blacks than for whites. In addition, the high incarceration rates experienced by poor minority neighborhoods may reduce neighborhood employment rates. Studies of urban poverty show that neighborhood concentrations of crime, alcohol and drug use, and low educational attainment can promote such outcomes in individuals.[9] Similar neighborhood effects could also influence employment. Poor urban communities with high incarceration rates are likely to have large numbers of idle young men recently released from prison or jail. These men may form peer groups or reference groups that offer the community few normative or social links to legitimate employment.

IMPLICATIONS AND CONCLUSIONS

The great irony of the prison boom is that it comes at a time when policy makers have set out to decrease the role of government in the lives of the disadvantaged. Despite antigovernment rhetoric in policy debates, the government has not regulated the lives of unskilled minority men so intensively since the Depression or wartime. The policy offensive was wide-ranging, affecting policing, sentencing, prison construction, post-release supervision, and a variety of other measures at the state and federal levels of government. The sheer commitment of public resources is comparable in magnitude to social welfare efforts in the 1960s and 1970s. Unlike antipoverty policy, however, the punitive trend in criminal justice policy conceals and deepens economic inequality between blacks and whites.

This represents a significant departure from the thrust of public policy through the twenty-five years following World War II. Beginning in the 1950s, school desegregation led to improved quality of schooling for black children, ultimately raising the relative wages of black workers. Bars on discrimination resulting from the Civil Rights Act, affirmative action, and equal employment opportunity all narrowed the economic gap between blacks and whites. Black workers also found secure employment in public sector jobs, which helped create the basis for a well-paid black middle class. For much of the postwar period, public policy played an important progressive role that helped offset the negative effects of declining manufacturing industries in urban labor markets. Weighed against these achievements, the prison boom can be seen as one of the most important developments in American race relations in the last thirty years. Whereas we often consider how welfare, employment, and education policy affect inequality, criminal justice policy is usually judged by other standards.

Much of the analysis of this chapter treats prison and jail inmates simply as disadvantaged and not as dangerous. Yet critics will warn that residents of the penal system should be thought of as criminal first, and poor second. From this perspective, nearly half the prison population are violent offenders. Many prisoners are also repeat (although not violent) offenders. For partisans in the war on crime, incarceration may affect economic inequality, but the criminal propensity of most young black and white men with little schooling demands an aggressive policy response. The inegalitarian effects of criminal justice policy must be balanced against the goal of public safety.

This counterargument raises a complex question: Can public safety be achieved by policies that deepen social inequality? To answer this question, much depends on the link between inequality and crime. If inequality causes crime—and a large research literature indicates that it does—the recent reliance on punishment as the first option in criminal justice policy may be a self-defeating route to public safety. The connection between crime and inequality is well-trodden ground for students of criminology. The prison boom and its effects on racial inequality give this question renewed urgency. In earlier research and policy, the contours of social inequality were viewed as fixed and external to the patterns of crime that they generated. Our new challenge involves viewing inequality as, in part, a product of the expansion of the American system of punishment.

The Problem with "Addition by Subtraction": The Prison-Crime Relationship in Low-Income Communities

Todd R. Clear

A s a theory of public safety, incarceration is based on the premise of "addition by subtraction." It is a social policy that removes people from their communities, subtracting from those places whatever deficits were exacted by their presence. The hard-and-fast assumption of incarceration as a tool of public safety is that removing these people from their communities subtracts only (or primarily) the problems they represented for their places, and thereby leaves those places better. Any assets that are removed pose a problem for the theory.

Two points regarding this routine assumption of incarceration policy are worth noting. First, the idea that removing criminals has primarily the effect of eliminating community deficits comports closely with dominant public opinion about criminals: they are viewed as people whose net contribution to community life is negative, and so not much will be lost by their being gone. Second, neither the broad policy assumption nor the common public wisdom has been subjected to direct empirical test.

Even though the traditional theory of incarceration for public safety is one of the most uniformly held ideas in contemporary and popular crime policy, there is good reason to question both the common wisdom and the policy assumption of "addition by subtraction." I argue that very high concentrations of incarceration may well have a negative impact on public safety by leaving communities less capable of sustaining the informal social control that undergirds public safety. This happens not only because incarceration, experienced at high levels, has the inevitable result of removing valuable assets from the community, but also because the concentration of incarceration affects the community capacity of those who are left behind.

COERCIVE MOBILITY AND CRIME CONTROL

The argument in this chapter is based on a continuing line of research studies undertaken by my colleague, Dina Rose, and me. In the initial paper[1] we explained a theory of "coercive mobility," based on a review of research conducted outside the criminal justice context. Taken as a whole, this suggests that high rates of incarceration can destabilize communities in ways that make them vulnerable to crime. The argument draws upon social disorganization theory, which has long held that in areas where residents are highly outwardly mobile, crime will flourish, because those locations will lack the stable infrastructure that is required as a foundation of informal social control.

Three related studies, all using data from Tallahassee, Florida, have provided support for the "coercive mobility" hypothesis. A second paper[2] showed that people who have personal experience with incarceration, either directly or through a close associate or family member, are more likely to have a low assessment of informal social control when they already have a low opinion of formal control, and makes nonblacks just as likely as blacks to hold a negative assessment of informal social control. An analysis of crime rates[3] found that neighborhoods with the highest levels of incarceration in one year had higher-than-expected crime rates in the following year, compared with other Tallahassee neighborhoods (and controlling for poverty, racial composition, and mobility). A third study[4] in which over one hundred residents and civic leaders in two high-incarceration neighborhoods were interviewed, showed that those who live or work in such areas can point to a number of ways in which the incarceration experience has damaged the quality of life in their neighborhood.

I should emphasize that this model of "coercive mobility" applies to the highest levels of incarceration in poor and disadvantaged neighborhoods. This is not a general theory of incarceration; rather, it is a theory that applies to particular dynamics of incarceration in places that lack social capital to begin with. Indeed, we find evidence that low levels of incarceration seem to benefit neighborhoods' public safety. But when incarceration reaches a certain level in an area that already struggles for assets, the effects of imprisonment undermine the building blocks of social order. This is, for these neighborhoods, a kind of double whammy. First, they suffer the disruptions that occur when large numbers of residents are coercively removed and imprisoned. Then, they struggle with the pressures that occur when large numbers of former convicts return to community life. Both processes—removal and return—are important, but because the latter gets far more attention than the former, I will focus on the effects of removal in this essay.

CONCENTRATION OF INCARCERATION

For the last thirty years, one aspect of corrections has overshadowed all others: growth. The decade of the 1970s began with barely 200,000 Americans in prison, and an incarceration rate around 100 per 100,000 citizens. Beginning in 1972, the prison population started a pattern of unrelenting growth in annual increments, lasting for over a generation and continuing today. This sustained growth in imprisonment has occurred with little relationship to crime rates (which have both risen and fallen during this period), economic patterns (which have cycled through good times and bad), and population demographics (which have seen the number of crime-aged males in the population both increase and decrease). Today, a 500 percent increase in prisoners leaves the country with over 1.3 million citizens in prison (counting those in jail, almost 2 million are confined) and an incarceration rate of nearly 700 per 100,000. This is not the place to offer a full-scale explanation of the growth of Americans in prison; suffice it to say that at no time in human history has there been such a sustained, systematic increase in the use of confinement as a tool of social control.

For our purposes, it is important to recognize that the growth of incarceration has been concentrated among certain groups and in certain locations. Men, for example, are eight times more likely to go to prison than women. The lifetime probabilities of spending time in prison are 28.5 per 100 for African-American males and 16 per 100 for Hispanic males, about six and four times higher respectively, than for white males.[5] Incarceration is far more an issue for minority communities than in white communities, especially among men.

Because poor men of color live in concentrations in neighborhoods that are racially and economically homogeneous, some of the places where these men live are particularly hard-hit by incarceration. Depending upon the size of the neighborhood and the method of counting, studies have estimated that up to 25 percent of the adult male residents in particular neighborhoods are locked up on any given day,[6] up to 13 percent of adult males enter prison or jail in a given year,[7] and up to 2 percent of all residents enter prison in a given year.[8] To be sure, incarceration affects all social groups and can happen in any neighborhood; but it is far more prevalent among some groups and in some areas than in others.

The dynamics of growing concentrations of the residents of certain neighborhoods going to prison (and jail) are not insignificant for these locations. Imagine, for a moment, living in an area where one in eight parent-aged males is removed for confinement each year, and one in four is locked up at any given time. It is not difficult to see that this social process, over time, would be one of the truly important aspects of community life. The question is, how does this level of concentrated coercive mobility affect public safety through its impact on the building blocks of social order?

BUILDING BLOCKS OF PUBLIC SAFETY

We are used to the idea that public safety is the task of criminal justice. Yet upon minimal reflection, we are bound to realize that the lion's share of public safety comes about not from the actions or practices of public agencies of government but from the everyday decisions and perspectives of citizens. When places become unsafe, it is not primarily due to a breakdown in the formal social controls of the state, but because of the limitations of the informal social controls operating in those places. This is a routine sociological insight.

Over the years, sociologists have developed numerous ways of describing the nature of informal social controls and how they work. In previous writing on the impact of incarceration on community, Dina Rose and I have borrowed mainly from the works of Hunter,[9] Hirschi,[10] and Shaw and McKay.[11] These are established control theories in criminology, and they remain useful to any understanding of the nature of informal social control and the limits of formal social control. For this chapter, I want to stray a bit from these established theories and offer a simplified idea of three levels of informal social control that promote safer places: what people do privately with intimate relations; what people do collectively in social relations; and the normative views people adopt regarding criminal conduct. I will describe each of these levels of control, and illustrate how they work to promote safer places. Then I will show how high levels of incarceration might undermine the capacity of each level.

Before I begin this line of analysis, I want to briefly note four important sociological ideas that work their way throughout this essay, explicitly and implicitly. *Human capital* refers to the talents a person brings to social life, innate and acquired. *Social capital* is the capacity of a person to accomplish important personal aims through that person's connections to others. Where human capital is an attribute of a person in detachment from others, social capital is an attribute that refers to the quality and potency of interpersonal attachments, and thus may be an attribute both of individuals and of the groups to which they belong. *Social networks* are webs of relationships through which social action occurs. Social networks occur in a wide variety of ways and have an even wider variety of capacities: they may be dense or shallow, intimate or impersonal, weak or strong, and a host of other comparable attributes. It is through the potency of one's social networks that one's social capital is realized. Finally, *collective efficacy* (a new term coined by Robert Sampson and his colleagues)[12] refers to the ability of an aggregate to put shared expectations for their community into action and to achieve desired qualities of community life.

These terms are of enduring importance to an understanding of public safety. People who suffer limited human capital will be able to exercise few personal choices in their pursuit of whatever desires guide their lives; they will instead rely upon available social capital to advance their personal aims. Places where social networks are weak or thin will provide little basis upon which social capital may be produced. The worst situation a person can confront is to possess little in the way of human capital, suffer a dearth of network relationships, and hence have little social capital to call upon for personal aims. Such a person will face a life of limited choices, indeed. Concentrate a large number of such people in a particular area, and there will be little basis for generating collective efficacy, the translation of social capital into social action. My comments below will make a few points about how incarceration, in concentrated levels, works on community life through the way it affects these attributes.

Having laid this conceptual foundation, let us now consider the three mechanisms of informal social control that help a place become safer, and how high levels of incarceration affect them.

What people do privately with intimate relations. There is no more important source of public safety than the family unit. It is from their families that children learn behavioral norms and experience the first consequences of disobeying those norms. Families also structure the time of young people in childhood and especially in adolescence. It is safe to postulate that children who grow up under prosocial normative expectations and structured availability of time will be less inclined to engage in criminal conduct. Thus, the first way in which private social control operates as an important source of public safety is through the processes of child rearing in family units. Important elements of child rearing are normative socialization and basic supervision.

In addition, families establish the framework for a person's human capital and eventual social capital. They support or impede education; they help develop or retard personal skills. Young people who hail from families that invest in the child's human capital grow up in a web of informal social controls that are not experienced otherwise. The social network of the parents also frames the child's initial social capital: "connections" can lead to job opportunities, and this in turn provides the network of controls that reinforce prosocial choices.

Intimates provide informal social control in other ways. Close associates reinforce values learned in childhood, and they share activities with one another. When those values and activities are prosocial, they serve as effective mechanisms of informal social control. In this way, intimate associations carry on the social control functions of the family into later life. Intimates can also become key components of potential new networks of social relations because their networks (and their resulting social capital) may be tapped through the interpersonal connection. A close friend will help someone get a job; a family member's friend will help someone deal with legal trouble through connections to the legal system.

This discussion illustrates a central point made a half-generation ago by Albert Hunter.[13] Much of the work of social control is performed in private, interpersonal relations. Family members and close friends are sources of a person's association to the larger society, and they form the most basic source of informal social control. It is a plain fact that, aside from the importance of these relations, not everyone has them in equal abundance. Some children are born into families that provide less support for human capital formation, offer fewer networks of relations that can promote social capital, and supply a much more limited foundation upon which informal social control can be built. These children are well known to us; we call them "at risk."

The way concentrated neighborhood levels of incarceration affect these "private" sources of social control is at once obvious and also subtle. Families that lack adult male role members are known, on average, to face economic stresses and provide reduced levels of child supervision. When these families live in settings where the absence of adult males is common, there are widespread problems in recruiting males as fathers, mentors, providers, and role models.

The efforts of many women who raise families with absent fathers is heroic, and the immense capacity of many women to lead their families despite missing men is an undeniable fact. But to understand the significance of incarceration, we have to recognize that it is not just some families who are affected in high concentration locations, but nearly all families. Almost every family faces the loss of male role-takers, and a large number of additional families face the burden of female members in confinement. Anthropologists who study these areas describe a reality in which a child being raised with stable male and female adult supports is the exception rather than the rule.

High incarceration locations are always places where poor people live. In the face of the dearth of resources, incarceration in wholesale amounts exacerbates the limits of social support. Here is the blunt reality. Children who grow up in areas where substantial amounts of human capital are not easily acquired struggle with inadequate schools, limited leisure time choices, and insufficient formative supports. The systematic absence or weakening of male sources of support for human capital formation makes a bad situation worse and adds a further impediment to overcoming these disadvantages of birth.

Concentrated incarceration also impedes the formation of social capital in impoverished locations. Social capital is most enhanced by expansive networks that include "weak" ties—that is, broad networks that interact with numerous other networks in simple ways.[14] Poor locations tend to produce "strong" ties—kinship and similar relational ties that are sustained by close contact—in smaller networks that are isolated from other networks. This lack of connection between poor peoples' networks and others' outside narrow environs explains the very limited capacity these networks have for their members' social capital. A middle-class person, for instance, can call upon relationships with a wide variety of acquaintances for various types of assistance and support, but a poverty-stricken person living in the impoverished inner city has a limited list of people—mostly family and a few close friends—who may be tapped for help. When these limited networks of mostly "strong" ties become saturated with people who have been incarcerated, the capacity of the networks is hampered further. Being poor is associated with problematic social ties, and experiencing incarceration aggravates that difficulty.

What people do collectively in social relations. People are social animals, and their drive for social interaction is what forms a society. Between the formal controls of the state and the informal controls of the family and intimates exists a range of socializing associations and groups. Just to mention a few of these shows how important they might become in a person's life: churches, social clubs, business leagues, volunteer groups, organized youth groups, neighborhood associations, and even patterned social get-togethers. One of the primary ways many people spend their time is in personal collective social relations that go beyond family ties. These social controls are intermediate, in that they fall between the private sources of control offered by the family and other intimates and the public forms of control managed by the state. Because these forms of control are often products of social arrangements particular to a group or neighborhood location, they have been called "parochial" controls.[15]

Parochial social control contributes to public safety in three ways. At its most basic, these associations occupy free time for those who engage in them, thereby reducing the amount of time that remains available for other activities, including antisocial behavior. The old saw "idleness is the devil's playground" is not without merit. Second, parochial social controls can substitute for absent or limited parental contact. This is one of the reasons so much importance is placed on summer and after-school activities for youth who otherwise would lack adult supervision. Finally, the range of parochial associations operating in a given area creates a social web of relationships that influence behavior. Attending church, belonging to a social club, sharing leisure pursuits with a regular group, knowing the local store owner personally—all these patterned relationships act as controls on behavior.

In the poor places that contribute residents to the prison system in large numbers, there are already limits in the capacity of parochial social control. One of the effects of high mobility, for example, is that these informal community relationships are less likely to form and less likely to thrive.[16] Mobility is not the only culprit. Studies show that crime leads people to isolate themselves from their neighbors and therefore inhibits the social activity that promotes parochial social control.[17] People who have to struggle to make ends meet simply do not have the time to devote to the intermediate social activities that create the interpersonal networks of parochial social control. People who fear their neighbors and feel unsafe on the streets where they live do not venture out to frequent whatever intermediate social interactions are offered. For the most part, those who live in unsafe places also face economic hardship, and this poses a double-edged challenge to the ability of these places to develop new forms of intermediate social controls and sustain those that might already exist.

High incarceration rates exacerbate these dynamics. When primary (private) social control systems, principally families, are impaired by the instability of adults flowing into and out of prisons, they become less capable of participating in the intermediate social activity that underpins parochial social control. Thus, coercive mobility imposed by the state begins to have the same destabilizing effects on neighborhood social structures that have been observed for voluntary mobility, with the added problem that those who remain may have a weakened capacity for this form of social activity. One study[18] interviewed residents in two high-incarceration areas in Tallahassee, Florida. These people reported that the levels of imprisonment in their neighborhoods created problems in children's self-esteem and supervision, and led neighbors to isolate themselves further from one another due to the social stigma associated with imprisonment. Stories were told of incarceration of a family member leading to the family's estrangement from churches, neighbors, and social groups. And while a general ethic of a willingness to forgive and accept back home was expressed regarding most locals who run afoul of the law, it was also clear that families who send a loved one to prison often face a social crisis with their neighbors. In this way, incarceration affects not just those who go to prison, but those who are left behind as well.

The normative views people develop regarding criminal conduct. Collective efficacy, which studies show is one of the sources of public safety, is founded on normative cohesion. That is, people who share common values and know that these values will be supported create a place where people feel free to act publicly to uphold those standards of conduct. When this is true, people collectively create a public order through their expectations of one another's conduct and their actions to reinforce those expectations. Thus, a critical component of ordered societies is a level of consensus about the values of social order and a belief in the legitimacy of social order.

Researchers have long known that direct personal experience with the criminal justice system affects how a person evaluates the system. Two general patterns of findings are worth noting. First, people of color report they are more likely to experience unfair treatment at the hands of the police.[19] Second, people who feel they have been unfairly treated by the justice system feel less obligation to obey the law.[20] This may explain why so many people of color have such negative attitudes toward the criminal justice system: they believe it is unfairly biased against them.

The importance of personal experience has a neighborhood component. Sampson and Jeglum-Bertusch[21] show that people who live in places where social control fails and social disorder thrives express a strong distrust of formal social control and a greater degree of tolerance for those who engage in deviance. It may well be that a sustained, collective experience with criminal justice in these troubled areas promotes a negative view about the justice system, a nuanced view about offenders, and a cynical view about social control. Rose and Clear[22] found, for example, that people who know someone personally who has been incarcerated and feel negatively about formal social control also hold more negative views about the capacity of informal social control in the areas where they live.

It would not be surprising to learn that places sustaining high levels of incarceration are home to residents who feel unjustly treated by the criminal justice system. When they see their ex-convict family members caught up in a cycle that keeps them jobless, drug-dependent, and at the edge of recidivism, they blame the system for making things worse. Indeed, residents interviewed in Tallahassee are quick to identify racism as one of the causes of the high levels of incarceration they experience and one of the consequences of the way incarceration affects their lives.[23] This antagonistic view of the work of formal social control systems undermines the capacity of informal social control by sustaining an attitude of "we-versus-they." It makes the neighbors less inclined to trust the aims of representatives of formal social control systems, and it pits friends, family members, and formal agents of control against one another. Under such conditions, collective efficacy is not possible.

A COMMENT ON THE COUNTERFACTUAL

This has been an argument that high incarceration rates destabilize community life and undermine the community forces that promote public safety. It is a subtle set of forces; less a scissor that slices social fabric and more a straw that breaks the back of social control. Each of the dynamics described above is modest in its own right; together, they add up to a significant social force. In neighborhoods that suffer large numbers of offenders removed from incarceration and then returning from prison, these small effects are so common as to become a major dynamic of community life.

The idea that incarceration becomes problematic for some communities is deeply counterintuitive in today's public opinion climate. It seems beyond debate that any policy that removes people who do bad things leaves those who remain better off; it seems laughable to say that "incarceration causes crime." It is important, then, to be clear about what is being argued and what is not. The line of analysis developed above is *not* meant to say that "incarceration causes crime." The relationship between amounts of incarceration and levels of crime is complicated, and it would be far-fetched to claim that incarceration makes no contribution to public safety. It surely does in specific cases and under particular conditions.

The argument made here is a much more narrow one. Well-established theory and a solid body of evidence indicate that high levels of incarceration concentrated in impoverished communities has a destabilizing effect on community life, so that the most basic underpinnings of informal social control are damaged. This, in turn, reproduces the very dynamics that sustain crime.

There are, of course, plenty of families that rally in the face of a loved one being sent to prison, finding ways to strengthen child-rearing and locating substitute resources to replace the lost family member. There are plenty of families, too, that benefit from the temporary reprieve from what may well have been a damaging member of the household. Nothing in this theory of "coercive mobility" should detract from the large numbers of valiant adults and children who rise to the challenge of incarceration in their lives by finding ways to overcome the effects and not only survive, but become stronger. There are such families; there are, one can suppose, such neighborhoods. Yet, these stories are the exception rather than the rule. On average, the effects of very high levels of incarceration are destabilizing in the aggregate, and they pose a problem even the strongest families must struggle to deal with. Too many families and too many neighborhoods fail the challenge.

PART V

Incarceration As Socially Corrosive

12

Building a Prison Economy
in Rural America

Tracy Huling

*We struggled, myself and a brother, two sisters, my mother there, to keep the farm
in the family and keep it going. And we barely made a living. So that's what made
me appreciate the job so much, that it was a lot easier and the money was secure.
Before I even started the job, they was always telling me, the worse things get out in
the world, the better things get in jail. You'll always have a job.*
     Ted Flegel, family farmer and retired prison guard, Coxsackie, New York[1]

I n the United States today there are more prisoners than farmers.[2]
And while most prisoners in America are from urban communities,
most prisons are now in rural areas. During the last two decades the
large-scale use of incarceration to solve social problems has combined
with the fall-out of globalization to produce an ominous trend: prisons
have become a "growth industry" in rural America.

Communities suffering from declines in farming, mining, timber-
work, and manufacturing are now begging for prisons to be built in their
backyards. The economic restructuring that began in the troubled decade of the 1980s has had dramatic social and economic consequences
for rural communities and small towns. Together the farm crises, factory
closings, corporate downsizing, shift to service sector employment, and
the substitution of major regional and national chains for local, main-
street businesses have triggered profound change in these areas. The
aquisition of prisons as a conscious economic development strategy for
depressed rural communities and small towns in the United States has
become widespread. Hundreds of small rural towns and several whole
regions have become dependent on an industry that itself is dependent
on the continuation of crime-producing conditions.

Ironically, while rural areas pursue prisons as a growth strategy, whether this is a wise or effective strategy is far from clear. Increasing evidence suggests that by many measures, prisons do not produce economic growth for local economies and can, over the long term, have detrimental effects on the social fabric and environment of rural communities. Moreover, this massive penetration of prisons into rural America portends dramatic consequences for the entire nation as huge numbers of inmates from urban areas become rural residents for the purposes of Census-based formulas used to allocate government dollars and political representation.

A RURAL GROWTH INDUSTRY

Since 1980, the majority of new prisons built to accommodate the expanding U.S. prison population have been placed in non-metropolitan areas, with the result that the majority of prisoners are now housed in rural America. By contrast, prior to 1980, only 36 percent of prisons were located in rural communities and small towns. Calvin Beale, a senior demographer with the Economic Research Service of the U.S. Department of Agriculture, reports that throughout the 1960s and '70s, an average of just four new prisons had been built in rural areas each year. During the 1980s that figure increased to an annual average of sixteen, and in the 1990s, it jumped to twenty-five new prisons annually.[3] Between 1990 and 1999, 245 prisons were built in rural and small town communities—with a prison opening somewhere in rural America every fifteen days.[4]

Some of the most depressed rural areas in the United States have had significant infusions of prisons and prison work:

- On the west Texas plains, where both farmwork and oil field jobs were in full retreat in the 1990s, eleven rural counties acquired prisons, where earlier only one prison existed. Overall, one of every five new rural prisons in the 1990s opened in Texas, which had the largest number of new rural prisons by far, with forty-nine.

- The Mississippi Delta picked up seven prisons in the 1990s, added three in 2000–2001, with two more underway as of 2001.
- Nine prisons opened in the Southern coal fields region (Appalachia), and three new federal prisons were underway as of 2001.
- South-central Georgia has a contiguous string of fourteen rural counties with new prisons, and twenty-four altogether in the state.

The new rural prisons of the 1990s had about 235,000 inmates and employed 75,000 workers at the end of the decade—averaging thirty employees for every one hundred prisoners. All in all, about 350 rural counties have aquired new prisons since the start-up of the prison boom began in 1980, and more than half of all rural counties added prison work to their available employment mix during the final two decades of the century just past.[5]

PRISONS AS ECONOMIC DEVELOPMENT: BOOM OR BUST?

Despite a lack of studies documenting the effects of prisons on rural areas and small towns over time, prisons are now heralded by economic development professionals and politicians of all stripes as beneficial economic engines for depressed rural economies. Along with gambling casinos and huge animal confinement units for raising or processing hogs and poultry, prisons have become one of the three leading rural economic enterprises as states and localities seek industries that provide large-scale and quick opportunities.

The county economic development director in the small New York town of Romulus, for example, states that economic development experts throughout the state consider correctional facilities to be positive contributors to local economies, providing good-paying jobs and benefits in communities where employment is scarce.[6] Ernie Preate, a former

Pennsylvania attorney general and member of the advisory board for northeastern Pennsylvania's economic development council, says, "It is policy in Pennsylvania to pursue prisons as economic stimulation for depressed rural areas."[7] When announcing the potential siting of a federal prison in Northumberland County, Pennsylvania, in August 2001, Congressman Paul Kanjorski called the prison "the single largest public works project in the history of Northumberland."[8]

Prison officials go to great pains and often great expense to convince rural communities of the economic benefits of prisons. It is common for local officials to sponsor town meetings where prison officials and their supporters are invited to extol the benefits of prisons to communities. When proposed prisons are on the table, local newspapers are filled with articles reporting grand claims for economic salvation, and flyers flood into local coffeeshops, general stores, and mini-marts. The purported benefits are described by a California Department of Corrections official who states that "Prisons not only stabilize a local economy but can in fact rejuvenate it. There are no seasonal fluctuations, it is a non-polluting industry, and in many circumstances it is virtually invisible. . . . You've got people that are working there and spending their money there, so now these communities are able to have a Little League and all the kinds of activities that people want."[9]

As a result of such claims, the competition for prison "development projects" has become fierce and political. In order to be considered competitive in the bidding wars for public prisons, rural counties and small towns give up a lot in order to gain what they hope will be more: offering financial assistance and concessions such as donated land, upgraded sewer and water systems, housing subsidies, and, in the case of private prisons, property and other tax abatements.

In the all-out contest spurred by New York governor George Pataki's 1996 proposal to build three new maximum-security state prisons, the rural town of Altamont set aside one hundred acres of land to entice the state to locate a prison there. Antwerp, another small community in northern New York, applied for a $600,000 federal grant to rebuild their water supply system to increase their chances of winning a state prison.[10]

States also compete fiercely with one another for federal prisons. In 1997, Pennsylvania offered up to two hundred acres of prime state-owned farmland in rural Wayne County to the Federal Bureau of Prisons (FBOP) for a dollar. When a rural citizens group legally challenged the sale, the land—also evaluated as eligible for status as a National Historic Register District because of the historic remains on the site—was again transferred by the state to the FBOP as part of a "friendly condemnation." That transaction was also sealed for a dollar.

Despite the prevailing wisdom regarding prisons as economic panaceas, evidence suggests that prison boosters in rural America should be careful what they wish for.

The majority of public prison jobs, for example, do not go to people already living in the community. Higher-paying management and correctional officer jobs in public prisons come with educational and experience requirements that many rural residents do not have. Seniority (and, in some cases, union rules) in public corrections systems means that these prisons are typically activated with large cadres of veteran correctional personnel from other prisons. In addition, competition for jobs in depressed areas is fierce, so rural residents compete in a wider than normal market for available positions. The distances people drive to work at prisons are quite great, in most cases nearly double the average commuter range, according to Ruth Gilmore, a professor at UC-Berkeley. Gilmore's study of prison towns in California shows that less than 20 percent of jobs on average go to current residents of a town with a new state prison. Although that percentage increases over time, it is below 40 percent for all of California's new rural prison towns.[11]

The findings of Gilmore's study in California are echoed in reports from disappointed local officials in prison towns across the country. The 750 jobs that a state prison opened in 1999 brought to the tiny rural town of Malone, New York, went mostly to people from outside the town because of prison system seniority rules. According to the village's director of the Office of Community Development, "Did we get seven hundred fifty jobs? We didn't get a hundred."[12]

A significant development in rural incarceration is the advent of private prisons, which accounted for one-sixth of nonmetro prisons built in the 1990s.[13] Although private prisons do fill most jobs with new recruits when they open, and they sometimes give a hiring preference to local residents, they fail to provide a stable employment base in their host communities because they suffer extremely high rates of job turnover—three times higher than the rate for public prisons. Correctional officer turnover rates in for-profit facilities are 40.9 percent (compared with a turnover rate of 15.4 percent in government-run prisons), mostly because of poor training and low wages. This rapid turnover can create staffing problems that play out in understaffed shifts, low morale, and a sense of instability in the facility and the surrounding community.[14]

According to Thomas Johnson, an economist and professor of public affairs at the University of Missouri, prisons are not very good economic development strategies because they generate few linkages to the economy, failing to attract significant numbers of associated industries, as an auto plant might spark the development of delivery companies, radio assemblers, and electronic harness makers.[15]

Prisons may also fail to foster significant retail development. Because prisons, as a large-scale enterprise, attract chain stores, there is a "replacement" effect, with giants such as McDonald's and Wal-Mart pushing out locally owned enterprises. In Tehachapi, California, home to two state prisons, 741 locally owned businesses failed in the last decade of the 1990s, while retail and fast food chains absorbed the local markets. As a result, there may be no net increase in tax revenues, and, because profits made by chain stores are not locally reinvested in the way that locally owned profits may be, the circulation of dollars within a community may drop in absolute terms.

Anticipating that prisons will attract new people to live in the host community and that locals with prison jobs will be able to afford better housing, developers build new housing. But because today's prison employees often choose not to live in small rural towns, opting instead to commute from urban and suburban areas, speculation in housing development can end in disaster both for the speculator and for the town, as happened in the California prison towns of Corcoran and Avenal.

The impact of prisons on housing can also cause economic hardships for the poor and elderly in rural communities. Both land and rental values generally increase when a prison siting is authorized by a governmental or corporate entity; however, land values fall once the actual (low) number of locally gained jobs, and associated homeowners, becomes clear. This has the effect of placing additional burdens on poorer members of the community, particularly renters and elderly homeowners, since rents generally rise when real property prices rise, but landlords rarely reduce rents during economic downturns. As a result, renters, who are often the poorest members of communities, are made even poorer because their fixed costs increase while income does not change. This happened in Crescent City, California, when a state prison opened in 1989. For elderly homeowners, the rise and fall in prices during the period of speculative development ultimately devalued their homes.[16]

Prisoners themselves may also displace low-wage workers in struggling rural areas. One researcher assessing the impacts of prisons on host communities noted that "Prisons as industries do have the added plus of a captive workforce available for community projects."[17] Work projects performed by prisoners for local government, churches, hospitals, libraries, and many other kinds of organizations are very common in prisons located in rural communities and small towns, and prison officials tout them as good "community relations." This can lead to competition within the community for the services of inmates working both inside and outside the prison. In Coxsackie, New York, home to two state prisons and 3,000 prisoners, work performed for the community varies widely according to the prison guard coordinator of the inmate work crew: "We've done a lot of painting this year, painting a community center building in Athens, painted the inside of a church parish hall, put a roof on the town of New Baltimore town hall, had them sealing blacktop . . . just about everything. They get an industrial rate which amounts to 42 cents an hour."[18] Although local governments and other organizations save money on work they would otherwise have had to contract out to workers at a prevailing wage, prison labor may result in displacement of workers in these communities and can deepen local poverty.[19]

The "hidden" costs of doing prison business can be high for small communities. Local court and police systems are often the first to feel the impact. In many states, county or district public defenders are responsible for defending indigent inmates charged with committing crimes (e.g., assaults on guards and other inmates) within state prisons. In low-population counties with large numbers of prisoners, the prisoner share of a defender's caseload can be quite high, and the much higher rate of inmate assaults on staff and inmates at private prisons as compared with that in government-run facilities means this is a particular burden for towns with private prisons. Since private prison guards do not have the same police powers that state or federal correctional officers do, many disciplinary infractions in private prisons are handled by district or county courts. In Bent County, Colorado, filings in the county court increased an astonishing 99 percent after the opening of the privately operated Bent County Correctional Facility in Las Animas.[20]

The increasing practice of importing inmates from other states can exacerbate these costs. This poses serious problems since, in the event of a disturbance or escape, state and local law enforcement personnel can be left with the task of "cleaning up" when there is a problem. This happened in 1999 at the Correctional Service Corporation's Crowley County Correctional Facility (CCCF) in Olney Springs, Colorado, when inmates from Wyoming protested inadequate food service and state employees were called in to restore order. State investigators found that CCCF employees were not trained to detect possible problems, handle disturbances, or even properly use their radios.[21]

Though boosters claim that prisons are "recession-proof," in fact they are subject to downturns in the economy, and expected booms can change to busts for small towns. Bonne Terre, Missouri, chosen in 1995 as the home for the state's largest and costliest prison, learned that lesson the hard way. In 2001, six years after the announcement, the city was in debt, and new businesses nearly broke because state budget shortfalls delayed the opening of the prison. As with many small communities trying to replace dead or dying industries with prisons, Bonne Terre, once one of the nation's top lead-mining towns, gave a lot to get what they hoped would be more. The town purchased the land for the prison and issued bonds to help pay for $14 million in improvements that included new roads, and sewer and water lines. But the town has been forced to pay back the debt on these loans without the expected increases in revenue from the prison. Businesses such as a Texaco convenience store and gas station, car washes, and fast-food outlets that opened in anticipation of the prison found themselves in a similar bind. One local land developer, unable to get more than one business to commit to a 240-acre site that he bought and cleared, estimated that businesses in Bonne Terre lost millions of dollars.[22]

The effects of the recession begun in March, 2001 also show that Bonne Terre's experience may look good compared with that of other prison towns in such states as California, Ohio, Michigan, and Illinois, which have announced their intentions to close existing prisons. States faced with choices between spending on corrections and spending in other areas are now up against a wall, shelving prison-building plans for the near future and laying off hundreds of prison employees. As one North Dakota legislator put it, "For every dollar that you're spending on corrections, you're not spending that on primary and secondary education, you're not spending it on the colleges or tourism. It's just money down a rat hole, basically."[23]

Prisons can also discourage other kinds of economic development. The lack of amenities in a town, coupled with the dominance of a prison on its social and economic horizon, may discourage other industries from locating in the town that might, for all other purposes, be perfectly suitable. In California, all new prison towns have had great difficulty attracting other industries. Explanations for this difficulty range from the "spectre" of prison as an undesirable neighbor, to the fact that prisons are not necessarily required to conform to all environmental and other controls. Thus, in California prison towns Tehachapi and Avenal, water quantity and quality have become major issues.[24]

The town of Malone, New York, is another small community in the throes of realizing its future as a prison town. Despite having three state prisons, a hoped-for food processing plant to serve the prisons hasn't materialized, and a $4.5 million expansion of the sewage-treatment plant, paid for by the state to accommodate the third prison opened in 1999, has increased the amount of nitrates dumped on a daily basis into the Salmon River, a beautiful trout stream treasured by the community. Because the loans to build the sewage plant and a new water system for the prison were based on the village's, not the state's, borrowing capacity, taxes have gone up, and the payments were estimated to be more than $1 million in 2000.

Boyce Sherwin, the town's industrial recruiter who was born and reared in Malone, deplores the prison boomlet. "It will institutionalize a degraded environment and quality of life," he states. "Is this our legacy to our children?" The executive director of Friends of the North Country, a community development group that has opposed prison-building, believes "Once you have the reputation of a prison town, you won't become a Fortune 500 company town, or an Internet or software company town, or even a diverse tourism and company town." Sherwin sees a dream that has gone sour: "It was get a prison and your community is set," he says. "But look around, is this heaven?"[25]

NORMAN ROCKWELL MEETS QUENTIN TARANTINO

In response to increased difficulty in attracting other industries, local officials in towns with one prison often opt or are forced to lobby for more prisons, creating a "one-company town" scenario over time. The tendency of states—including Texas, Arizona, New York, Pennsylvania, Illinois, Michigan, Colorado, Florida, and California, among many others—to "cluster" prisons in distinct rural regions has created dozens of rural penal colonies where prisons dominate the community's economic, social, political, and cultural landscape with myriad and profound effects.

In the small town of Ionia, in a rural region of Michigan, a sixth state prison was due to open in 2002, tying it with Huntsville, Texas, for most lockups in a U.S. city. The prisons cover two square miles and comprise a third of the city's size. They hold 5,094 prisoners and have 1,584 workers. According to a *Detroit News* reporter, "When this world of servitude collides with that of freedom, Ionia takes on the look of a Norman Rockwell painting defaced by Quentin Tarantino." He noted that prison supervisors belong to the chamber of commerce and are regulars at Rotary. One warden serves on the city council, and another was president of the city's fair association. It's not uncommon to come across an inmate in his prison blues pruning bushes at police headquarters or, during the winter, shoveling snow for seniors. Teams in city leagues drive into lower security prisons to play softball against inmates.[26]

Although the local government and business leaders of Ionia express contentment with its prison-town identity, there's no shortage of anecdotal evidence of increased rates of divorce, alcoholism and substance abuse, suicide, health problems, family violence, and other crimes associated with multigenerational prison communities, suggesting that below the surfaces of local power structures, people in these communities are suffering.[27] The stress of work in prisons, though not a subject of open discussion in most prison towns, is well documented and most recently made the subject of popular discussion with the publication of journalist Ted Conover's book, an account of a year working as a prison guard inside one of America's most famous prisons.[28] A quick perusal of the letters Conover has received from prison guards and their family members from across the nation speaks to the dehumanization of both prisoners and guards that inevitably takes place behind bars and to the toll on the loved ones, neighbors, and friends of correctional officers.[29]

The impact of this process of soul-death on a small community is suggested in remarks made by Richard Purdue, a former mayor of Ossining, New York, the prison town that changed its name from Sing Sing in an attempt to alter the perceptions of the town by outsiders. In a letter written in 1997 addressing New York's proposal to locate a maximum-security prison in the tiny town of Tupper Lake in the state's Adirondack Mountain region, Purdue says, "A state prison is a disadvantage to a small community. A maximum security prison in particular drags on the public perception of a town and quietly injures a town's perception of itself. The State Legislature still can turn back the Tupper Lake proposal. For Tupper Lake and for the Adirondacks, this could initiate a period of progress, rather than a dismal retreat into the industry of incarceration."[30]

PERPETUATING RACISM

Racial hatred behind and beyond prison walls is another deeply troubling consequence of the increasing dependence of rural communities on prisons. While racism is not a new feature of the U.S. prison system, efforts to address the problem are undermined by the trend toward building prisons in rural areas where the work force is predominantly white and prisoners are predominantly people of color. Calling racism pervasive in rural prisons, author, researcher, and former corrections officer Kelsey Kauffman has gathered extensive documentation on both individual and organized acts of racist activity in rural prisons throughout states as diverse as Indiana, New York, Virginia, Florida, New Jersey, Illinois, Colorado, California, Maine, and Michigan.[31]

Individual acts of racism in prisons include the wearing of Klan-style robes or hoods at work and the wearing or displaying of Confederate or skinhead flags or insignias by employees inside prisons. The problem becomes one of organized or organizational racism when excuses like "Hey, it was just a joke," or, "That's my heritage" are accepted and translated by prison management as, "White boys will be white boys."[32]

In at least six states, guards have appeared in mock Klan attire in recent years. Guards have also been accused of race-based threats, beatings and shootings in ten states. Lawsuits have been filed in at least thirteen states by black guards alleging racist harrassment or violence from white colleauges. And uncounted settlements have been reached in civil cases filed by guards or inmates, where damages are sealed by court order.[33]

The Florida NAACP has joined more than a hundred black employees in filing suit against the state Department of Corrections for harboring and condoning overt racism in the state's prisons. Black officers and prisoners have accused white officers of carrying so-called "nigger knots" (small knotted nooses on their key chains worn as symbols of solidarity); of wearing and displaying racist symbols (such as Klan tattoos) at work; of routinely using racist epithets; and of retaliating against employees—black and white—who challenge these practices.[34]

In the late 1990s, two separate lawsuits by African-American correctional officers were filed against the Department of Corrections in Washington, where individual and organized racist activity among white prison guards has been a widely reported problem in rural prisons throughout the state. In 2000, the Washington Department of Corrections paid $250,000 in an out-of-court settlement to black officers who had accused it of condoning racist behavior at the Clallam Bay Corrections Center located in a remote northwest corner of the state, where most of the prison guards are white, formerly unemployed loggers.[35]

"The people we work with out there are ex-loggers," said former guard Doris Washington, a plaintiff in the Clallam Bay suit. "They have never come into contact with the outside world per se. They don't know how to deal with us because they've never been around us." Though Clallam Bay's prisoner population is 48 percent minority, only 4 of of its 326 employees are black. The lawsuit stated that black officers were denied promotions, subject to threats and racial epithets like "coon," and that minority prisoners were harassed and set up for beatings. Some white guards had taken to calling Martin Luther King, Jr., Day "Happy Nigger Day" and a handful of guards openly bragged about associations with hate groups such as the Ku Klux Klan. A similiar lawsuit filed in 1999 by black employees of Washington Correctional Center in Shelton also included complaints about organized neo-Nazi activities, including "Heil Hitler" salutes among some white officers and distribution of hate literature inside the prison.[36]

In other instances, prison officials would like to sanction employees who are prominently associated with white supremacist organizations outside the prison but can't because these employees have clean records inside. And although there have also been cases where correctional officers who are leaders in their local white supremacist organizations have been fired when they openly recruited at work, others who flaunt their white supremacy at work keep their jobs.

"Such situations are highly corrosive for those who work in rural prisons, for those who live in them, for the communities around them, and ultimately for the nation as a whole," says Kauffman, who recommends the first course of action to address this problem is to stop building prisons in rural areas: "Beyond the obvious parallels that we are once again using black bodies to sustain white rural economies, we are setting ourselves up, over the long term, for greater racial tensions in this country. Prison walls cannot and will not contain the racial hatreds generated within them."[37]

REDISTRIBUTING WEALTH AND POLITICAL POWER

The shock waves of the prison-building spree in rural America are now penetrating the inner core of our nation's large cities and threatening dramatic and troubling changes in the way the nation allocates resources and political representation. The near-doubling of the prison population and the rural prison boom during the 1990s portends a substantial transfer of dollars from urban to rural America because prison inmates are counted in the populations of the towns and counties in which they are incarcerated and not in their home neighborhoods. The result? Inner-city communities, home to large numbers of prisoners, will lose out. The prisoner "share" of the nearly $2 trillion in federal funds tied to population counts distributed nationwide during this decade will go to the mostly rural hometowns of their keepers.[38]

Ironically, it is prisons that are reversing long-standing trends of population loss in rural counties. Sussex County, Virginia, a 496-square-mile patch of peanuts, cotton, and hog farms, was recently declared the fastest growing county in the United States. The reason? Between 1998 and 1999, two new maximum security prisons increased its population by 23 percent. As rural communities gain inmates, they harvest federal cash. In Coxsackie, New York, prisoners make the community more "competitive" for federal antipoverty funds distributed on a per capita basis. Because they earn little or no money, prisoners in the town's two correctional facilities—who made up 27.5 percent of Coxsackie's 1990 population—drove down its median income on the census and made it eligible to receive more funding from the federal Department of Housing and Urban Development. Since that time, the number of Coxsackie's prisoners has continued to grow, and local officials acknowledge that Coxsackie will benefit even more from the final 2000 census count.[39]

As the cutoff for that census approached, localities rushed to get their piece of the pie. In 1998, an Arizona law permitting municipalities to annex prisons set off a bidding war between the towns of Gila Bend and Buckeye for neighboring adult and juvenile prisons. Buckeye won, and as a result expects to reap $600 per inmate every year, amounting to over $10 million in Census-tied subsidies in this decade.[40] Florence, Arizona, with five prisons, employed an even more novel approach when it paid the Census Bureau thousands of dollars for mid-decade population tabulations to adjust for new prisons built there—assuring that its "fair share" of Census-tied federal and state dollars would flow into the town before the results of the 2000 Census were in.[41]

The big losers in this shift will be urban communities of color. Half of all U.S. prisoners are African American, and one-sixth are Latino. The vast majority are from places like East New York and South Central Los Angeles. As a result, these neighborhoods—which have already sustained years of economic and social crises and loss—stand to lose more money in coming years.

These communities also stand to lose political representation and power as a result of the prison boom in rural America. Political districts are based on population size and determine the number of Congressional, state, and local representatives. When political boundaries are redrawn to conform with Census figures, the huge numbers of urban people imprisoned will be reapportioned to the rural areas hosting their prisons.

We are thus on the verge of a national crisis, particularly in situations where the communities that "win" are predominantly white, and the communities that "lose" are predominantly minority. In Florida, for example, including the state's growing inmate population could greatly affect political boundaries in sparsely populated North Florida counties, where prisons have cropped up like mushrooms over the past decade. Gulf County has two new prisons accounting for a significant percentage of its 13,000 residents; a prison built in Gadsden County could help move state legislative boundaries that affect Tallahassee and other Big Bend counties. Opinions issued by Florida's attorney general in August 2001 said county commissions and school boards must include prisoners when redistricting.[42]

So, while they can't vote, Florida's 82,000 prison inmates may figure heavily in the state's redrawing of political boundaries. Therein lies another major dilemma: because prisoners in forty-eight states are disenfranchised, if prisoners are allowed to be counted in the region of their imprisonment for the purposes of political representation, then their votes are effectively given to those who happen to live near a prison, thus diluting the voting power of the predominately black, Hispanic, and urban prison population and giving it to mostly white, rural regions.[43]

Among political gatekeepers, concerns about these potentially significant impacts are growing. In 1999, Republican Congressman Mark Green of Wisconsin introduced a bill that would allow states to count for Census purposes the state and federal prisoners exported to other states. The congressman was concerned that Wisconsin could lose one of its nine Congressional seats after the 2000 census count.[44]

CONCLUSION

Although the growth in prisoner populations and new prisons slowed somewhat in the late 1990s, without other interventions such as changes in mandatory sentencing laws and parole policies, or more extensive use of alternatives to incarceration, prisoner populations and prison-building may climb upward again.

As well, the use of prisons as moneymakers for struggling rural communities has become a major force driving criminal justice policy toward mass incarceration of the urban poor regardless of policy rationales like rising crime and prison overcrowding. As former New York State legislator Daniel Feldman observed, "When legislators cry 'Lock 'em up!' they often mean 'Lock 'em up in my district!' "[45] Indeed, the rural prison boom during the decade of the 1990s occurred at a time of falling crime rates, and experience shows that the federal and state governments are reluctant to pull the plug on the many interests that now lobby for and feed off prisons. Allowed to continue, this cycle will have catastrophic consequences for the health and welfare of individuals, families, and communities in urban and rural areas, and indeed for the nation.

13

The Impact of Mass Incarceration on Immigration Policy

Teresa A. Miller *

P rior to the 1980s, wide-scale detention of aliens by the Immigration and Naturalization Service was highly unusual. The conventional policy for dealing with undocumented aliens seeking to reside in the United States was exclusion at the border or deportation of those who had already crossed the border illegally, with liberal provision for bail, release on one's own recognizance, and other forms of relief from detention. Aliens who were legally residing in the United States but who had committed acts subjecting them to deportation likewise had options other than detention. Yet today, immigration detainees represent the fastest growing segment of the jail population in the United States.[1] The INS contracts out to local and municipal jails the care, custody, and control of approximately 60 percent of all its detainees.[2] Fifty-five hundred detainees were held in INS custody in 1994. In 1997, as the rapid increase in the number of federal and states inmates actually slowed—to 5.2 percent from a decade-long average of 7 percent growth—the number of detainees in INS custody rose to 16,000, representing a tripling over a period of four years.[3] During the 2000 fiscal year, the INS detained close to 190,000 aliens. By 2001, the INS was detaining on average 19,500 non-U.S. citizens on any given day.[4]

In the custody of the INS, these detainees are little more than prisoners. Detainees who may have done nothing more serious than come to the United States without documentation seeking asylum or who overstay their visas are housed with maximum-security criminal offenders in federal prisons and local county jails. Detainees are required to wear prison uniforms and spend most of their time in cells. They are transported in handcuffs and shackles, strip-searched, and disciplined harshly, even though their failure to conform to prison rules may result not from belligerence but from poor English comprehension and cultural differences.[5]

Although the conditions under which detainees are confined may resemble that of their criminal counterparts, they are, in fact, far worse. Detainees have fewer due process rights than are granted to American prisoners. Aliens have no right to court-appointed counsel. This means that if a detainee cannot afford legal services, he must go without. In fact, the Executive Office for Immigration Review has reported that less than 11 percent of detainees receive attorney assistance.[6] Detainees are also cut off from services simply because they do not speak the language. INS usually provides detainees with translators only in the event of an emergency or a medical examination, and often these are provided by phone.[7] The few services detainees do have access to are threatened by the explosion in the number of INS detainees. INS is sending more aliens to detention centers that are already overcrowded and understaffed.

This burgeoning new segment of the prison population is a product of immigration policies that have grown increasingly punitive over the past decade, culminating in the enactment in 1996 of two harsh federal laws that enhance the government's ability to remove undesirable aliens from the country: the Anti-Terrorism and Effective Death Penalty Act (AEDPA) and the Illegal Immigration Reform and Immigrant Responsibility Act (IIRIRA). These laws criminalized immigration violations to an extraordinary degree. They impose criminal penalties for immigration violations that were civil under prior law, and heightened penalties for violations that were already considered crimes. These laws also mandate the detention—and eventual deportation[8]—of non-U.S. citizens with even minor criminal convictions. They foreclose most avenues of relief from detention, and provide for the expedited removal of inadmissible aliens by the INS without any form of judicial review.

Crime policy in the United States has profoundly influenced immigration detention policy. Mass incarceration policies and practices have provided a template for the widespread detention of immigrants who lack proper documentation or have criminal convictions in their pasts.

Moreover, "get tough" policies within the criminal justice system and the immigration system have common roots. Both mass incarceration of criminal offenders and the broader detention of immigrants emerge from negative perceptions of the welfare system, racial prejudice, hysteria about people seeming to be culturally inassimilable, and economic expedience. The template fashioned during the unprecedented expansion of the prison system that began with longer and fixed sentencing policies in the 1970s then served as a model for the subsequent reconfiguration of the immigration detention system in the 1990s. Increasingly, the immigration system functions—like the criminal justice system—to socially control through confinement in secure, disciplinary facilities the unpopular and the powerless, which in this case are undocumented people of color.[9]

The exponential expansion of criminal incarceration within the past thirty years is characterized by enhanced "zero tolerance" law enforcement leading to higher rates of prosecution; increasingly harsh criminal penalties and dramatic expansion of prison capacity; unprecedented increases in the number of people incarcerated in prisons and jails for longer terms; incarceration of those traditionally controlled by processes and agencies outside the criminal justice system (e.g., drug addicts, women, juveniles, and the mentally ill); increased privatization of a traditionally government function; and a growing managerial emphasis on incarceration as a vehicle of risk management.

Many of the same policies that defined mass incarceration in the criminal justice system are reconfiguring the contours of the U.S. immigration system—so much so that the immigration system is becoming a replica of the criminal justice system. First, immigration has become increasingly criminalized.[10] In sharp contrast to its traditional functions of preserving opportunities for legal immigrants, refugees, and asylees to resettle in the United States, assisting undocumented immigrants in their pursuit of naturalization,[11] and preserving family unity, the immigration system has instead over the past decade become increasingly punitive.

The criminalization of immigration law has also led to elimination of avenues of relief from detention previously available, including waiver, bond, and release on the alien's own recognizance. Consequently, the number of people detained in INS processing centers and local jails increased dramatically, along with the length of detention. For example, in 1981, the average stay in an INS detention facility was less than four days.[12] By 1990, it grew to twenty-three days, with many individuals detained for more than a year,[13] and a year later it had more than doubled to fifty-four days.[14] After the enactment of the 1996 legislation, the range of time in detention expanded greatly. By 1998, the average length of detention had dropped to thirty-four days,[15] primarily reflecting the expedited removal of large numbers of Mexican nationals at the southern border. After 1996, far greater numbers of aliens were moving through the detention system, ranging from a mere two days to several years. The numbers reflect not only the increasing volume of detainees, but a broader scope of detention as well. The numbers further reflect the fact that the INS began to detain categories of immigrants—such as lawful permanent residents, women, children, and families—it had traditionally released in the past.

Immigration policies also reflect an increasingly managerial approach to immigrants consistent with what postmodern criminological theorists have dubbed the "new penology."[16] This is particularly true for so-called "criminal aliens." As the INS increasingly targets for removal immigrants who are lawfully in the country (some of whom have lived in the United States most of their lives) and excludes at the border individuals who are not eligible for admission, it takes on the role of policing society from within as well as from without.

Traditional penology emphasizes punishing and correcting individual offenders. In the past thirty years, however, the criminal justice system has embraced a new set of values aimed at reducing the risks that specific criminal subpopulations (e.g., drug addicts, violent juveniles) pose to the broader society by more effectively controlling these groups. The new penology emphasizes efficiency, management, and control rather than the traditional penological techniques of individualized justice and personal transformation. As one commentator points out, the result is that the criminal justice system "recycles human beings from one form of custodial management to another without attempting to impose justice or to reintegrate offenders into society."[17] As the influence of criminal justice policies on the immigration system becomes more evident, the impact of the new penology on immigration policies is clear. Legislation mandating the detention and deportation of criminal aliens aims to cleanse society of foreigners with criminal histories. Their vulnerable citizenship status makes this possible. The INS conforms to the new penology both by emphasizing enforcement and detention rather than social service, and resorting to the processing of large aggregates of foreigners, specifically targeting nationalities such as Cubans, Haitians, Jamaicans, and, most recently, Arabs.[18] Over the past three decades, crime legislation and policies have made the stigma of criminal prosecution far harder to escape. And for someone who is not a U.S. citizen, involvement with the criminal justice system is an indelible mark—a prelude to banishment.

All three of these recent trends in the law of immigration detention—heightened criminal penalties, decreased alternatives to detention, and managerialism—reflect the influence of mass incarceration policies on immigration. The treatment of criminal aliens in particular illustrates the new, punitive emphasis in immigration law and the profound influence the criminal justice system exerts on the immigration system. Within the past fifteen years, various state and federal laws were passed that facilitate the deportation of long-term permanent resident aliens with criminal histories.[19] One-third to one-half of removals of noncitizens from the United States in the late 1990s have been criminal aliens. The mandatory detention provisions of the 1996 immigration reforms are also responsible for the long-term detention of criminal aliens whose countries will not permit them to be repatriated. Even after the Supreme Court held that the indefinite, potentially permanent, detention of immigration detainees was unconstitutional in *Zadvydas v. Davis*,[20] some "dangerous" criminal aliens will remain in indefinite detention, and the meaningfulness of the "reasonable time" limitation imposed by the Court will remain in question.

THE HARSH IMPACT OF 1996 IMMIGRATION LEGISLATION

Enacted in April 1996, AEDPA amended the Immigration and Nationality Act, relying heavily upon a distorted notion of "criminality" to justify confining and expelling thousands of immigrants. The IIRIRA was passed five months later to fill gaps in the hastily passed AEDPA. These two federal acts treat immigrants with unprecedented harshness. Even green card holders (technically known as lawful permanent residents) lost a great deal of their relatively insulated status as immigrants generally regarded as being on the fast track toward naturalization. One of the most significant aspects of the 1996 legislation is that it mandated detention without the possibility of release on bond for virtually all non-U.S. citizens with a criminal conviction in their past (so-called "criminal aliens") pending deportation proceedings against them. Prior to the enactment of the AEDPA, only excludable aliens (those who had not technically "entered" the United States) could be detained if the examining immigration officer doubted their admissibility.[21] And in such cases, parole was frequently granted for reasons ranging from pregnancy, youthfulness, and illness to the absence of a public interest served by continued detention. However, the AEDPA explicitly limited agency discretion to ensure fairness and prevent unconscionable results.

The 1996 legislation drastically expanded the litany of crimes that subject immigrants to detention and deportation. Aliens seeking to enter the United States have long been excludable and deportable as a result of committing certain categories of crimes: crimes of moral turpitude, drug trafficking, weapons offenses, prostitution, etc. The Anti–Drug Abuse Act of 1988 created three categories of aggravated felony crimes: murder, drug trafficking, and weapon trafficking. Congressional legislation passed in 1990 (the Immigration Act of 1990) expanded the scope of the term "aggravated felony" to include crimes of violence for which the alien received a prison sentence of at least five years, and made deportation and other penalties flowing from the conviction apply retrospectively. In 1994, the definition of an aggravated felony was further expanded to include certain fraud and money-laundering crimes.

Since the passage of AEDPA and IIRIRA in 1996, however, the scope of the aggravated felonies now encompasses fifty different categories of crimes, and subjects to deportation (and mandatory detention prior to deportation) any non-U.S. citizen who may have had a relatively minor criminal conviction in the past.[22] For some categories of crimes, a mere misdemeanor conviction of at least one year constitutes an aggravated felony. As a result of the 1996 legislation, a lawful permanent resident who pleads guilty to attempted sexual misconduct in New York State (a Class B misdemeanor) can be removed as an aggravated felon. Mandatory detention followed by deportation is triggered by minor offenses such as first-time shoplifting convictions, gambling offenses, and perjury, and do not incorporate the moderating influence of judicial discretion and procedural protections within criminal proceedings that often impact upon the conviction. Many crimes considered to be "aggravated felonies" within the meaning of AEDPA bear little relation to their menacing title. Perjury, forgery, reentering the country after being deported on the basis of an aggravated felony conviction, or failing to appear in court to answer to a felony charge are all crimes considered to be "aggravated felonies" in the context of immigration that would not be aggravated felonies in the criminal context. In effect, an aggravated felony within the meaning of the AEDPA bears little resemblance to an aggravated felony in the context of the criminal law.

The impact of the broadened scope of aggravated felonies is magnified by the retroactivity of the legislation since the IIRIRA applied the expanded definition of an "aggravated felony" to convictions "before, on, or after" September 30, 1996.[23] Since the amendments operate retroactively, they apply to crimes committed decades before. Many of these crimes did not constitute grounds for deportation when they were committed; therefore, the foreign defendants may have pled guilty to a lesser crime rather than risk deportation on a more serious charge. Many of these older crimes were not even considered "aggravated felonies" when they were committed. The retroactivity of the mandatory detention provisions combined with the vastly expanded categories of offenses which subject non-U.S. citizens to deportation are primarily responsible for the threefold increase in the numbers of non-U.S. citizens in federal immigration detention.

IIRIRA and AEDPA demonstrate how the immigration system has adopted methods of socially controlling society's "undesirables" by redefining the boundaries of criminality. These acts broadened the net in which aliens are confined by expanding (some would say exaggerating) categories of criminal offenses, criminal conduct, and notions of what constitutes a threat to society. Much like zero tolerance of drugs, this legislation takes a zero tolerance posture toward noncitizens with criminal histories, even histories of minor crime. With the passage of IIRIRA and AEDPA, the federal government brought immigrants squarely under the locus of control it has applied to prisoners for decades.

Since their enactment, the 1996 laws have had a predictably harsh impact on families, undocumented minors, asylum-seekers, border communities, and others. Examples of egregious, inordinately harsh results abound. In Georgia, a lawful permanent resident from Nigeria and the mother of two American children was ordered deported for shoplifting $14.99 worth of baby clothes six years earlier. Although she received only a suspended sentence of one year in circumstances that suggested she was not guilty, she was nevertheless deported.[24] A California man who was a lawful permanent resident for twenty-nine years was deported to Colombia for the sale of a $10 bag of marijuana ten years before, despite the fact that he received only a ninety-day sentence for his crime. His teenage son—a U.S. citizen—committed suicide the day after his father's deportation.[25] A thirty-three-year-old lawful permanent resident from Colombia who immigrated to the United States when she was six was convicted of criminal facilitation in a drug purchase, a felony, and sentenced to three to nine years. She was released after two years. She went on to earn a college degree, work as a secretary to former New York City mayor David Dinkins, and became a social worker. Returning from her mother's funeral in Colombia, she was arrested at the airport and immediately put in detention pending deportation.[26]

In spite of the overwhelming support AEDPA and IIRIRA garnered in Congress, there was wide consensus among immigrant advocates and high-ranking INS officials alike that the legislation was too aggressive; that it all too broadly mandated detention and deportation of all non-U.S. citizens previously convicted of a crime no matter how long ago and how minor.[27] The terrorist attacks on the World Trade Center and the Pentagon on September 11, 2001, provoked a public outcry against loopholes and laxity in immigration controls that virtually ensures that the 1996 legislation will stay on the books for a long time to come. Moreover the USA PATRIOT Act,[28] enacted by Congress a little over six weeks after the attacks on September 11, confers on the government broad authority to detect, exclude, prosecute, and detain[29] undesirable foreigners in the investigation of terrorism. Unlike criminal aliens who can be detained and deported based upon past (and, in some instances, quite minor) criminal acts, foreigners rounded up in the aftermath of September 11 were preventively detained in a deliberate strategy to disrupt communities thought to be sympathetic to terrorism and, by association, Islamic fundamentalism. Thus, in spite of justifiable concern about the scope of detention after AEDPA and IIRIRA, subsequent legislation passed to combat terrorism goes even further in expanding the authority of INS to detain aliens.

DRUG POLICY, IMMIGRATION, AND INCARCERATION

The "war on drugs" has been a central component of the expanding incarceration of both prisoners and immigrants. Crime policy in the United States changed dramatically when efforts to reduce the possession, use, and distribution of controlled substances such as marijuana, cocaine, and heroin escalated to the status of a war. By raising the stakes, the drug "war" has been used to justify inordinately harsh, punitive treatment of those suspected of involvement in drug trafficking. The same war that is being waged on the streets of America's inner cities is being fought at the U.S. border as well. Indeed the "war on drugs" has been waged disproportionately on noncitizens.[30] The present crackdown on criminal aliens emerged from a broad consensus on the need to reform illegal immigration. By adopting a "zero tolerance" policy toward non-U.S. citizens with criminal records, Congress harnessed the broader plenary power of the immigration system in meeting law enforcement objectives—apprehending, detaining, and deporting individuals thought to pose a risk to society by virtue of their past criminal conduct. In fact, many of the criminal alien provisions of the 1996 Illegal Immigration Reform and Immigrant Responsibility Act are directed toward aliens with histories of controlled substance violations.

THE INTERSECTION OF WELFARE REFORM AND IMMIGRATION POLICIES

Changing attitudes toward welfare also figure prominently in the expansive incarceration of both prisoners and immigrants. The "tough on crime" era began during a massive repeal of welfare legislation. The Reagan-Bush era of national leadership (1981–1992) ushered in a major philosophical shift on crime policy consistent with the conservative commitment to reduce the role of "big government." The rhetoric of individuals taking personal responsibility for their own destinies in a land of tremendous opportunity was employed to supplant the notion that societal problems were the appropriate subject of governmental intervention.[31] Punishing the criminal offender, rather than focusing money and energy on preventing crime or reforming criminal offenders, became the official policy.[32] Public supports to buffer the impact of economic deprivation and social exclusion on urban minority populations were derided as efforts to expand the welfare state. Conservatives argued that government efforts to reduce poverty and disadvantage not only had no effect on crime, but that the expansion of the welfare state itself was to blame for high crime rates.[33] Huge sums of money were diverted into prison construction. And over the past twenty years, these corporate and political interests became invested in the continued growth of a lucrative incarceration industry.

A marked increase in hostility toward welfare recipients in the past two decades has likewise contributed to increasingly punitive immigration policies, including mandatory deportation. In the mid-1990s, antiwelfare sentiment crested for a variety of reasons. The Clinton administration proposed legislation that would drastically reduce and restructure public benefits—the Personal Responsibility and Work Opportunity Reconciliation Act of 1996. The act was passed by the same Congress that enacted the IIRIRA and the AEDPA, during the same session. All three statutes advance key goals of the 104th Congress: restoring values of work, family, personal responsibility, and self-sufficiency; and ending the cycle of welfare dependency.

Mass incarceration policies may not have been designed with class and racial containment as their sole aim. However, within the social and economic context of the 1980s—deindustrialization, domestic insecurity, a broad sense of social breakdown evidenced by increasing poverty, emerging homelessness, and rising crime rates—racial minorities and the poor came under "renewed ideological assault."[34] "People of color were cast as parasites and violent predators, pilfering middle-class (read white) Americans by means of such Great Society programs as AFDC [Aid to Families with Dependent Children] and Head Start."[35] Indeed as the image of the criminal offender as an urban black or Latino male hardened into public consciousness, support for punitive approaches to social problems increased exponentially.[36]

Welfare reform peaked at the same time consensus emerged on the need to reform illegal immigration. Proposition 187 galvanized welfare reform with popular notions of illegal immigrants draining California's resources. Similar to the Bush-era stereotype of urban, black welfare mothers and "welfare queens" defrauding honest taxpayers of hard-earned dollars, so too, were poor, Mexican immigrant women stereotyped as illegally entering the country, having their babies in U.S. hospitals, sending children without English proficiency to public schools, and leaving taxpayers to pick up the tab.

The Illegal Immigration Reform and Immigrant Responsibility Act's harsh penalties for non-U.S. citizens with criminal histories were imposed in the same term that significant restrictions on federal direct aid were codified in the Personal Responsibility Act. These two acts have been referred to as the "one-two" punch of legislative reform in 1996.[37] In concert, these two acts reversed a long-standing policy orientation toward helping legal immigrants obtain benefits. The emphasis is on preventing illegal immigrants from obtaining benefits by requiring all immigrants (even naturalized U.S. citizens) to participate in a process designed to screen out illegal immigrants.

Since 1996, the INS's threshold for detaining and deporting criminal aliens has been drastically reduced. The criminal justice system takes advantage of the immigration system's relatively permissive standard for detaining aliens to detain suspects who happen to lack citizenship for the purpose of conducting criminal investigations. The criminal investigation into the terrorist attacks on September 11, 2001, is a case in point. The FBI relied heavily upon the power of the INS to detain noncitizens without placing them under arrest. Within a month after the attacks, the United States had more than a thousand alien suspects in custody. If they were criminally charged, these aliens would be entitled to due process that they are not afforded as immigration detainees. The criminal justice system not only profoundly influences the immigration system—it also functionally uses the immigration system to extend its own authority.

RACIAL DISCRIMINATION AND IMMIGRATION DETENTION

In May 1981, the INS adopted a formal policy of categorically detaining undocumented Haitians on military bases, in federal prisons, and in secure INS detention facilities run like prisons. This was a radical departure from the existing practice of regularly releasing Haitian aliens, making detention the rule rather than the exception. Moreover, it contrasted dramatically with the contemporaneous treatment of undocumented aliens from other, mostly Communist countries. The policy of incarcerating Haitians, the vast majority of whom were seeking political asylum from a repressive military dictatorship, opened the door to the broader use of detention for subsequent immigrant groups whom the U.S. government views as undesirable.

The immigration system's radical shift to detaining undocumented aliens that began with the detention of Haitian refugees was immediately preceded by the mass incarceration of prisoners by the criminal justice system. Although drug policy did not shape the U.S. response to Haitian immigration to the same extent that it drove mass incarceration, the biases and processes that facilitated mass incarceration similarly facilitated the mass detention of Haitian refugees and subsequent groups of immigrants arriving in the United States en masse. Indeed, the unconventional incarceration of Haitian refugees can only be fully understood in light of several key factors that facilitated mass criminal incarceration: criminal investigation, arrest, and sentencing policies that had a disproportionately negative impact upon poor, black communities; hostility toward welfare and a growing consensus that the disadvantaged are deserving of their plight; and cultural hysteria that perceived impoverished people of color as criminally dangerous, inassimilable others. In effect, the criminal justice system's engagement in the "war on drugs" made available to the INS (a fellow law enforcement agency) a new tool with which to combat mass migrations of undesirable immigrants. That tool is secure detention in disciplinary, prison-like facilities.

Haitians were detained en masse largely as a result of the same factors that contributed to the mass incarceration of poor, uneducated, mostly African-American communities in the "war on drugs." The role of racial discrimination in the mass detention of Haitian refugees is evidenced by the disproportionately punitive treatment of Haitian refugees in comparison with other nonblack contemporaneous refugees from the Caribbean Basin. The influence of zealous welfare reform on the mass detention of Haitian refugees is evidenced by political movements such as the SOS (Save Our State) movement in California that endorsed Proposition 187 for the purpose of divesting illegal immigrants of public supports such as public education and health care. And the role of cultural hysteria is evident in political rhetoric labeling Haitian immigrants as dangerously inassimilable.

A. *"First-Wave" Cuban Refugees: Affirmative Action*

For twenty-five years prior to the 1980s, the INS maintained a policy of detaining only persons who posed a risk to security or were likely to abscond. Indeed, the 1950s and 60s represent a high point in the warm reception of aliens. More than 215,000 so-called "first-wave" Cuban immigrants arrived in the United States between January 1959 and October 1962.[38] The influx consisted of supporters of the U.S.-backed Batista dictatorship who were fleeing Fidel Castro's rise to power. All of European extraction, these refugees were large landholders, industrialists, and managers of expropriated U.S. businesses, professionals, merchants, and middle management employees.[39] They arrived at the peak of the Cold War and in the middle of the civil rights movement, when anti-Communist sentiment and domestic racial tensions were pronounced. This was the first time the United States became a country of first asylum for refugees arriving directly from their home country without passing through third countries.[40]

This "first wave" of Cuban refugees along with subsequent waves of Cubanos that arrived through the 1970s were encouraged to resettle in the United States and given generous assistance to aid in that process. In the most elaborately funded refugee assistance effort ever undertaken, the $1.4 billion federally funded Cuban Refugee Program, these refugees were given a spectrum of benefits including free medical care (including outpatient services, dental, maternal, and child health), bilingual education (for children and adults), vocational training, federally subsidized college and university education for professional retraining, and surplus food distribution. By all appearances the program largely succeeded in assimilating Cuban refugees who arrived during the 1960s and 70s into the American middle class.

B. *Mariel Cubans: Open Arms*

Mariel Cubans were an influx of illegal aliens who arrived in the United States by boat from about April to September of 1980. Frequently referred to as the "fifth wave" of Cuban migration, Mariel Cubans represented an influx of poor and working-class Cubans launched from Mariel Harbor in a ploy by Castro to undermine the political currency of the U.S. government's claim that Cubans were desperate to escape Communism and were trapped in Cuba by a ruthless dictator. On April 20, 1980, Castro opened Mariel Harbor to hundreds of boats piloted by Cuban exiles arriving to take friends and relatives back to the United States "illegally," and to makeshift boats and rafts filed with those wishing to leave Cuba. Declaring that "anybody who wishes to go to any other country where he is received, good riddance,"[41] Castro hoped to embarrass the Carter administration by creating a chaotic, disorderly flood of illegal immigration from Cuba while appearing to be grandiose. It worked. Nearly nine thousand Cubans arrived in Key West on the first two days, and thousands continued to arrive daily in a wave of immigration that would exceed 120,000.[42]

Mariel Cubans differed from earlier waves of Cuban immigrants in that they were less affluent, lacked strong claims to political persecution, and were more racially mixed than the "first-wave" Cubans who were uniformly of European extraction. Yet because Spanish was their first language, they were considered Hispanic within the United States. Many were relatives of Cubans who came to the United States in earlier waves of migration, although some 60,000 Mariels arrived without family or friends in the United States, eager to live in the "land of opportunity." The Carter administration dealt with the massive influx of illegal aliens by declaring a state of emergency in Florida and erecting a "tent city" in Miami's Orange Bowl Stadium to accommodate thousands of homeless Cubans until they could be paroled to friends or relatives living in the United States. Many were flown to military bases for temporary housing until they were claimed by family members or sponsors. Only a small percentage of Mariels were detained on more than a temporary basis. Indeed, of the 120,737 illegal Cubans processed by the INS in 1980, all but 1,050 were paroled and released to their families or private charity groups.[43] The fraction of Mariels[44] who became long-term detainees had committed serious crimes in Cuba, were considered seri ous threats to security within the United States (and thus too dangerous to be paroled with their fellow refugees), and were not allowed to return to Cuba. Thus, through their involvement in serious crime and Castro's refusal to take them back, some Mariel Cubans were confined indefinitely in federal prisons.

C. Haitians: Closed Door

In addition to the 125,000 Mariel refugees who arrived in Florida during the Mariel boatlift of 1980, an estimated 25,000 Haitian refugees arrived illegally in South Florida during the same period and in similar fashion.[45] In contrast to the professional and skilled workers who migrated to the United States and Canada from Haiti in the 1960s, these new refugees were largely uneducated, unskilled, Creole speakers with dark brown complexions. Unlike the "first-wave" Cubans, who were given generous public benefits to support their resettlement, Haitians were denied public supports and were left to rely upon charitable organizations and a black community in Miami that had no cultural affinity with the francophone refugees. Indeed, rather like the 1,050 Mariels whose prior serious crimes or mental health status landed them in federal prison in Atlanta, undocumented Haitian refugees who arrived in the United States after May 1981 were incarcerated on military bases and in federal correctional centers across the United States in spite of the fact that they were neither criminal nor mentally ill. In marked contrast with the treatment of Cuban refugees, the primary response of the U.S. government to the influx of Haitians was detention, interdiction, and accelerated deportation. Known as the Haitian Program, this three-pronged approach was a deliberate effort by the INS to expel Haitians from the Miami area and to discourage other Haitians from coming to the United States regardless of the substance of their claims to asylum.[46]

For aliens who have not received authorization to immigrate to the United States before they leave their countries of origin (e.g., through visas), only three legal avenues exist by which people fleeing their country may gain entrance to the United States: as refugees, as members of a group to whom parole has been granted, or as asylum seekers. Two of the three avenues were closed to Haitians. Haitians were not eligible for admission as refugees because U.S. foreign policy dictates what countries are annually designated as ones from which the United States will accept refugees. As an ally of the Duvalier military dictatorship, the U.S. government did not allocate refugee slots to Haiti.

Neither were Haitians eligible for parole after May 18, 1981. Congress and the Executive Branch can establish parole programs for refugee groups. These programs supplement ordinary channels of immigration. Cuban refugees have historically benefited from a variety of parole programs designed to persons fleeing Communist regimes to remain in the United States. Haitians have been paroled into the United States on only one occassion: from 1972 to 1980.[47] After the Mariel boatlift, Haitians were granted parole by the Cuban-Haitian Entrant Act, which allowed both Cubans and Haitians entering the country before January 1, 1981, to stay in the country on a two-year trial basis. Although Haitians benefited in the short-term from the legislation, the parole program did not apply to the subsequent refugees who continued to arrive in South Florida at a rate of 10,000 a year.[48] Nor was it likely that parole would have been granted at all had Haitians not been swept in on the coattails of the Freedom Flotilla.[49]

The only direct avenue of immigration open to Haitians after Mariel was political asylum. Asylum-seekers must prove that they have a well-founded fear of persecution in their country of origin based upon race, religion, nationality, membership in a particular social group, or political opinion. Aliens granted asylum can become lawful permanent residents (also known as "green card" holders) after one year of residence in the United States.[50] But applying for asylum is a time-consuming, rigorous, case-by-case process never intended to accommodate mass migration. Although many Haitians could demonstrate a well-founded fear of persecution, the INS concluded that Haitians were, in the aggregate, "economic refugees" who were not entitled to political asylum. Ignoring blatant human rights violations, the State Department generally likened

Haitians to Mexicans, leaving an impoverished country to seek better opportunities in the United States.[51] Having thus dismissed the gravity of persecution in Haiti, the INS did everything in its power to assure that Haitians were not admitted to the United States.

The construction of Haitians as low-wage labor migrants provided political support for a dubious legal distinction. Many Cubans and Haitians—if considered individually—could demonstrate a credible fear of persecution, and would, therefore, have been eligible for refugee status. On the other hand, there were Cubans and Haitians who could not make such a showing. Despite the fact that their freedom had been restricted by governments that were both nondemocratic and repressive, some could not claim to have been persecuted. Yet because Cuban and Haitian refugees were treated as groups, notwithstanding their individual motives for seeking asylum in the United States, Cubans received generous assistance for resettlement as "political" refugees while Haitians were excluded and detained as "economic" refugees. In light of the flagrant human rights abuses in Haiti, the United States played up the dire poverty and low standard of living in Haiti while downplaying the vicious political repression. At a time when Californians passed a state referendum divesting illegal immigrants of public benefits such as education and health care, politicians easily sold the message to the American public that Haitians constituted a major threat to an already weakened economy. Within the context of a conservative Republican administration and a weak economy, this strategy had the intended effect.

A cultural hysteria about the impact of waves of poor, black immigrants arriving in the United States generally, and Florida, in particular, similarly added legitimacy to a distorted refugee policy. Haitians were associated with all sorts of negative impacts on the United States. Because of a higher incidence of AIDS in Haiti than in the United States, Haitian refugees were stigmatized as disease-ridden carriers of the disease.[52] In the late 1980s, when scientists first discovered the deadly virus, Americans were alarmed and particularly susceptible to AIDS-based hysteria. In a move that was ultimately retracted, the U.S. Food and Drug Administration went so far as to recommend that Haitians be excluded from donating blood, for fear they would contaminate the nation's blood supply.[53] In a television interview in 1991, former presidential candidate Patrick Buchanan made a blatantly racist argument against Haitian immigration based upon the inability of Haitians to assimilate in America. Buchanan posited the following question: "If we had to take a million immigrants in, say Zulus, next year, or Englishmen, and put them up in Virginia, what group would be easier to assimilate and would cause less problems for the people of Virginia?"[54]

In the consciousness of the American public, Haitians were an extension of the problems America had with its own African-American community. In the mid-1980s, white Americans were fleeing to the suburbs and disinvesting in inner cities that were deteriorating while growing monolithically poor and black. Drugs and drug-related crime dominated these once vibrant, now abandoned neighborhoods. Racially biased policing of drug possession and sales led to a dramatic increase in the representation of African Americans in prisons and jails. On the basis of race and poverty, Haitians became subject to the same practices as African Americans, despite obvious differences.

The mass detention of Haitians set an unprecedented policy of incarcerating aliens and established a new norm of punitiveness that influenced the reception of subsequent immigrant groups. Between 1979 and 1985, over half a million Salvadorans, Guatemalans, and Nicaraguans came to the United States fleeing political violence perpetrated by repressive governments responding, at least in part, to U.S.-supported insurgency. In response to the influx of undocumented Central Americans, the Bush administration confined them to detention centers in South Texas. And again in 1994, when a collapsing Cuban economy sent thousands of Cuban *balseros* to Florida, the Clinton administration extended the Haitian interdiction project to counteract the flood.[55]

THE IMPACT OF SEPTEMBER 11, 2001,
ON IMMIGRATION POLICY

September 11, 2001, will long be remembered as the day that changed everything. The events that unfolded that morning radically changed Americans' perceptions of the security they enjoy within the territorial boundaries of the United States. The perceived risks associated with air travel would be redefined, as well as conventional wisdom regarding the conceivable outcomes of a skyjacking. Indeed, Americans would ironically breathe a sigh of relief that a "wake vortex" emerged as the culprit in the investigation of another devastating airplane disaster in New York City—this time in Queens—nine weeks later. The terrorist attacks on the World Trade Center and the Pentagon guaranteed a deep economic recession that was only speculative at the time, and derailed an immigration initiative that would have granted legal status to millions of undocumented aliens crossing America's southern border. Fear of anthrax and other biochemical weapons, sporadic announcements by the government ominously alerting the public to immediate threats of potential terrorism, the highest nationwide job loss in one month since 1980, and racial profiling of Middle Eastern men are all inextricably linked to the alarming erasure of the Twin Towers from the skyline of New York City.

One could argue that the one thing that remained unchanged by the events of September 11 was the United States' system of immigration detention. After all, it remains one of the most punitive forms of civil confinement employed in the United States. It continues to broadly mandate the incarceration of diverse categories of foreigners in a one-size-fits-all approach to deterring illegal immigration and socially sanitizing the population of legal immigrants residing in the United States, frequently treating most harshly those whose cases are the most sympathetic. And it remains, at least for the foreseeable future, a key element of the legal response to the devastation of September 11. The reforms that were implemented in response to the September 11 attacks belie this simple assertion.

The detention of non-U.S. citizens intensified as government leaders broadly reevaluated America's immigration policies. The Justice Department authorized the detention of hundreds of foreigners for minor, technical violations of immigration procedures that were previously overlooked in order to apprehend suspected terrorists and neutralize sympathizers in a law enforcement dragnet. Practices such as detaining aliens incommunicado without access to lawyers or translators were broadly adopted in the name of national security. The U.S. attorney general expanded the Justice Department's detention authority by doubling to forty-eight hours the amount of time the INS could hold aliens without bringing them before an immigration judge, and extending the limit where necessary.[56] The attorney general further imposed new powers to detain noncitizens for an unspecified period of time without filing charges against them in "emergency" or other "extraordinary circumstances."[57] Even the delegated authority of the INS to apprehend and detain suspicious foreigners was broadened under counterterrorism legislation, while the authority of courts to review the INS's detention decisions was further stripped away.

The deadliest attack on U.S. soil could not have come at a less certain time in the evolution of immigration detention law and policy. Two decades after the Reagan administration authorized the unprecedented detention of Haitian "boat people" on U.S. military bases and in refugee detention centers and camps, the standard policy of the INS was to employ secure detention as a method of deterring large numbers of excludable aliens from coming to the United States and ensuring that candidates for removal from the United States appeared at their deportation hearings. This policy was codified by Congressional legislation passed in 1996 that mandated detention without the possibility of release on bond for virtually all foreigners with a criminal conviction in their past until their actual deportation. "Court stripping" provisions of the same legislation nearly eliminated judicial review of final orders to deport these so-called "criminal aliens." Yet only weeks before the attack, the contours of the immigration service's massive and harsh detention policy were being remolded by judicial decree. In June 2001, the

U.S. Supreme Court declared indefinite detention to be unconstitutional, and limited to six months the amount of time "unremovable" aliens[58] may be detained before the government must present evidence to the effect that removal is reasonably foreseeable in the near future.[59] The Supreme Court similarly reversed the "court-stripping" provisions of the 1996 legislation, reasserting its authority to review the habeas corpus petitions of detained aliens.[60] In the face of a well-established, statutorily mandated policy of detaining criminal aliens, judicial challenges to the 1996 legislation nevertheless injected a note of uncertainty.

In the midst of this uncertainty, federal law enforcement authorities investigating the attacks began using the INS's sweeping detention imperative to justify the detention of large numbers of aliens in civil custody for questioning by the FBI. More than 1,200 aliens were detained in the first ten weeks after the attacks,[61] either as material witnesses, for immigration violations, or on federal, state, or local criminal charges unrelated to the attacks.[62] Furthermore, antiterrorism legislation such as the USA PATRIOT Act of 2001[63] enacted shortly after the attacks, and proposed legislation circulating on Capitol Hill, virtually ensure that the detention power of the INS will be increasingly invoked to facilitate the apprehension of suspected terrorists and those who assist them. After all, according to one former INS attorney, "It's perfectly legal to hold someone on an immigration charge if the government's real interest is a criminal investigation—as long as the underlying charge is legitimate.[64] The potential for abuse, however, is great. Resident aliens enjoy far fewer due process and other constitutional rights than the criminally accused. They are subject to civil penalties as extreme as incarceration (e.g., deportation) for far less culpable conduct. Deploying the INS's broad plenary powers over immigration to evade greater protections afforded the criminally accused is clearly abusive.

Although the most extreme measures proposed by the Bush administration were ameliorated by the opposition of civil liberties advocates and the threat of judicial invalidation on constitutional grounds, the USA PATRIOT Act nonetheless casts such a broad net that it permits the detention and deportation of people arguably engaged in constitutionally protected speech and the indefinite detention of immigrants and non-citizens who are not terrorists.[65] Within days after the attacks, the Justice Department had 352 people in custody, a third of whom were being detained under suspicion of violating immigration laws.[66] By the end of the month following the attacks, over 1,000 foreigners had been detained.[67] The total was 1,182 before the Justice Department abruptly announced that it would no longer issue a running tally of the number of people detained across the country pursuant to the investigation of the September 11 attacks.[68]

In its legal response to the terrorist attacks of September 11, the Justice Department deployed weapons developed to punish criminal aliens and those created to advance the war on terrorism. The Justice Department's response to the September 11 attacks incorporated policies and procedures established for the detention and deportation of criminal aliens. Yet the punitive and policy dimensions of immigration detention before September 11 are distinct from those after September 11 in several significant ways. Prior to September 11, purging the country of foreigners with criminal backgrounds was the primary reason for detaining and deporting foreigners already admitted to the United States. AEDPA and IIRIRA effectively imposed a zero-tolerance policy for non-U.S. citizens with histories of criminal prosecution by expanding the scope of conduct triggering detention and deportation to crimes potentially punishable by a year or more in prison. This lower threshold combined with harsh state and federal laws imposing long mandatory sentences for relatively minor—usually drug-related—crimes dramatically increased the volume of non-citizens detained and deported by the INS. Criminal aliens are disproportionately detained for drug-related crimes, reflecting the general trend in criminal prosecution over the past three decades. They are an ethnically and racially diverse group, although people of color are overrepresented (likewise reflecting trends in the policing and prosecuting of crime over the past three decades).

After September 11, the detention and deportation of aliens for past criminal conduct continued but was overshadowed by a new criminal justice imperative-detaining aliens involved in, or possessing information about, an ongoing criminal investigation. Terrorism is a crime of a magnitude far greater than the crimes for which criminal aliens are typically detained. It threatens national security to a degree not contemplated by Congress in the drafting of the AEDPA and IIRIRA. In contrast with the detention of criminal aliens prior to September 11, aliens detained pursuant to the terrorism investigation were overwhelmingly men of Middle Eastern descent, detained in secrecy and as part of a broader law enforcement and national security plan to prevent further terrorist attacks from occurring.

CONCLUSION

The INS's current policy of detaining masses of immigrants with criminal convictions in their pasts is a result of converging policies regulating criminals and immigrants. In the past fifty years, as waves of undocumented refugees of color have increasingly come to the United States from Latin America and the Caribbean Basin en masse, the response of the U.S. government has been increasingly punitive. Once reserved for extreme circumstances, locking up these immigrants in prisons and prison-like facilities has become a policy that mirrors mass incarceration in its heavy-handed response to even minor crimes, its racially disproportionate impact, its abandonment of individualized notions of justice, and its social sanitation of "undesirables."

As crime and immigration policies have converged, the criminal justice system has increasingly deployed immigration policies to accomplish law enforcement objectives. The latest, and strongest, evidence of this is the preventive detention of Middle Eastern men in the wake of the September 11 attacks.

Mass incarceration has provided a template for locking up large numbers of poor people of color whose citizenship status and past involvement in crime, even minor crime, makes them vulnerable to incarceration without the full-blown process guaranteed to the criminally accused. By using past brushes with crime as a "hook" for reincarcerating and deporting non-U.S. citizens in the absence of subsequent criminal involvement, the criminal justice system has furnished the immigration system with a potent weapon with which to control access to opportunities in the world's wealthiest economy. In turn, the immigration system adopted many of the processes and objectives of the criminal justice system—racial profiling, prison expansion, zero tolerance—and supplemented rural economies by filling empty prison beds. In light of the fact that the prison population dropped slightly for the first time in nearly three decades in the latter half of 2000, the immigration system is well positioned to compensate for the decline.

14

The House of the Dead: Tuberculosis and Incarceration

Paul Farmer

Incarceration is a prosperous industry, and one with a glowing future—as is true of all the others linked to the great hiding away of the American poor.
Loïc Wacquant, *Les Prisons de la Misère,* 1999

In his penetrating analysis of prisons in the United States, sociologist Loïc Wacquant remarks that the state of New York counts more men of color in its prisons than in its public universities.[1] In these prisons, social inequalities—most notably, racism—and a series of ill-advised and unjust policies are the chief ingredients for epidemics of infectious disease that have claimed the lives of scores of prisoners (and a number of wardens). Several of the worst outbreaks of tuberculosis documented in the United States in recent decades have their roots in prisons and jails. For example, the most well-known outbreak—an epidemic of drug-resistant tuberculosis in New York City—began in the late 1980s within prisons and jails, spreading in time to hospitals and homeless shelters and beyond. At the height of this epidemic, Rikers Island prison registered rates of tuberculosis that exceeded those seen in most developing countries. Hundreds died of a disease thought by many Americans to have been vanquished years ago.

Some estimate that it took more than a billion dollars to bring the New York epidemic to an end. New isolation facilities were installed in many prisons, and, in the end, no effort was spared to diagnose, isolate, and treat patients with drug-resistant tuberculosis. In many circles, the tuberculosis outbreaks were attributed to a single factor: The arrival of a new epidemic, AIDS, which had weakened the immune system of many

of those who later died of tuberculosis. But the epidemic was less a consequence of HIV than of the rapid rise of incarceration as a means of responding to social ills ranging from addiction and petty crime to housing
shortages and racism. The United States has been willing to invest billions of dollars in maintaining—indeed, enlarging—the vast prison network that now detains a proportion of its population that is larger than
any other country on the face of this earth. Its only close competitor in
this grim race to incarcerate has been the Russian Federation. This chapter will explore the relationship between prison and TB, with a special
look at the latest developments in the United States and Russia.

TUBERCULOSIS AS PUNISHMENT

It's easy to find, in the long and grim history of punishment, inventive
ways of making prisoners suffer. The crudest of these are usually known
as penal torture, a practice roundly condemned by all governments—and
practiced, still, by many. Here I will discuss *tuberculosis as punishment.*

Tuberculosis has a long history of association with prisons. In the
prechemotherapeutic era, "consumption" was in many settings the
major cause of prison mortality. In the mid-nineteenth century, for example, TB was estimated to cause up to 80 percent of all U.S. prison
deaths. In Boston, Philadelphia, and New York, about 10 percent of all
prisoners died from the disease.[2] In our own postantibiotic era, prisoners continue to endure TB risks well in excess of those not in prison. In
most countries, rates five to ten times the national average are not uncommon, and outbreaks can lead rapidly to TB rates more than one-
hundred times the national average.[3]

As society and human behavior have changed, *Mycobacterium tuberculosis,* the organism that causes TB, has changed, too. Multidrug-
resistant tuberculosis (MDRTB) is a relatively recent development, one
that has emerged only in the past two decades as a frightening concomi-
tant of drug development. Unfortunately, the TB bacillus has mutated
more quickly than our own ability to respond with new and effective

drugs. And MDRTB is difficult to treat and carries a high case-fatality rate when not treated. It is also stubbornly entrenched in many of the prisons of the former Soviet Union. And even though TB treatment is available for the fortunate few, others, including most prisoners, are summarily informed that their affliction is incurable.

DRUG RESISTANCE, CHEMOTHERAPY, AND AMPLIFICATION

Patients who relapse after TB therapy do not necessarily have MDRTB; indeed, most of them do not. "MDRTB" implies resistance to at least isoniazid (INH) and rifampin (RIF), the two most powerful antituberculous drugs. When a patient infected with a TB strain resistant to INH and RIF is treated with a regimen based on these two first-line agents, he or she is unlikely to be cured. Unfortunately, many experts have advocated one-size-fits-all empiric regimens based on first-line drugs—even in the middle of MDRTB outbreaks. Such recommendations are often made because the second-line drugs that might cure patients with MDRTB are held to be too expensive for use in precisely those countries or settings in which they are most needed. They are not "cost-effective," in the confused and morally flabby jargon of our day.

Not only do INH/RIF-based regimens fail to cure patients with MDRTB, they may also lead to iatrogenic worsening of individual patients' patterns of resistance. That is, the infecting strain is exposed to brief courses of drugs that do not kill the microbe but can induce further resistance, rendering even carefully designed subsequent regimens less effective. In our work, we've called this the "amplifier effect" of short-course chemotherapy.[4]

There are other ways to amplify the problem as well. TB is an airborne pathogen, coughed into the air in what are known as "droplet nuclei" that may be inhaled by anyone who shares air with an infectious person. The number of droplet nuclei coughed into the air and rate of ventilation (air changes per unit of time) are key determinants of risk of infection. Complex mathematical formulae describe transmission dynamics; overcrowded prisons with poor ventilation are particularly effective amplification systems for the spread of TB whenever prompt diagnosis and effective therapy are unavailable. Adding HIV to the equation increases the likelihood that new infections will progress to active and contagious TB, further amplifying outbreaks and driving up mortality.

Prisons have gates, but they are highly permeable institutions, with a great deal of interaction with surrounding communities (the "outside world"). This occurs not only through guards, other employees, and visitors, but also because detention is often brief. In the United States, for example, about 14 million people pass through prisons or jails each year.[5] So what goes on inside these institutions is of great relevance to the public's health, as we'll see in examining data from the United States and Russia. It is for all of these reasons that certain correctional facilities have been termed "infectious prisons."[6]

Acquired MDRTB occurs when patients do not or cannot adhere to therapy, and intermittent selective pressures allow drug-resistant mutants to become the dominant infecting strain. *Primary* MDRTB occurs when others are infected and fall ill with MDR strains. When poorly conceived regimens further amplify preexisting resistance, primary MDRTB may be misdiagnosed as acquired MDRTB. The difference is critical in prisons, as we shall see.

A review of the literature reveals many discrepant claims about the nature of the prison-tuberculosis association.[7] For example, while one survey argues that prisons are "particularly difficult environments" in which to treat TB, and that prisoner education is "often hopeless," another review concludes more hopefully that, "with on-site services and confined patients, [correctional institutions] are all suited for public health interventions, health professional education and epidemiologic study."[8] And although the literature seems to show that TB treatment outcomes among prisoners are often poor, there's little agreement as to why. First, few if any studies have examined the contribution of endemic drug resistance to poor clinical outcomes in prisons. Some commentators argue that poor treatment outcomes are the result of the structural constraints of working within underfunded prison systems; others seem to blame the prisoners, often by focusing on alleged psychological or even "cultural" traits. Still others refer to the fragility of the patient-doctor relationship when the latter works for the system that is punishing the former.

THE TUBERCULOSIS-PRISON NEXUS:
THE UNITED STATES AND RUSSIA

The United States and Russia hold world records in many prison statistics, taking the prize, most notably, for the highest per capita rates of imprisonment in the world. In recent years, the United States has surpassed Russia to become the uncontested world leader in detention. Of every 100,000 U.S. citizens, approximately 700 are in prison; 644 per 100,000 Russians are incarcerated. (In many European countries, fewer than 100 per 100,000 citizens are in prison.)[9]

What do we know about epidemics of MDRTB in U.S. prisons? First, several of what are termed institutional outbreaks began in prisons, not hospitals. In the largest U.S. outbreak of MDRTB in New York City in 1989, fully 80 percent of all index cases could be traced to jails and prisons.[10] The U.S. Centers for Disease Control (CDC) had sounded the alarm even before the New York MDRTB epidemic, noting the steady and dramatic rise in TB incidence within prisons. In the New York state correctional system, for example, average annual TB incidence went from 15.4 per 100,000 inmates in 1976–78 to 105.5 per 100,000 in 1986.[11] Much of the rise was associated with HIV, but intramural TB transmission was clearly affecting HIV-negative inmates, wardens, visitors, and surrounding communities: There were at least eleven prison outbreaks between 1985 and 1989.[12]

These warnings went largely unheeded, as did new guidelines to prevent intramural transmission.[13] By 1991, the Rikers Island jail, which during the course of the 1980s had experienced a threefold increase in census, had one of the highest TB case rates in the nation: 400 to 500 cases per 100,000 population.[14] The record shows a dozen more prison epidemics, many with fatalities, between December 1990 and December 1992. By the time the dust settled, it was clear that a strain of *M. tuberculosis* resistant to all five first-line drugs was implicated in most of the deaths. In the New York prison system, for example, MDRTB was diagnosed in at least thirty-three inmates, of whom 84 percent died of the disease; one correctional officer was fatally afflicted.[15]

HIV further fueled these prison epidemics. At the time of the outbreaks, New York inmates were already saddled with the nation's highest reported rates of HIV infection.[16] But the explosion of TB in prisons was even more intimately tied to government policies, most notably those of the Reagan and Bush administrations. In addition to the dismantling of the country's TB infrastructure—budgets were slashed throughout the 1970s—the "war on drugs" was declared in 1982. One of the newer ruses for managing inequality and criminalizing poverty, the "war on drugs" is in large part a war on drug users and petty traffickers rather than on those who run or finance the drug trade, and rates of drug-related arrest and imprisonment skyrocketed during the first decade of the program.[17] In 1980, there were approximately 10,000 new commitments for drug offenses; in 1990, over 100,000. The inequalities of U.S. society were mirrored in sentencing: By 1995, some 7 percent of all African-American adult males[18] were interned.[19] As noted, these trends reflect changes in policy rather than changes in behavior.

These policies have had a profound impact. By 1990, some 2.35 percent of the U.S. adult population—4.3 million men and women—were in prison or jail, or on probation or parole. This was a 63 percent increase over 1984, and left most U.S. detention facilities well over design capacity. Prisons without proper ventilation were soon crammed with inmates with high baseline rates of infection with both HIV and *M. tuberculosis*. As noted in a 1993 review. "Expansion of physical facilities has not kept pace with the doubling of prison and jail populations in the past decade, nor did it contemplate the risk of transmission of airborne disease."[20]

Yet the connection between the "war on drugs" and drug-resistant tuberculosis was noted early on by those working in the correctional system.[21] Just as detention facilities were not designed to warehouse such large numbers of prisoners, so too was the prison medical system ill-prepared to manage the resulting TB crisis. A lack of TB diagnostic capabilities was further compounded by HIV co-infection, which was associated with atypical presentations of active TB.[22] More critically, overburdened providers could not track adherence to anti-tuberculous therapy, leading to increased rates of acquired resistance to first-line drugs. In the sardine-can atmosphere of 1980s prisons, MDRTB transmission soon led to high rates of primary MDRTB infection in a vulnerable and captive population.

HIV and prison are thus two reasons for the male preponderance of U.S. tuberculosis case rates: More than 70 percent of new "excess" TB cases were diagnosed among men, most of them poor blacks and Latinos living in cities.[23] Among urban African-American males, for example, rates of TB jumped *over 1500 percent* between 1985 and 1990.[24] Many of those afflicted lived in shared spaces: prisons, jails, homeless shelters, drug-treatment programs, and public hospitals. Molecular epidemiology subsequently showed that TB outbreaks tied such institutions together in a vast chain, conveying the mutant strains rapidly across the nation.[25]

There was little public outcry, it has been noted, until prison wardens, health professionals, and other such "innocent" parties began to fall ill. Then, as Laurie Garrett notes, "panic broke out."[26] Articles began to appear in newspapers and other print media.[27] "This publicity caused such alarm in one upstate New York community," note the authors of one review, "that its hospitals refused to care for inmates, even in life-threatening emergencies."[28] With unions of health-care workers and prison employees pressing for their own protection (more than for that of the incarcerated), OSHA (Occupational Safety and Health Administration) and other regulatory bodies laid down guidelines designed to contain institutional transmission. Court-ordered caps on the number of inmates were issued to several of the key prisons and jails.[29] Several detention facilities were upgraded. Others were built to permit respiratory

isolation. Enhanced awareness and surveillance led to earlier identification of drug-resistant cases, and improved outcomes ensued. Culture
and drug-susceptibility testing on all isolates of *M. tuberculosis* were recommended by the CDC (reversing a previous recommendation that had
termed such testing "no longer cost-effective").

These tardy interventions were, in the end, effective. But what was the
cost of the delay? The MDRTB outbreaks—to an important extent the
result of imprudent cost-cutting and ill-advised public policy—led to a
massive outlay of public monies, especially in New York City. In addition to treatment costs, the upgrading of hospitals and detention facilities cost big money: A new facility for Rikers Island alone cost $113
million. In a helpful review, Garrett writes:

> When all the costs of the 1989–94 MDR-TB epidemic were totaled it was clear that
> more than $1 billion was spent to rein in the mutant mycobacteria. Saving perhaps
> $200 million in budget cuts during the 1980s eventually cost America an enormous
> sum, not only in direct funds but also in lost productivity and, of course, human lives.[30]

The MDRTB misadventures also led many professionals to reevalu-
ate the "war on drugs," widely regarded as totally ineffectual by both the
medical and jurisprudence communities. "Prisons are terrible institutions," observed Dr. Robert Cohen, whose experience as medical director of the Rikers Island facility forever changed his views on prisons and
on drug policy. "The problem of drug abuse is much better approached
with a medical model than with a crime-and-punishment model."[31]

Crime-and-punishment models bring us to modern Russia, where
prison conditions perhaps recall Kafka more than Dostoyevsky. As
noted, the tuberculosis-prison story is even grimmer in Russia than in
the United States, recently demoted to developing-country status and
embracing, according to many observers, "Western" (read, American)
ways of managing inequality. Writing of the growing influence of U.S.
penal policy in Europe, Wacquant notes in passing that "the influence of
Washington, on both economic and penal fronts, is felt even more
strongly in Latin America and—supreme irony of history—in numerous

countries of the former Soviet Empire."[32] As rates of incarceration rose, so too did rates of tuberculosis, with both trends tightly linked to economic decline. In 1990, TB incidence in Moscow was 27 per 100,000 population; by 1993, it had almost doubled, to 50 per 100,000. The situation was worse in Siberia, where incidence went from 43 to 94 per 100,000 during the same period.[33]

And the degradation continues. International health officials announced, at a March 24, 1998, news conference in Copenhagen, that TB incidence had risen another 50 percent in Russia between 1994 and 1996. "We have never seen such an increase before," commented Arata Kochi, director of the World Health Organization's Global TB Programme. About a quarter of a million cases were announced in 1996, and officials further warned that these infections respected no borders: From Scandinavia to Israel, new cases of drug-resistant tuberculosis were diagnosed in immigrants from the Baltic states or elsewhere in the former Soviet Union.[34] By the close of the millennium, rates had surpassed 100 per 100,000 in many parts of the Russian Federation.

Russia's increase in TB rates cannot be attributed to HIV or to ill-conceived drug policy. Nor can it be attributed to the attitudes and practices of the local TB specialists, who have had their funding cut, in many instances, by more than 90 percent. The collapse of the public-health system, a part of the broader social disruption registered there, is the heart of the problem; and prisons, it transpires, are central to both the amplification of the TB problem and to the mortality trends. "In the Russian Federation," notes one recent review, "there is evidence from tuberculosis control programmes in the community that a high proportion of patients have served time in prisons, and that having been in jail is a major risk factor for the development of multidrug resistant strains of *M. tuberculosis.*" The same report pegs tuberculosis death rates as high as 24 percent, with the disease causing from 50 to 80 percent of all prison deaths.[35] The problem is not denied by prison officials. As one of them recently remarked, "The three major problems facing our correctional system are underfunding, overcrowding, and tuberculosis. Simply being in prison is one of Russia's biggest risk factors for TB."[36]

With so many TB deaths in prison and with such a high rate of imprisonment, it is less surprising to learn that tuberculosis has become the single leading contributor to increased mortality among young Russian men. Why are these patients dying from an eminently treatable disease? Although HIV has recently been introduced to the formula, it remains, at this writing, a potential contributor to the problem.[37] Some Russian patients die because they have no access to therapy; others die because they have access to the wrong kind of therapy. As in the U.S. outbreaks, many of these prisoners have MDRTB, but in Russia many are receiving the very medications to which their infecting strains are already resistant. Still others, it is said, are dispirited enough to give up. Poor conditions in Russian jails and prisons led to prison riots in 1992, and these were harshly repressed. If anything, conditions have gotten worse since.

Overcrowding in Russian prisons is now far greater than in U.S. facilities. In the United States, legislation was passed to ensure that each prisoner was allotted 80 square feet. In Russia, the same allotment was increased recently from 27 to 43 square feet.[38] But site visits to prisons and jails reveal the actual parameter to be far below 27—especially in pretrial detention centers, where some 216,700 people currently languish.[39] And more and more of those detained have or develop active tuberculosis. In these conditions, even brief pretrial detention often means intense bombardment with viable TB bacilli. The average duration of *pretrial* detention is now ten months. One journalist recently observed that, in these crowded holding centers, "a death sentence stalks people who have not yet been convicted of a crime."[40]

Pretrial detention, certainly, is more Kafka-esque than Dostoyevskean. The criminal-justice bureaucracy, though large and complex, cannot begin to keep up with the current demand. Matrosskaya Tishina, a jail in central Moscow built for 2000, currently holds 5,000—no small number of them with active tuberculosis. Moscow's chief of corrections reports that, within the jail, seventy detainees died in the first nine months of 1996—a majority of them from tuberculosis. And the problem has since worsened. For example, Mischa Chukanov, then twenty-two years old, was arrested in February, 1997, for petty larceny—

he and another young man were accused of stealing a crate of watches from a Moscow warehouse—and waited seventeen months for his case to come to trial. But shortly prior to his first post-arrest encounter with a judge, Mischa was diagnosed with active pulmonary tuberculosis. After almost four months of treatment he remained "smear-positive"—with evidence of tubercle bacilli in his sputum—suggesting that he might never respond to conventional therapy. By his own account, he felt worse than ever and had lost almost thirty pounds since his arrest. Tried and convicted in absentia, he was slated for transfer from the Matrosskaya Tishina sick bay to a TB prison colony. "It can't be worse than here," he said.[41]

What are the TB penal colonies like? Russia has about fifty. They house almost 71,000 prisoners—half of them under twenty-five years of age. Mischa Chukanov is to be transferred to a colony located in a town of about 30,000, about 100 kilometers east of Moscow—a trip of two hours through well-tended fields and through thick forests of birch and fir. The colony's dreary barracks, when I saw them, were of course depressing and overcrowded. Prisoners with tuberculosis were allotted 4 square meters per person. But the facility was clean, the guards and correctional officials cooperative, and the prisoners did not appear malnourished.

The colony's medical director explained that of 909 prisoners, well over 800 suffered from active tuberculosis. Mean age was forty and falling, though teenagers were sent to another facility. The prison had been designed, she explained, for patients who had already received the "intensive phase" of treatment and who, smear-negative, were slated to complete therapy in the colony. In recent years, however, patients arrived with nothing more than a diagnosis. They were transferred, smear-positive, from the facility in which they'd been diagnosed. To tend to these sick prisoners, she had an ancillary staff of forty-three, most of them from the community and several of them prisoners themselves. HIV was not yet a problem, although hepatitis B and syphilis were endemic among the prisoners. "Our medical capacity," she told me, "is altogether inadequate."

Asked about TB outcomes, the medical director was very forthcoming: Cure rates were low. Why? She denied that prisoners showed widespread reluctance to be treated:

> On the contrary, the patients are very interested in treatment. They want to recover—especially the younger ones. A very small percentage of them refuse treatment, and usually do so because of some extenuating circumstance or misunderstanding. For example, some patients with liver disease are under the impression that they cannot tolerate the drugs. With a minimal amount of explanation, they too accept TB therapy.

Furthermore, all patients, she insisted, receive directly observed therapy. The explanation for low cure rates lay elsewhere. "We know how to manage the cases," she explained wearily, "even the drug-resistant ones. But we don't have the resources." An annual medication budget of 14,000 rubles—not much more than $2,000—meant an irregular supply of first-line drugs, and no supply whatsoever of second-line drugs, even though many patients, especially those infected in prison, were known to have drug-resistant disease.[42] Although no survey of drug susceptibility had ever been conducted, the medical director estimated that fully half of all prisoners had drug-resistant TB.

Just how low are the cure rates? The colony's general plan is to treat patients with active TB and then transfer them back to regular prisons. But fewer than one-hundred prisoners were transferred in 2000, reported the chief warden as he listened quietly to his medical director. Far more common is another scenario: the prisoners remain in the colony until they are released. The warden informed us that of thirty prisoners slated for release that month, twenty-seven were known to have active, infectious TB. "We can't really cure them," added the doctor, "so we do our best to keep them alive."

Post-release care is not under correctional-system jurisdiction, and there is little coordination between the Ministry of Interior and the Ministry of Health. "They're released, and many have not finished therapy," continued the prison doctor. "We send them out with prescriptions rather than the medications. By law, they have a right to the medications for free. But that's on paper. In reality, we know that the medications are no longer available for free. Sometimes they are not available at all." Asked about transmission to family members, she replied, "We have no statistics, but we fear the worst. We certainly have cases in which a father comes here as a convict, and we later meet his son—also a convict, and also with active TB."

Concern about this state of affairs was visible in the prisoners' faces. Take, for example, the case of Viktor, a thirty-two-year-old man arrested in Eastern Siberia in 1988. He is now only four months away from the end of an eleven-year sentence for fraud. He was diagnosed with TB while working in the TB infirmary, a job he earned for good behavior. He was treated, but he relapsed later in the course of his sentence. He is now slated to return to his wife and children in Siberia, but he's still sick. "Of course I'm worried I won't be better by the time my sentence is up," he said, "and that I will give my illness to my family."

The double jeopardy faced by Russian detainees is not lost on those working on their behalf. One penal reform activist recently observed, "Sometimes, the prison officers and medical staff are doing the best they can, and the inmates understand that poor conditions are not the fault of the prison staff but rather of the whole criminal justice system." [43] A former dissident, also now a prisoners' rights activist, agrees, but his assessment is even more dour: "During my six years in Soviet prisons, I lived through many horrors." But "it is certain," he adds, "that conditions in normal jails were not this bad even under Stalin." [44] The Ministry of Justice—now responsible for the penitentiary system—has deplored prison conditions quite publicly. "We do not wish to house prisoners in such awful conditions," noted Vice-Minister Yuri Ivanovitch Kalinin in January 2000. "It makes no sense for anyone concerned with justice, to see young men arrested for minor crimes condemned to die of tuberculosis."

In summary, the collapse of the Soviet Union, with its infamous gulags and "psychiatric prisons," has lead to a *worsening* of TB care for prisoners, even as it has increased their risk of contracting the disease. The cost of this degradation is in some ways incalculable, and not merely in terms of human lives. The virtual disappearance of social services and a blatant disregard for human dignity fuel a growing cynicism in Russia, weakening chances for the development of a truly open society.

WHAT SHOULD BE DONE?

There is no doubt, then, that MDRTB in prisons—a subset of the problem of tuberculosis in prisons—is a significant public-health problem and also a peculiarly modern human-rights challenge. How have the public-health and human-rights communities responded? It is not hyperbole to say that much commentary on the problem reveals both a lack of vision and an ignorance of MDRTB management. Many international-health experts throw up their hands, as if the ongoing spread of MDRTB and the mounting death toll are reflections of a *force majeure,* beyond the scope of human intervention. Although there is evidence to the contrary, one of the most commonly heard excuses is that MDRTB is simply untreatable.[45] Since drug stockouts are a major problem, it's also argued that drugs are "unavailable," or "too expensive." But is it really a question of drug distribution, when Coca-Cola and McDonald's have introduced their products into the far reaches of Siberia without much difficulty?

Other excuses abound. Here are some we have heard in Peru, the United States, Geneva, and Russia: The patients refuse treatment; they're noncompliant; they hide drugs in their mouths and spit them out later; they falsify lab results. Some have argued that prisoners with TB are simply "too antisocial to be treated." It's also been said that "prison culture" in Russia undermines efforts to treat—another example of the conflation of structural violence and cultural difference. When these excuses are heard from international experts or from those responsible for addressing tuberculosis in prisons, one fears that hunches and impressions and prejudices are being translated into public policy. Permanent isolation without treatment has been proposed as a "solution," with little objection from human-rights activists. Indeed, international humanitarian organizations have in some instances been the primary architects of isolation schemes in some Russian oblasts.

What about those who propose action on behalf of prisoners with tuberculosis? Even in these circles, we're offered long lists of pitfalls. For example, Reyes and Coninx report on the Red Cross experience in six Ethiopian prisons, in which a TB program was abandoned because of a high defaulter rate—62 percent of patients in the Addis Ababa prison defaulted. And these partially treated prisoners were unlikely, notes the report, to receive therapy elsewhere: "the national tuberculosis program for the general population was unable to provide treatment."[46] The situation in Russia is depicted as singularly discouraging. There, even laboratory results must be regarded with suspicion, since "wealthy prisoners" may "put pressure on laboratory technicians to find bacilli in negative sputum samples" in order to have access to antituberculous drugs that can be sold in the prison black market.[47]

Recognizing the gravity of the situation, the International Committee of the Red Cross, working with the World Health Organization, called a meeting in Baku, Azerbaijan, in 2000, where an estimated 700 prisoners were sick with TB. Many of them, it is clear, have MDRTB. Disturbingly, 89 percent of the patients whose sputum did not convert after they had received first-line drugs were found to have MDRTB. Furthermore, fully 24 percent of patients initiating therapy were found to have MRDTB. It is not clear from the report what therapy was offered to these prisoners, but the "Baku Declaration" issued there called upon "Governments, ministries of justice and interior and state security and health to work together towards providing prisoners with adequate health care and the means to cure tuberculosis, and prison health services to implement DOTS [directly observed treatment, short course]."[48] DOTS refers to a program strategy based on directly observed therapy using short course regimens. Unfortunately, this strategy will not work well in the Baku prisons. If 24 percent of all comers already have MDRTB, and the majority have drug-resistant disease, DOTS will not afford a "means to cure tuberculosis." Empiric short-course regimens of first-line drugs are the wrong prescription for what ails a substantial fraction of these prisoners.

A robust human-rights discourse must be underpinned by technically adequate recommendations. So what, then, is to be done? Alexander Paterson, British prison commissioner in the 1930s, put it well: "Men are sent to prison *as* punishment, not *for* punishment."[49] Paterson's aphorism reminds us that we're faced with an enormous challenge: to identify prisoners with tuberculosis, to remove them from conditions in which treatment is unrealistic, and to initiate effective therapy. In so doing, we will halt the ongoing spread of this disease, reducing the risk of making detention tantamount to a sentence of tuberculosis. And thus we will also respond, at last, to the mandate of protecting the public's health.

To enact this plan of action requires a great deal of collaboration and goodwill, and it will require resources. Surveillance of drug resistance is critical, for it alone helps to steer choice of empiric regimens, when and if empiric regimens are warranted. New field tools for rapid detection of resistance to INH and RIF are becoming available, and should be deployed where they are most needed. Once patients with MDRTB are identified, further testing will be necessary to design treatment regimens, and technical assistance will be critical if good outcomes are desired. It is difficult to abort prison TB epidemics through effective therapy, but it is possible with the existing tools. This has been proven in the United States, a country hardly known for progressive prison policies. Only after the situation got totally out of hand were ample resources made available, but in the end they came bursting forth. Ironically, some prison health experts now deplore a lack of funding for TB *outside* of U.S. prisons.[50]

Above all, we must avoid the temptation to throw our hands up, for that is the stance that has led us to the current impasse in Russia and elsewhere. In fact, some years of engagement with this problem lead me to conclude that the biggest pitfall of all may be resignation—not that of the prisoners, but rather our own. It's for this reason that we cannot find, in either the published literature or in public-health circles, a blueprint for action that would help us to respond effectively to the problem of drug-resistant tuberculosis in prisons. Nowhere can we find recommendations arguing that prisoners, precisely because they are wards of the State, must be protected from undue risk of infection. Nowhere can we find recommendations arguing that prisoners have the right to top-of-the-line therapy in part because they are prisoners, and may have contracted their malady in prison. Instead, calls for effective therapy of MDRTB are often dismissed as "utopian," "unrealistic," "pie in the sky," not "cost-effective."

Whether or not universal TB care sounds "utopian," it is clear that the problem will not improve without it, and most prison officials in Russia and Central Europe appear to want the problem brought under control. Many prison physicians and nurses are competent and, indeed, compassionate advocates for prisoners sick with TB. Furthermore, many of the prisoners are afraid of TB and more than willing to undergo rigorous treatment. Finally, the propositions now before us—continued directly observed therapy with short-course empiric regimens—simply will not work wherever MDRTB is already a problem.

Prison medicine is most legitimate when it is humane. Medical interventions are most powerful when they are effective. Human-rights arguments are most powerful if we really believe that all humans are equally valuable. When we do believe this, we are less likely to accept second-rate interventions, and more likely to remediate the inequalities that are each day brought more clearly into view by a globalizing economy.

EPIDEMIC TUBERCULOSIS AND PENAL POLICY

> The branch that breaks
> Is called rotten, but
> Wasn't there snow on it?
> —*Bertolt Brecht, "On Sterility"*[51]

"Contracting tuberculosis in prison," observes a recent report, "is most certainly not part of a prisoner's sentence."[52] But in many places, as we have seen, it most certainly is. As long as prison serves as amplifier, as long as effective treatment is not assured, tuberculosis is part of the punishment—a package deal of new corporality. In his history of French penology, Michel Foucault charts a "displacement of the very object of the punitive operation" from the body of the offender to his "soul" or "psyche."[53] Does tuberculosis as punishment signal a return to a sort of laissez-faire penal torture, a reembodiment of discipline? Does the State's apparent impotence before the problem mean that no one is to blame for ongoing, fatal outbreaks of drug-resistant tuberculosis in prisons? That such outbreaks are accidents? Freakish natural events, microbial El Niños?

As long as there have been states, states have arrogated the power to punish. In all societies, government reserves the right to strip of their agency those deemed miscreant; in some societies, including certain self-declared democracies, it reserves the right to kill criminals. But even prisoners on death row are regarded as having certain rights, including freedom from undue risk of disease. The U.S. Supreme Court has in recent times reminded us that "deliberate indifference to the serious medical needs of prisoners constitutes the unnecessary and wanton infliction of pain proscribed by the Eighth Amendment."[54]

For what it's worth, then, allowing prisoners to die of tuberculosis is illegal in the United States. While many of those who died in recent U.S. prison outbreaks were poor and voiceless, it did not take long for prisoners' rights groups to see that many detainees had been exposed, through poor planning and carelessness, to unnecessary risks. In 1981, in *Lareau v. Manson,* a group of pretrial detainees and inmates brought suit against the Hartford (Connecticut) Community Correctional Center for exposing them to tuberculosis and other transmissible pathogens. A district circuit court ruled that failure to screen detainees for communicable diseases not only violates the Eighth Amendment's due process clause protecting pretrial detainees but also constitutes "cruel and unusual punishment" for all inmates.[55] The ruling was subsequently upheld by a federal circuit court. In 1992, a group of inmates in Pennsylvania argued that the prison's lack of an adequate TB-control strategy violated the rights guaranteed them under the Eighth and Fourteenth Amendments. A federal district court ruled in their favor, mandating the prompt implementation of an effective TB-control program.[56]

A large number of similar cases have been reviewed in the literature, and many other cases are still pending.[57] The point is simply this: Since history reveals our persistent inability to protect prisoners on principle, we must entrap ourselves into decency through public policy. The call for better policy is not an argument against human-rights discourse. On the contrary, it is an argument to gird such discourse with the power to enforce.

15

Media on Prisons:
Censorship and Stereotypes

Peter Y. Sussman

Prisons are surrounded by high walls—walls of concrete and razor wire, of course, but also walls of secrecy and stereotype. The public is protected from whatever physical danger might be presented by prisoners, but it is also "protected," less legitimately, from the knowledge of what goes on behind those walls. The secretiveness that has come to characterize many of our country's prison systems hampers the public's ability to help shape government policy, to correct abuses, to understand crime, to evaluate prison programs and practices, and generally to reassess our costly and ineffectual system of criminal justice sanctions.

It is the special role of the news media, guaranteed explicitly by the U.S. Constitution, to operate freely so that governmental officials and institutions, including prisons, may be subjected to public scrutiny. In recent years, the news media have failed to meet their responsibilities to explore fully the operation of prisons. Much of the blame can be placed on government censorship, operating in various overt and covert ways— well before the administration of George W. Bush upped the ante by putting an impenetrable blanket of secrecy over legions of detainees in its notorious terrorism investigation. But the news media themselves must share some of the blame; they have often indulged in distortion and self-censorship in their coverage of crime, prisons, and prisoners, sometimes in response to presumed demands of the marketplace.

On the government side of the ledger, the problem may originate with the increasing politicization of prisons. No longer is incarceration an issue of public protection alone. Politicians at national, state, and local levels have come to see "criminals" as one of the most effective political weapons in their electoral arsenal. The now infamous television ad with which George H. W. Bush furthered his presidential campaign at the expense of furloughed prisoner Willie Horton was hardly the first time a politician played "the fear card," but its successful use in that instance undoubtedly helped persuade others of its effectiveness as a powerful advertising tool.

Coming out four-square against criminals is easy pickings; who could object? So in federal races and in state after state, politicians try to outgun one another in their indignant denunciation of crime and criminals and in their passionate support for ever-longer sentences, sometimes for minor offenses that had been featured briefly on newspaper front pages. Once elected, the politicians must respond to the fears and expectations they generated when campaigning for office. At the federal level, crimes that had formerly been classified as local are "federalized" to fulfill extravagant tough-on-crime campaign pledges by candidates for federal offices. Because of such political dynamics, legislators at all levels "solve" more and more social problems with a single blunt tool: longer prison sentences.

In view of the superheated emotions generated by the electoral uses of crime, any thoughtful attention paid to prisoners themselves—by the news media or the public—becomes a politically charged issue. The shorthand word for such attention is "coddling." It has become almost fashionable for local penal officials to vie with one another in dreaming up creative new ways to pander to public hysteria by further debasing prisoners and stripping them of their remaining vestiges of personal dignity. Chain gangs, tents in the desert, and striped clothing are just a few of the ways in which already dehumanized men and women have been deprived of whatever individuality they had left and of the inner resources that might help them someday to make a go of it on the outside.

In the 1990s, as the politicization of crime increased and the resulting prison population boom began careening out of control, prison and government officials in the United States started tightening up on news media interviews and other contacts between prisoners and journalists—just as they had done in a previous period when prisons became politicized, in the early 1970s. Even in jurisdictions that didn't tighten access rules for the news media, preexisting regulations were often murky, leaving interpretation—and media access—to the whim of individual wardens or lower-level officials, many of whom seemed more inclined than formerly to exercise such arbitrary powers—even, or perhaps especially, when journalists' interest focused on the actions of the very people who were controlling news media access. Prison administrators were granted, or usurped for themselves, a latitude accorded no other government officials to control the coverage of their own activities and misdeeds.

Consider the following examples:

- California prison newspaper editor Robert "Boston" Woodard was punished in 1996 for the contents of a letter he wrote openly to a journalist. The charge: "circumventing policies"—policies that didn't exist in writing at the time he was convicted of "circumventing" them. Regulations issued by California prison authorities months later placed new restrictions on interviews with journalists but would not have prohibited letters such as Woodard's. In short, the policies he was convicted of circumventing didn't exist. The prisoner later sued the state Department of Corrections, which elected to settle the suit to the prisoner's satisfaction after losing several preliminary skirmishes in court.
- Two prisoners, Shearwood Fleming and Charles Ervin, were sent to special detention at another California prison, for supposedly "impugning the credibility" of a prison program—a garment manufacturing operation run jointly by a private company and the California prison system. Again, no such infraction is listed in prison regulations. The suspected "impugning"—which could also be thought of as "criticizing" a government program—was accomplished, the charge papers said, "by contacting the news media." The prisoners were also told that they were being investigated for "a conspiracy to mastermind a sabotage effort to *discredit* [emphasis added] a joint venture project at this institution" and later were

transferred to other prisons because of "the sensitive nature of the Joint Venture [garment manufacturing] Program and a negative impact the news media placed on this program." That "negative impact" could only have referred to a news report on a San Diego television station, broadcast shortly before Fleming and Ervin were sent to segregation, in which two unnamed prisoners, with voices disguised, said that prisoners in the garment factory had been ordered to remove "Made in Honduras" labels from prefabricated T-shirts and to replace them with "Made in USA" labels.

• An attorney for a *parolee*—no longer incarcerated at the time—named Leslie White was told by California Department of Corrections authorities that he was being denied permission to publish an op-ed essay he wrote that had already been accepted for publication by the *Los Angeles Times*. In the essay manuscript, which parole authorities insisted on reviewing, White opposed "three strikes" legislation and criticized then-governor Pete Wilson. The reasons given for the publication denial, which was reversed after White's attorney threatened legal action, were that the article was "inflammatory" and "not in the best interests of the State."

All these actions came during a period in the mid-1990s when abuses in the California prison system were the subject of a great deal of press attention and prisoner litigation. The news media and lawsuits spotlighted, among other issues of legitimate public concern, the treatment of the mentally ill in the California prison system; severe psychological and physical abuse of prisoners at the "super-max" prison in Pelican Bay; an unprecedented number of incidents in which guards shot prisoners to death at Corcoran state prison; and harsh new criminal penalties such as "three strikes" legislation, passed by the state legislature and later by the public, in a statewide initiative, in 1994.

It was during this same period that the state Department of Corrections issued regulations restricting the ability that journalists had enjoyed during the previous two decades to interview specified prisoners face-to-face. The new regulations were designed to prevent journalists from conducting one-on-one interviews with willing individual prisoners with the use of cameras, tape recorders, or even, for a period of time, pencil and paper. As a result, exposure of abuses was dependent at times on the ability of reporters to gain access to prisoners through subterfuge, through tenuous, monitored phone calls, or through "visits" in which they literally tried to memorize prisoners' comments, in the hopes of re-creating portions of the interview later. Following issuance of the regulations, one prison reporter began taking a colleague with him when he visited an inmate, with each trying to memorize the prisoner's words so they could try to reconstruct key portions of the interview after they ran back to confer in their car in the prison parking lot. Another reporter says he stopped at a nearby coffee shop to try to reconstruct his memories of a critical interview.

Even after the state's regulations were clarified—under news media pressure—to permit reporters' use of paper and pencils that they found in the visiting room and that were available to all other visitors, "freelancing" officials, imbued with the secrecy culture that dominates most prisons, tried to do on their own what the Department of Corrections had been persuaded not to do on a statewide basis. One reporter had a pencil and napkins confiscated from him by two guards on the grounds that he wasn't an ordinary visitor—who would have been entitled to use them—but a journalist conducting an interview and taking notes on the napkins. A guard stood over this journalist for the remaining hour of his interview with a sixty-one-year-old female prisoner. The story the reporter was trying to research concerned an important public issue, the system of parole for prisoners suffering from battered women syndrome. Without access to quotations and details of the woman's complicated life story, the feature that this reporter ultimately wrote for his readers was "not the story it would have been," he says. "No way. No way."

Similar restrictions on interviews were issued in other states, some of them influenced by California's example. Shortly after a court ruled that Pennsylvania death row resident Mumia Abu-Jamal could not be singled out for denial of press interviews, the state's rules were tightened to restrict in-person interviews with *all* of the state's prisoners. Michigan, too, came up with regulations restricting taped interviews with all prisoners. In that state, the regulations were drafted after a trial court ruled that ABC could not be denied an on-camera interview with one willing interviewee, Jack Kevorkian, at a time when regulations included no general prohibition on such interviews.

Other court cases have involved a prisoner in Idaho who was punished for talking to the news media about an HIV problem at his prison, and a North Dakota prisoner who was punished for failing to obtain her warden's permission prior to telephoning a newspaper reporter. The North Dakota prisoner said that prison officials had previously taken no action in response to her complaint of a sexual assault by a guard. The prison's media contact rule was repealed as part of the settlement of the prisoner's lawsuit.

In state after state, prison officials who have tightened media access to prisoners cite not security concerns as they were once understood but the "celebrity" of prisoners, especially "notorious" prisoners. California prison officials have even established a tighter custody category based on the "notoriety" or "public interest" of prisoners; that is, the fact that the prisoner had generated "extensive attention by the public, media, or lawmakers" was used as justification to place the prisoner in tighter security. The worry was not the security danger per se of the prisoner's contacts with the news media but the content of the resulting news reports and/or public reactions to them.

The California Department of Corrections justified some of its restrictions on media access by pointing to the need to protect the public—not "physical" protection in the traditional sense, it said, but the "*emotional* well-being" of victims and others. In short, information that had been available to the public through the press was to be restricted based on the possible emotional impact of whatever the press reported from the prison. Corrections officials thus took it upon themselves to safeguard citizens' emotional well-being, and they elevated that self-appointed duty above the press's constitutionally protected right to inform the public on the operation of public institutions.

As Supreme Court Justice John Paul Stevens wrote in an unrelated case: "The First Amendment directs us to be especially skeptical of regulations that seek to keep people in the dark for what the government perceives to be their own good."

According to the publication *Prison Legal News,* jail officials in Seattle, in a move analogous to California's, have classified some prisoners as "ultra high security" and isolated them from contact with other prisoners based at least in part on the widespread media attention paid to their offenses—another clear attempt to punish prisoners based on their interest to the press and public.

Prison officials eager to squelch interviews frequently point to the need to keep prisoners like the oft-cited Charles Manson from gaining undue celebrity outside the prison walls (as if Manson didn't arrive in prison with a lifetime's worth of celebrity). As the California Department of Corrections' tortured reasoning goes, "Media interviews tend to glamorize crime and criminals by making inmates television 'stars' and thus undermine the severity of the penalties designed to deter crime. For example, sales of recordings and Tee-shirts concerning inmate Charles Manson have no doubt been aided by frequent interviews with this inmate." The department did not provide evidence to substantiate its assertion of a linkage between Manson's prison interviews and his celebrity, much less between press interviews and T-shirt sales. Nor did it offer any evidence that the "star" quality of prisoners like Manson undermined criminal penalties that deter crime. Again, the focus of the California Department of Corrections was clearly on the free-world social impact of whatever news stories might be written based on interviews. The graphics on T-shirts worn by nonprisoners would seem to any neutral observer to be far beyond the province of prison custodians.

There's a further irony in the "celebrity" argument. One prominent prison reporter notes that officials at Corcoran state prison have sometimes gone out of their way to tour visiting journalists through the unit where their famous prisoners are kept. Said the reporter, "They took us by this protective housing unit, which is where all the stars of the system are. There's Charlie Manson next to Sirhan Sirhan next to Juan Corona. And they take everybody through. And it's almost like—it reminded me of being at the San Diego Zoo, and they took you by Ling Ling, the panda bears. . . . They're just showing off; the prison system is showing off its stars."

Interview restrictions in many other states are also tied specifically to the presumed content of the ensuing news story. Restrictions on content have long been considered a violation of the Constitution's free-speech and free-press clauses, but in Connecticut, for example, journalists have been required to include in their written requests for access to prisoners "a statement of any perceived benefit to law enforcement agencies" resulting from the interview. One can surmise that journalists would have a harder time justifying interviews with prisoners who intended to "impugn" or "discredit" prison policies or practices, however corrupt. The Connecticut regulation carries an uncomfortable, Orwellian echo of the ruling that temporarily silenced parolee Leslie White's expression of political opinions in California: "not in the best interests of the State."

As part of the California rule-making process, the Department of Corrections characterized news media interviews as "a public forum in which [prisoners] can espouse their often sociopathic philosophies," as if free-world citizens could not be trusted to hear and evaluate for themselves those "philosophies" that prison administrators chose to characterize as sociopathic. The argument betrays a disturbing distrust of the "marketplace of ideas" assumed by the First Amendment.

Many of the arguments for regulations to restrict interviews with prisoners are based ultimately on the fallacy that the purpose of prison journalism is to serve as a public relations vehicle for prisoners. In fact, journalistic interviews are necessary to assess the truthfulness of prisoner assertions or to elicit new information of public interest, not simply to pass along the self-interested and undigested assertions of a prisoner.

State restrictions on interviews and news coverage bear some rhetorical resemblance to the capricious rules of an autocratic third-world country, although the punishments for violation are not nearly as harsh. Compare them, for example, to the press law of the Democratic Republic of Congo. There, according to the Committee to Protect Journalists, the news media are required to back the government's war efforts. The death penalty is prescribed for "insulting the army" (impugning its credibility?) and "demoralizing the nation" (not in the best interests of the State?). Scratch deep enough, and there's not much theoretical difference between the concern that news stories might insult the army of the Congo and the requirement that journalists justify that their stories will be a benefit to law enforcement agencies in Connecticut.

Although journalists in this country are not subject to execution for their prison coverage, they are not immune from retaliation by the state. In an attempt to defend itself against a prisoner's civil rights lawsuit, California subpoenaed all of this writer's notes and other documents on the issue of media access to prisoners. Before the state capitulated and settled—without receiving the documents it had demanded—efforts were initiated to subpoena my e-mail provider to gain access to my electronic correspondence on the subject matter of this chapter, journalists' prison coverage. I was subjected to nearly fourteen hours of interrogation in depositions, with numerous questions focusing on my political advocacy, the nature of my future publishing plans, and the subject matter of past articles. I was asked, for instance, whether I had "written anything for Pacific News Service, whether published or not, regarding then-Governor Wilson" and "what plans" I had to write about the lawsuit's plaintiff, a prisoner, "in the future." I was asked, "What is the subject of [my upcoming] book contract?" and "Are you involved in lobbying for or supporting any of that legislation" on inmate-specific interviews in California prisons and "in what capacity" was I "involved in lobbying for or supporting that legislation?"

Restrictions on press access to prisoners tend to be strictest where the resulting news stories could be of greatest public significance. In many states, in-person interviews with death row prisoners are either forbidden or more restricted than those with other inmates. Such restrictions shut off one of the main vehicles for correcting abuses that have led to the execution of people who may well have been innocent of the crimes for which they were killed. Many other prisoners on death rows across the country have been exonerated perilously close to their execution dates, often through the investigative efforts of the news media. In such last-chance situations, it would seem to be wise public policy—if only to affirm the justice of the legal process—to *encourage* effective press coverage of potentially irreversible judicial mistakes that carry the direst of consequences. Yet Arizona, for example, orders that no interviews of any kind be permitted with prisoners after they've been moved to the "death watch," fourteen days before execution. Other states subject reporters to hurdles in reaching death row prisoners that are far more difficult to surmount than the restrictions placed on contact with prisoners in general custody. Is it possible that this higher level of restriction, like so much else that happens in prisons, is based on the increasingly political nature of the death penalty?

A number of high-profile mistakes have underlined the press's important responsibility to investigate the possibility that the legal system has dispatched innocent people to death row. In November 1998, the National Conference on Wrongful Convictions and the Death Penalty at Northwestern University Law School was attended by several dozen of the seventy-five formerly condemned inmates who, in the previous two decades, had been exonerated and released not only from death row but from prison. A little over a year later, when George Ryan, the Republican governor of Illinois, declared a moratorium on executions, that state had exonerated more men on death row than it had executed—an imbalance that chillingly illustrated the extent of error that has crept into the criminal justice system.

The execution lottery that has led to so many erroneous convictions has been buttressed by new laws and court rulings limiting judicial appeals by the condemned. With avenues for judicial review thus constricted, the role of the press is all the more important in righting potentially fatal government mistakes. The news media are—now more than ever before—the court of last resort. With access to prisoners further restricted, the press is not able to be as effective as it must now be in its traditional and vitally important oversight role.

Yet one Virginia prison spokesman told a newspaper in that state,

"Prison is not the place for media productions. We are under no obligation to provide a platform for inmates to profess their innocence or make allegations against the prison system."

Aside from the issue of execution-by-mistake in individual cases, there are many questions about the validity and fairness of the death penalty, with mounting evidence that racial and other extraneous considerations sometimes determine whom the state puts to death and whom it doesn't. It is vital that the public discuss such life-and-death issues with all the information it can bring to the debate, including information that only the condemned can provide. It is up to the press to fulfill that awesome responsibility, and it ought to be the government's obligation to facilitate that process.

The problem of wrongful conviction is not confined to those facing the death penalty, of course. Onetime Black Panther Party leader Elmer (Geronimo) Pratt is a celebrated example of a prisoner who was imprisoned for decades for a murder before his conviction was overturned because of new evidence. It was confirmed many years after his conviction that the primary witness against Pratt had been a police and FBI informant who lied about that fact under oath and that prosecutors had withheld this critical evidence. After his release, Pratt won a multimillion-dollar settlement of his lawsuit for false imprisonment and violation of civil rights.

Pratt had long maintained that he was punished while in prison for his contacts with reporters who were investigating his claims of innocence. California's crackdown on in-person media interviews surfaced soon after several investigative reporters began to take a close look at the questionable circumstances leading to Pratt's conviction. These reporters say that the first prisoner with whom they were denied on-camera interviews was Pratt. Although no one has offered definitive proof, the reporters suspect a direct connection between the renewed press interest in Pratt's innocence and the more general media restrictions that followed soon thereafter—as well as the official jeremiads against "celebrity prisoners."

Critical concerns about prison justice go well beyond the validity of death penalty verdicts or other claims of innocence. The routine hostility and brutality of life in many of the nation's prisons is also a matter of social equity—and certainly is of interest to the U.S. public and government when similar treatment is documented in other countries' prisons. But beyond that, years-long subjection to the coarse cruelties of everyday life in prison leaves an indelible mark on the people whom we cycle in and out of the prison system and on their families. In this country, a disproportionate number of those people represent racial and ethnic minorities. The harsh, spiteful ways so many people are treated in our prisons degrade the level of our culture generally, even when prisoners don't emerge so embittered by their experiences that a life of continuing crime and drug abuse seems the only feasible anodyne or "payback." The public deserves to know about such conditions and understand their consequences while there is still an opportunity to change them.

Other issues of public policy that the press has a responsibility to investigate inside the prisons include sentencing policy. In California, the restrictions on press interviews were instituted at about the time the state enacted one of the country's harshest "three strikes" laws. Many of those subjected to the twenty-five-years-to-life penalty were put away after committing petty thefts; others had lifelong histories of mental illness or retardation; still others suffered from debilitating drug addictions for which they could get no treatment. Enactment of the "three strikes" legislation was more than an issue of academic public interest. The penalty was presented to the public on a statewide ballot; it was an electoral issue. So the circumstances of the lives and crimes of people facing the penalty were legitimate components of the public decision-making process.

After passage of the California initiative, the effectiveness of that electoral decision—and possible modification of its provisions—continued to be an issue of importance for the voters and legislators of the state. Who was going to prison under the law? Were they the people the electorate intended to put away? And what was the effect of prison on them and on crime patterns? The news media cannot answer such critical questions without effective access to prisons and prisoners. Yet many reporters who tried to tell the stories of prisoners who ran afoul of the law's inflexible, arithmetical criteria were thwarted by the state's new, tougher interview restrictions. When reporters can't get access to their subjects for interviews, the stories they would have told often remain untold. Policy debates are thus cut off from their informational roots. Several reporters have complained of having to abandon projects on "third strikers" because of access restrictions.

There are, of course, many other reasons why citizens might want— or need—journalistically screened information that only prisoners possess. Issues that originate in prisons include the uses and limits of prison labor (the issue that got the San Diego prisoners sent to "the hole" for "impugning"). Some prisoners are uniquely qualified to enhance our understanding of corruption—governmental and otherwise—in the world outside; this is especially true of government officials who have been imprisoned for corruption and come to understand criminal justice issues from complementary perspectives, as both policy makers and offenders. But surely it is in the setting of criminal penalties and the investigation of human rights abuses that prisoners' information is of greatest use in a democracy.

One class of prisoners whose stories frequently cannot be told are those in heightened detention—in prisons-within-prisons often called "administrative segregation" but known colloquially as "solitary" or "the hole." Prison officials say they place their toughest, most incorrigible convicts in administrative segregation. Prisoners in these units have fewer visiting and telephone privileges than those in the general prison population, if they have any. Administrative segregation is often the first stop for those who have violated prison rules, but it is also a convenient place to "hide" prisoners who have objected to prison practices or had conflicts with staff members. In any other government institution, some of these in-house critics might be known as "whistle-blowers." In the closed, airless world of prisons, they are written up for offenses and effectively isolated from fellow prisoners and the press. In some cases, the very offenses that got them sent to "ad seg" were contact with the news media to alert them to abuses or convey what, on the outside, would be constitutionally protected opinions on government programs. Such was the case with the San Diego prisoners suspected of "impugning" a prison program. Dannie Martin, a federal prisoner, was punished by a trip to administrative segregation for a story he wrote that I had published in the *San Francisco Chronicle*.

Restrictions on journalistic access are especially onerous for reporters working in visual media—television and documentary films. If there's no film or videotape, there's no story. And increasingly, in states across the country, there is no film or tape because of stricter access restrictions. Connecticut, for example, allows no videotaped interviews and no transmission by any visual medium. Pennsylvania: no still or video cameras and no tape recorders. New Hampshire: no cameras, tape recorders, or "videotaping machines." South Carolina: No recording tools of any kind, including pencil and paper. Similar restrictions exist in other states.

If restrictions such as those had been in effect in Texas, the public would likely not have learned the full story of the wrongful conviction of Randall Adams for the killing of a police officer. Adams gained his freedom after documentary filmmaker Errol Morris brought the injustice to public attention in his now-celebrated film *The Thin Blue Line*.

There are many stories that simply can't be told without use of a camera. When *60 Minutes* aired an interview with a convict witness to a killing by prison guards at Corcoran prison—a witness whom they could interview only because he was in protective custody in a federal prison, where on-camera interviews were allowed—a key component of the story was an official prison video of the shooting. The interviewee pointed to the scene on a monitor, showing his position and those of the shooters and the shooting victim, Preston Tate. As the producer of the segment later noted wryly, "You can't do [that] in print." No camera, no story.

One reporter who has written many prison stories says that the barriers set up by the prison system are "a major disincentive to doing these stories." He adds, "This is a big reason why not many reporters are doing these stories." But it is not the only reason. The news media themselves must share some of the blame.

Just as many politicians have stoked public fears about crime and prisoners to serve their own electoral interests, so the news media often cater to and perpetuate the same fears to serve their commercial interests. With the news media increasingly concentrated in a few publicly traded megacorporations (some of them owned by conventional entertainment conglomerates) and under greater pressure to meet inflated profit goals comparable with growth stocks, they give undue emphasis to "what sells"—and fear sells.

Journalists are often pressured, too, to be entertaining, to cater to the lowest common denominator in order to boost the circulation and Nielsen ratings that translate into higher ad rates. Again, the effect is distortion of their purely journalistic focus—sometimes through news writing that is more colorful or simplistic than the circumstances of a story warrant; sometimes through excessive emphasis on rare or minor crimes or criminals and sometimes through suppression of prison stories altogether.

Prison officials in California and elsewhere have latched on to the increasing "entertainment" focus on the news media, using it improperly as a pretext to justify exclusionary policies for legitimate journalists. In recent years, at least two highly regarded broadcast news magazines have been informed that prison officials consider them entertainment shows. The New Hampshire Department of Corrections turned down a *60 Minutes* interview for that reason, and California prison officials informed a producer for NBC's *Dateline* that it was shows like his—"the next thing to tabloids"—that led to the system-wide ban on interviewing specified prisoners on camera. It would be illegal to base news interview restrictions on a department's assessment of the program's content, so California and many other states—using such innovative logic as California's "inmate television stars" theory—have chosen to hobble television journalists by denying them the use of the cameras they need effectively to report stories involving individual prisoners.

Despite the illegitimate use that some prisons have made of this trend, the journalistic distortion of crime and prison for the purposes of ratings and profits is a serious social concern.

One of the effects of the trend toward a journalism that doubles as entertainment is the commodification of many prison stories. The news from the joint tends to be reduced to certain presumably crowd-pleasing categories that serve as easily digestible substitutes for uncomfortable realities and soothing anesthetics for fears of social dislocation. You have your shocking-escape story, your monster-behind-bars story, your barbarian-riots story. Most such stories are based on actual prison occurrences, of course, but they are isolated and sensationalized to satisfy the same kind of illicit thrill some people presumably get from "action movies." For ease of identification, they make use of stereotypes of the good-versus-evil variety. The ultimate take-home message for the consumer is, "I'm okay; he's not."

Entertainment values are inherently nonjournalistic. In entertainment, what we read or hear or see becomes important for the feelings with which it leaves us and not for its accuracy or importance. And nothing satisfies more readily than the easily understandable, the simple emotional reaction based on familiarity. In other words, stereotyping— that convenient shorthand by which we falsify experience—substitutes for news judgment.

Prison stereotypes remove all nuance from prisons and prisoners, underscoring the comforting notion that "we" have nothing in common with "them." They underline the menacing violence of prison life and ignore the nobility and pathos that also characterize many prisoners, traits that are familiar to many lawyers, teachers, pastors, and social workers who have spent a lot of time in these remote institutions.

Academic studies have documented that far greater journalistic attention has been devoted to crime at precisely the time when crime incidence actually declined. Journalists sum up the trend toward increasingly lurid TV news coverage with the adage "If it bleeds, it leads" (leads off the broadcast). Prison stories, however—especially those that involve policy and not violence—are sometimes considered too dull or difficult to obtain to justify the expense necessary to cover them. That perpetuates the perception of prisons as places defined almost exclusively by violence. The horror stories of prison are widely known, but you are less likely to hear about prisoners who organize a drive to raise thousands of dollars for local child-abuse agencies, as a group of convicts did at one California prison. Nor is it likely to be explained to the reader or viewer that a high proportion of the nation's prisoners had childhoods of extreme abuse. Such nuanced human stories are of less and less interest to journalists, both in the raucous, high-voltage world of television news and in the newspapers that seem determined to compete with them by adopting the worst of their techniques.

Sometimes the inability to cover prisons with any complexity results from individual journalists' inability to see them with clarity. Many journalists are simply unable to imagine ways of looking at experiences that are not common in their own class or race. Yet, increasingly, imprisonment is becoming a matter of race and class. The populations of prisons are as poor and "minority" as newsroom populations are comfortable and white. Newspapers and other media have learned through error over recent decades how to cover some "minority" communities—largely the communities that their readers and viewers will bump into in the normal course of their lives. But they don't have the incentive to make comparable efforts to cover communities that are as voiceless, politically powerless, and invisible as those in our prisons. It's one thing to try to understand the motivations and interests of the people who demonstrate at city hall, and quite another to empathize with poor, black, or Hispanic dead-enders tucked into isolation cells in remote, rural prisons (as so many of them are). Nor is it easy to engage with—or even find—the families of those prisoners, who likely work long hours during the week and then trudge onto an all-night bus for a weekend visit with their loved one.

One can learn far more about crime and prisoners by spending time in the endless lines snaking into the visiting rooms of our jails and prisons than by spending an equivalent amount of time poring over budgets, academic reports, or computer databases. But you won't find many reporters on those prison lines. Not unexpectedly, reporters tend to cover the kinds of people they know and associate with daily, and much of their information—whether from casual news tips or carefully cultivated sources—also comes from people with whom they are comfortable socially.

Other obstacles to effective coverage are more institutional than individual. News budgets rarely include money for a prison beat. Journalists spend an inordinate amount of time covering crimes that take place in an instant and far less time covering the next step of the criminal justice system, the court trials that last days or, at most, weeks; and they devote virtually no time or resources to covering the jails and prisons where the convicted are psychologically transformed through months or years.

Another institutional bias is the market orientation of most media outlets. They are, after all, businesses, and the bottom line is more important to today's news media than it has ever been before. They hire consultants to tell them about market share and targeted advertising niches, but they don't generally hire consultants to tell them how to unearth social truths. There is certainly a generalized commitment to truth-telling, but except in extraordinary times, few are the top news executives who view that commitment as more than a means to a marketing end.

In short, whether through social habit, conscious policy, or business focus, the news media often end up mirroring politicians' self-interested stereotyping of prisoners and prison issues.

The bulk of the media-consuming public—its attention directed and its perceptions shaped by journalistic coverage—appears to be comfortable with the substitution of simplistic stereotypes for the complex personal and social dynamics of prisons and prisoners. It is far easier to barricade one's fears behind walls of concrete, rolls of razor wire, and reams of clichés than to deal with the realities of criminal experience in our troubled society. But the people society has put out of sight and out of mind continue to exist, and they are shaped—or warped—by the conditions to which we have relegated them.

Crime reporting is our new mythology, and sometimes it becomes almost Homeric as it weaves its tapestries of high drama to enthrall readers presumably bored by weightier fare. Take, for example, the mythic recounting of a girl's disappearance that ran on March 4, 1996, in the *San Francisco Chronicle,* datelined Hanford, Kings County. The page-one story began:

> This is one of those small towns where nothing really bad is ever supposed to happen.

So far, nothing about the missing girl. The story continued:

> Shady parks and playgrounds are easy to find. Schools and churches stand quietly around every other corner. Lemoore Naval Air Station, where pilots fly F-18 jet fighters a few miles west of here, seems to provide a sense of security and order.

Now, two paragraphs into the story, there is still no mention of that missing girl. It's all yarn-spinning atmospherics—a safe, upstanding rural enclave, protected from the dangers posed by modern social complexities and unstable outsiders. Indeed, this 1950s-model world is comfortingly protected by jet fighters.

It's not until the third paragraph that the reporter of this story finally alluded to the reason the story was being written:

> So when another girl disappears off the face of the earth—the third in the last two years from this area . . .

Later in the story, the reporter reinforced his idealized portrait, but this time with a discordant rhetorical twist:

> This community in the central San Joaquin Valley between Highways 5 and 99 is a prosperous town, surrounded by endless farms where cotton, alfalfa, grapes and dairy cows are raised. The snow-capped Sierra is clearly visible 50 miles to the east after the morning fog burns off.
>
> But residents clearly are aware that it is also surrounded by a world where life is sometimes cheap. There are four prisons nearby, including Corcoran State Prison 17 miles south, where Charles Manson, mass murderer Juan Corona, and Bobby Kennedy's assassin, Sirhan Sirhan, are housed.

Needless to say, Charles Manson, Juan Corona, and Sirhan Sirhan remained safely incarcerated and had nothing whatever to do with the girl's disappearance. Nor did the prison itself, which is, as the story said, 17 *miles* from the town where the girl vanished. Those notorious criminals and their famed lockup are evoked to provide a kind of lurid frame for a story that is totally unrelated to them. In short, the story titillates rather than educates. It uses notorious prisoners and other mythic stereotypes to pander to and reinforce widespread public fears instead of informing with a valid sense of context.

In fact, the remote farm area where the girl's disappearance occurred is no Eden. In some circles, it is as well known for its rural methamphetamine factories as for its cotton, alfalfa, grapes, and cows. But that fact might have ruined a good yarn. Furthermore, the suspect finally arrested in the case was a resident of this devout town—the father of the victim's twelve-year-old playmate—and not an evil outsider preying on its 1950s innocence.

In ways such as this, journalists often uncritically accept distorted public attitudes and self-serving political agendas, and in the process further distort public perceptions of both crime and prisons. It's an endless loop of misinformation and misunderstanding that's as destructive in its way as overt censorship by prison authorities.

Perhaps both journalists and prison administrators could refresh their sense of their obligations to the public by reading the Preamble to the Public Communications section of the policies and procedures of the Division of Prisons of North Carolina:

> Prisons are public institutions, operated at public expense for the protection of the public. All citizens of North Carolina have a right and a duty to know about conditions and operations of the State prison system. The governing authorities of this system desire to promote interest in and knowledge of our prisons and the care and treatment provided for the people in our custody. Our general policy is to facilitate access of the general public and mass media representatives to such knowledge by every practicable means, including visits to prisons and contacts with members of the State Correction Service and with the people in our custody. . . .

No wonder some of the best prison reporting in recent years—such as much of the "Crime and Punishment" series aired on *Nightline* in the summer of 1998—has been filmed in the prisons of North Carolina.

Whether the public is watching or not, it will be the public that must deal with the consequences of what happens in our nation's prisons. And the only feasible way for most of them to watch is through the news media. They deserve better than what they've been getting—both from the custodians of these flawed institutions and from the journalists whose duty it is to investigate them.

16

The International Impact of U.S. Policies

Vivien Stern[1]

. . . the expansion of prisons signifies the failure of the welfare state to prevent young people at risk drifting into a life of crime. If we, Europeans, want to avoid multiplying our prison cells manifold—like the USA—we are in need of a social policy that is genuinely accountable for prevention of crime.

Mrs. Winnie Sordrager, Netherlands Minister of Justice, 1997[2]

In an era when national borders are increasingly fluid and international communications are virtually instantaneous, U.S. criminal justice policies pose a challenge to other nations that have historically pursued less punitive approaches to the resolution of conflict. In contrast to the social welfare supports that have characterized much of Western Europe and other industrialized nations, the unprecedented rise in the use of imprisonment in the United States in recent decades presents a model to the world of a society committed to the use of punishment as a primary mechanism of crime control.

The extremes of U.S. policies to date have been such that in many parts of the industrialized world they have been seen as an aberration and have been met with resistance. Yet in other, sometimes more subtle, ways, these policies have begun to alter the political and cultural climate in which issues of crime and punishment are perceived in different nations. Such has been the case in regard to the leading international role of the United States in world forums in pressuring for a "war on drugs." We have also seen an increasing adoption of the prevailing U.S. model of viewing the poor as threats and politicizing the debate on crime policy in ways that discourage broader analyses of the complex causes of criminality. As we can see from this world survey, the means by which both industrialized and developing nations either acquiesce to or resist the

U.S. model in coming years will profoundly affect the shape of their crime and social policies for some time to come.

THE VIEW FROM EUROPE

Among mainstream politicians and commentators in Western Europe, it is a truism that the criminal justice system of the United States is an inexplicable deformity. Although specific aspects of it such as boot camps may arouse some interest in political circles, as a whole it presents a picture that arouses incredulity and incomprehension. There is incomprehension at the use of the death penalty for disproportionate numbers of poor people and minorities, for mentally retarded people, those who were juveniles at the time of their crime, and those whose trials were manifestly flawed. There is incredulity at the high and rising American rate of incarceration, now approaching 700 per 100,000 of the population when the West European norm is less than 100,[3] at the length of prison sentences, and at the treatment of prisoners.

The response of many European commentators is to struggle to understand how, for example, so many executions can take place, accompanied by a media circus, in a country that is so similar to European countries in many other ways. In her open letter of September 15, 2000, to the people of the United States of America, Nicole Fontaine, president of the European Parliament, said,

Within the EU Parliament, the voice of 370 million Europeans, a vast majority cannot understand why the United States is the only major democratic state in the world that carries out the death penalty.[4]

Writing in the *Washington Post,* the former U.S. ambassador to France, Felix G. Rohatyn, notes that during his time in France, no issue provoked as much "passion and as much protest as executions in the United States." There were repeated protests in front of the U.S. Embassy and a petition against the death penalty containing half a million signatures was delivered to the Embassy. Ambassador Rohatyn reports that his colleague in Germany had similar experiences.[5]

The commitment to punishment in the United States is seen most prominently in the context of the death penalty. To Europeans, it is regarded as abnormal and a result of a mistaken social policy choice that invests in prisons rather than in health care, education, and social services. It is a warning to other societies to not abandon their welfare states, and replace them with more police, courts, and prisons. No European political party of the left, center-right, or center-left advocates adoption of U.S. policies of mass incarceration.[6] Evidence presented to a Select Committee of the British House of Commons that England and Wales needed to at least triple its prison population to move toward U.S. levels received short shrift from the Members of Parliament. They "emphatically" rejected the "suggestion that a prison population of 200,000 is either desirable or feasible."[7] The Netherlands Ministry of Justice sets out their very different policy: "More prison sentences lead to more cells, more cells lead to still more incarcerations. How must this spiral be broken? Justice is striving for a broad range of penalties."[8] Denmark follows "the internationally recognized principle of using custodial sentences only when strictly necessary."[9]

Only on the farthest fringes of the right wing can any political support be found for following U.S. policies. The French National Front, for example, advocates a return of the death penalty for murder, terrorism, and major drug trafficking, a doubling of the justice budget, the construction of 15,000 more prison places, and severe penalties for even small drug dealers.[10] The British National Party advocates the death penalty for murder and for serious sex offenses against children.[11]

THE AMERICAS

Not just in Western Europe are U.S. policies seen as socially damaging. Canada has a public education policy about a sparing use of imprisonment based on the dangers that all can see of the policies followed by its southern neighbor. After substantial rises in the rate of imprisonment between 1991 and 1995, the Canadian government launched a strategy to combat prison population growth. The federal government and the ten provincial and three territorial governments were to work together to implement eleven recommendations to reduce the use of imprisonment.[12] In 1996, a reform of the law brought in measures to require any judge before imposing a custodial sentence to specify from a prescribed list what objectives such a sentence would achieve. A new conditional sentence was introduced as an alternative to prison for less serious offenders.[13]

The imprisonment rate in Canada fell from 115 per 100,000 in 1997/8[14] to 103 in 1999/2000.[15] At the same time, the level of imprisonment of its southern neighbor rose from 645 in 1997[16] to 702 in the year 2000.[17] This occurred in spite of the election of a provincial government in Ontario in 1995 and again in 1999 which followed policies more in line with the United States than any other in Canada.

Part of the Canadian project was a public education campaign to ensure that the public understood and would accept the program. The public education materials put out by the Canadian government cite the example of the United States.

One only has to look at the experience of the United States to see that relying solely on incarceration is a "dead end" street. The American incarceration rate is one of the highest in the world, but it has not made the United States a safer place to live. The murder rate in the United States, at 6.7 per 100,000, surpasses that of every other industrialized country in the world. Canada's murder rate by comparison, is barely 2 per 100,000. The United States is a good example of what happens when governments rely too heavily on incarceration. . . . When you consider that 1.6 million Americans are now behind bars; that four states spend more than $1 billion each year on corrections; that investing in education has taken a back seat to locking people up in California— then you understand why the Government has adopted a made-in-Canada approach.[18]

The countries to the south of the United States are generally no more enthusiastic than Canada about following the U.S. model. At the 2000 meeting of the justice ministers and attorneys general of the Organization of American States held in San Jose and attended by then–attorney general Janet Reno, a short debate on imprisonment concentrated on rehabilitation, prison health care, and reducing overcrowding.[19] The meeting invited "member states of the OAS to seek ways to reduce overcrowding in prisons, making use, inter alia, of alternatives to imprisonment."[20]

THE FORMER SOVIET UNION

The region of the world with incarceration rates nearest to the United States is the former Soviet Union, now the independent states of Eastern Europe and Central Asia. Since 1991, nineteen of the countries of the former Soviet bloc have joined the regional human rights body, the Council of Europe.[21] They have accepted therefore the jurisdiction of the European Convention on Human Rights and the requirement to move to abolish the death penalty and to humanize their penitentiary systems. All Council of Europe documents on criminal justice stress the treatment of prisoners within a human rights framework, the importance of social reintegration, and the need to use imprisonment as a last resort.[22] Most of the former Soviet bloc countries are therefore involved in extensive justice system reform programs with Council of Europe help. Many are decarcerating their prisoners, through amnesties, shorter pretrial periods, and the development of alternative sentencing. The United States hit the top of the world's imprisonment rate league in May 2000 when the Russian Parliament approved a prisoner amnesty that made up to 90,000 prisoners eligible for early release,[23] with as many as 350,000 additional prisoners to be subsequently released.[24] Penal Reform International is working with the Russian Ministry of Justice on the development of a model for alternatives to prison relevant to the Russian context.[25]

Since the beginning of 2000 there have been amnesties not only in Russia but also in Azerbaijan,[26] Kazakhstan, Kyrgyzstan,[27] Turkmenistan,[28] Ukraine,[29] and Uzbekistan,[30] with thousands of prisoners having been released. In Estonia, Latvia, and Slovakia, prison populations fell between 1997[31] and 1999.[32]

THE END OF REHABILITATION?

Other aspects of U.S. policies, such as the increased harshness of imprisonment and the removal of education opportunities and other programs, are not part of public policy elsewhere. Super-max prisons, where prisoners live for long periods in virtual solitary confinement, in bare concrete cells, with scarcely any access to activities,[33] have also not been adopted in other jurisdictions to any extent.

On the contrary, a group of English-speaking countries—Canada, the three jurisdictions of the United Kingdom, and Australia and New Zealand—are moving toward an intensification of rehabilitation efforts. Rather than removing prisoner programs, they are increasing them and reorganizing their structures in order to deliver individualized sentence planning, linking activities in the prison to reintegration into the community. In Canada, for instance, the federal prison system, which holds all prisoners serving two years or more, requires all prisoners to be assessed. On the basis of the assessment, a plan for programs and rehabilitative activities is drawn up and implemented under the supervision of a case manager. Policy requires this plan to be completed within seventy days of the prisoner's reception into prison. This policy has been developed in response to a ruling from the Canadian auditor-general. The auditor-general required the assessment plans to be ready for the parole board by the earliest possible date, arguing that parole releases represent good public administration.[34]

In France, too, there are major changes planned. Unsurprisingly, these are not in the direction of U.S. policies. The publication in 2000 of a book by a prison doctor from La Santé prison in Paris detailing squalid and inhuman treatment of prisoners caused a scandal.[35] Each chamber of the French Parliament set up an inquiry and began discussing reforms.[36] A commission set up to look at the way French prisons are controlled and decisions about prisoners' rights are made recommended new legislation that would enshrine the idea that a prisoner should have the status of a citizen, deprived only of freedom of movement.[37] Legislation setting out these changes was presented to Parliament.[38]

In the Netherlands, criminal justice policies certainly became harsher during the 1990s.[39] While the use of incarceration increased from 65 per 100,000 in 1995[40] to 87 in mid-2000,[41] the system's emphasis remains on reintegration. The prison system is being restructured toward a more neighborhood approach, with the prisons in the country being grouped into clusters that will cooperate with partner organizations to foster the successful reintegration of former prisoners. This will also mean that prisoners can progress through different types of prisons while staying in their home area.[42] In Belgium, one response to the mass public protests against the justice system failures in the Dutroux case (where the arrest of a sex offender who abducted two young girls was clouded with allegations of high-level corruption) was to introduce a new policy of restorative justice into prison administration.[43] All Belgian prisons now have a restorative justice counselor to help the prison consider how victims' needs can play a part in the prison sentence and what restorative activities can be carried out by the prisoner while in prison. These counselors are specifically trying to create possibilities for communication between the prisoner and the victim and between the prisoner and the community.[44]

U.S. policies are seemingly not being influential outside Europe, either. In China and Japan, where attitudes to prisoners have traditionally been very harsh, tentative steps toward humanization are being taken. It has been reported that conditions in Japanese prisons are easing with less strict enforcement of rules prohibiting eye contact and conversation. In 2000, a dialogue began between the Ministry of Justice and the Japan Federation of Bar Associations that was designed to lead to legislation regarding the treatment of convicted prisoners, including higher wages for work, expanded prison education, and a home leave policy.[45] China is engaged in a human rights dialogue with the European Union, and prison reform is part of that agenda.[46] A Canadian organization is working with Chinese partners to develop a parole system.[47] Even in Iran, where human rights abuses are common and horrific,[48] the head of the prison service has called for prison sentences to be used as a last resort and for more use of alternatives such as house arrest or rehabilitation workshops.[49] Penal Reform International has been invited to work in Iran on prison reform and the introduction of alternatives to prison for juveniles.[50]

In countries where planned change in criminal justice is underway, the package is not normally toward U.S.-style policies but toward better treatment of prisoners and less incarceration. In Chile, the reform program centers on improving prison management and humanization of prisons and introducing alternatives to prison.[51] In Kazakhstan, fundamental changes in the management of the penitentiary system and of criminal procedure are taking place alongside the development of alternative sentencing.[52] In Turkey, whose human rights record in regard to the treatment of prisoners has been regularly and strongly criticized by the Council of Europe, the Ministry of Justice has instituted a program of prison reform and is considering introducing independent monitoring of prisons by outside groups.[53] In the Republic of Georgia in the Caucasus a new government containing many former members of prison reform groups has developed a wide-ranging change program. One of their priorities is the introduction of a system of monitoring of prison conditions by outside bodies.[54]

At a major penal reform conference held in Kampala in 1996, many states in Sub-Saharan Africa accepted the need for penal reform and embarked on reform programs.[55] They are working to reform their criminal law to reduce imprisonment and make greater use of traditional African justice methods of reconciliation and restitution.[56] In Nigeria, the new democratic government has released large numbers of prisoners, instituted prison humanization, and is developing alternatives.[57] In Zimbabwe, the criminal justice system had been in a process of constant reform for nearly a decade until the recent political difficulties there.[58] In

Kenya, community service orders as an alternative to prison are now being extensively used.[59]

The privatization of prisons is also a part of the U.S. picture that causes alarm among reformers. Prison privatization first began to be developed in the United States when private companies took over the running of immigration detention centers and then moved on to running prisons. After a slow start, privatization got a large boost from the Reagan presidency.[60] In the 1990s, it took hold particularly in Australia, where 3,000 of Australia's 20,000 prisoners were in private prisons by 1999,[61] and in England and Wales under the Conservative government from 1992 onward.[62]

Yet, the overall growth of the prison privatization movement worldwide has been less than spectacular. In Australia, a private prison reverted to public control in the state of Victoria in October 2000.[63] In England and Wales, where 12 percent of prisoners are in privatized prisons, two recent competitions for existing prisons have been won by the public sector, and the prisons have been returned to public hands.[64] In Scotland there is one private prison out of fifteen prisons.[65] In New Zealand, a move toward privatization has been halted.[66]

Compared with the sell-offs of public transportation systems and utilities such as water and electricity in many industrialized nations, prison privatization has been marginal. In 1999, global privatization activity reached about $145 billion, up by about 10 percent over 1998.[67] In such a context, prison privatization looks very marginal. The U.S. model of incarceration as a new industry to replace the decline in manufacturing and revitalize economically depressed areas[68] has not yet been replicated elsewhere. Arguments about the unacceptable level of control over prisoners given to private companies have been dealt with by various means. Outside the United States models of privatization have been developed that give the state more control over what contractors provide. In England and Wales, contracts with the private sector provider require very high levels of programming and activities for prisoners. The delivery of the contract and the carrying out of statutory functions such as disciplining prisoners are in the hands of a government controller.[69] In France, no prisons have been privatized, but in twenty-one prisons, outside contractors provide all the services while state officials run the prisons.[70] The French method is also being followed in Chile, where ten new prisons are being built on this model.[71]

The private prison companies are now turning their marketing toward those states where the prisons are out of control or the government machinery is unable to deliver even a basic standard of care and protection to prisoners, such as South Africa,[72] Lesotho, and Venezuela.[73] It would seem that the campaigners against prison privatization have been very successful in putting together alliances against it, pointing out the deficiencies of the providers, the costs, and the dangers to the point where many governments have become wary of following that path.[74]

THE CASE OF THE UNITED KINGDOM

The foregoing does not mean that imprisonment levels have stabilized outside the United States, nor does it deny that there has been a hardening of attitudes and a lengthening of prison sentences. Throughout Europe there have been increases in imprisonment levels. The 1990s saw prison growth in twenty-seven out of forty-two European countries. South Africa's prison population rose by 33 percent, Brazil experienced a 16 percent rise over two years,[75] and in Thailand the prison population rose by 57 percent between 1997[76] and 2000.[77]

One jurisdiction in Europe where the U.S. influence can be seen clearly, though, is in England and Wales. The Conservative government of the mid-1990s cast aside a consensus about criminal justice policy that had been in place throughout the postwar era and set in motion a

process of discarding the received wisdom of both its Labor and Conservative predecessors. The notion that prison was ineffective and its use
should be minimized was replaced by the slogans "prison works" and
"more pensioners sleep safely in their beds because more criminals sleep
safely behind bars."[78] The presumption against the institutionalization
of children was reversed, and a plan to build secure prisons for children
from the age of twelve was developed.[79] In the face of great opposition
from the judiciary, mandatory sentencing for a second serious violent or
sex offense, a third offense of trafficking in hard drugs, and a third offense of housebreaking, was introduced.[80]

Perhaps with the lessons of the election of Bill Clinton in mind, the
opposition Labor Party came to power having ditched previous baggage
and policies on crime and offenders. The harsh Conservative line was
slightly modified into "tough on crime, tough on the causes of crime,"
but the policies adopted by the 1997 Labor administration have been an
extension of those of the Conservatives. More mandatory sentences
have been introduced.[81] Policies on juvenile offenders have become
much harsher,[82] and the number of prisoners has risen from 61,000 in
1997[83] to 67,000 in 2001.[84] Yet even in England there are doubts about
this course. Following the reelection of the Labor government in June
2001, a new line began to reemerge. As the new government minister said
in the House of Commons:

> . . . on that matter, we will be judged not by the [number of] people who end up in
> prison but by the number we prevent from having to be sent to prison. I want to get that
> on the record. There are now a record 66,500 people in prison—almost 50 percent
> higher than 10 years ago. That is not a record to emulate; it is a record to overcome.[85]

Also, a debate has started in the United Kingdom about the decriminalization of cannabis use. Police for the London area have decided that
those found in possession of small amounts of cannabis will be given a
warning only,[86] and a prominent Conservative politician has argued for
decriminalization of cannabis use.[87]

THE UNITED STATES IS UNIQUE

The United States' love affair with incarceration has not permeated other cultures and other political systems. The *2000 International Crime Victims Survey*, covering seventeen industrialized countries, asks a question about the percentage of people favoring imprisonment as the sentence for a repeat male burglar at age twenty-one. The number of those supporting a prison sentence in such a case varies considerably among countries. In France, 12 percent of those questioned favored a prison sentence. In England and Wales, the percentage was 51 percent. In the United States, the percentage was highest, at 56 percent.[88]

So, in spite of the wide reach of the U.S. news media and the influence of U.S. culture in many areas, penal justice seems to be susceptible to many other factors. U.S. models are not seen to resonate with the political culture, nor the social policy framework, of most other parts of the world. The United States and the specific policies it follows on incarceration are distinctively of the United States, and derive from its history, culture, traditions, and political structure. As criminologist Michael Tonry says of American incarceration rates,

> The scale of the phenomenon is distinctly American. It arises partly from American moralism and partly from structural characteristics of American government that provide little insulation from emotions generated by moral panics and long-term cycles of tolerance and intolerance.[89]

THE U.S. IMPACT

The specifics of U.S. policy have been too extreme to exert a major influence. Yet developments in the United States have undoubtedly had an impact. The first area derives from the war on drugs. The U.S. has played the leading role in world forums in demanding repressive measures to deal with all the substances that it has persuaded the international community to criminalize.[90] The effect of this policy emanating from the United States has been seriously damaging for the criminal justice systems of smaller and poorer states in the Americas and farther afield. On the Indian Ocean island of Mauritius, for instance, the criminalization of marijuana, which grew on the hillsides and was commonly used recreationally, has filled the prisons with poor drug users serving sentences of two years or more.[91] The prison population there immediately rose by 20 percent in six months.[92] The prison population rates of the islands of the Caribbean are among the highest in the world (Belize, 459 per 100,000, Dominica 420, St. Vincent 368, Suriname 437).[93] Heavy enforcement of drug laws by incarcerating small users and dealers to please the United States accounts for a proportion of these very high incarceration rates.

U.S. influence can also be seen in the changes that have taken place at a deeper level in the way Western industrialized societies look at crime and punishment. The United States has led the world toward free trade, the marketization of society, and the globalization of communications. U.S. cultural forms are widely disseminated. These forces have led to increased inequality, instability, and insecurity,[94] and crime levels have increased. A new view of crime and criminals is emerging from these changes. The way the United States sees the poor and marginalized as threats, the construction of crime as entertainment, and the use of crime and the fear of crime by politicians is spreading to other societies.

Criminologist David Garland suggests that "the distinctive combination of racial division, economic inequality, and lethal violence that marks contemporary America has given its penal response a scale and intensity that often seems wholly exceptional. A Western liberal democracy that routinely executes offenders and incarcerates its citizens at a rate that is six to ten times higher than comparable nations can easily seem so divergent from international norms as to defy useful comparison."[95] Yet Garland goes on to point out the underlying patterns of crime control that are influencing policy in Europe and suggests they are linked to "the cultural formation . . . that has grown up around crime at the end of the twentieth century."[96] The fear of crime has emerged as "a prominent cultural theme."[97] Victims have become politicized as righteous figures, symbols of a "problem of security that has become a defining feature of contemporary culture."[98] Justice has become a commodity "increasingly rendered in the currency of consumer society."[99]

These changes have permeated other countries. In the United Kingdom, the language in which crime and criminals are discussed has changed. A new language of rejection and stigma is used. That symbol of the politicization of victims, calling a law by the name of a well-publicized victim, rarely happens outside the United States, although in Ontario, Canada, there is a "Christopher's law"[100] and in England there was much talk of a "Sarah's law" after the murder of an eight-year-old girl. The interviewing of the victim or victim's relatives after a sentence has been passed to ask their opinion of its severity is now commonplace in the United Kingdom. The analysis of what causes criminality—poverty and bad social conditions or individual wickedness—has now shifted toward individual wickedness.

CONCLUSION

U.S. policies on criminal justice have not been widely adopted in other parts of the world because of the difference in culture and also because of the main institutions that mediate in the political arena. The UN human rights machinery is still respected and seen as a norm in many regions of the world. The influence of the European Convention on Human Rights and the Council of Europe covers forty-three European countries stretching from Lisbon to Vladivostok. The European Union aims at a model of economic growth that minimizes social exclusion. In some societies, churches and other organizations of civil society can be vociferous. This will not be of much comfort to U.S. reformers who have none of these protections. But there are worthwhile lessons to be drawn from looking at U.S. policies in a world context and support to be drawn from the experience of other nations.

Notes

INTRODUCTION

1. American Bar Association, Task Force on Collateral Sanctions, *Introduction, Proposed Standards on Collateral Sanctions and Administrative Disqualification of Convicted Persons*, Draft, January 18, 2002.
2. Jonathan Simon, "Governing Through Crime," in George Fisher and Lawrence Friedman, eds., *The Crime Conundrum: Essays on Criminal Justice* (Boulder: Westview, 1997), pp. 171–190.
3. Lisa Freeman and Robert Gangi, "Following the Dollars: Where New York State Spends Its Prison Money," City Project, March 2000, p. 4.
4. William Spelman, "The Limited Importance of Prison Expansion," in Alfred Blumstein and Joel Wallman, eds., *The Crime Drop in America* (New York: Cambridge University Press, 2000), pp. 97–129; and Richard Rosenfeld, "Patterns in Adult Homicide," in Blumstein and Wallman, pp. 130–163.
5. Spelman, p. 129.
6. Elliott Currie, "Reflections on Crime and Criminology at the Millennium," *Western Criminology Review*, Vol. 2, No. 1, 1999, pp. 1–16.
7. With the exception of about one-sixth who are awaiting trial in local jails.
8. See, for example, William Chambliss, *Power, Politics and Crime* (Boulder: Westview, 2000).

CHAPTER 1: INVISIBLE PUNISHMENT: AN INSTRUMENT OF SOCIAL EXCLUSION

1. Senior Fellow, The Urban Institute. The views reflected here are the author's and do not necessarily represent those of The Urban Institute, its officers, or trustees. The author would like to thank Sarah Lawrence, Margaret Colgate Love, Marc Mauer, Daniel Mears, Debbie Mukamal, Amy Solomon, and Michelle Waul for their comments on early drafts of this article.
2. U.S. Department of Justice, Bureau of Justice Statistics, Probation and Parole Data Survey. In 2000, there were an estimated 4.6 million adults on probation or parole, up from 1.3 million in 1980.
3. Professor Gabriel J. Chin captures the same thought this way: "Collateral consequences are now the system's secret sentences." Gabriel J. Chin and Richard Holmes, *Effective Assistance of Counsel and the Consequences of Guilty Pleas*, 87 *Cornell Law Review* (2002).
4. For a critique of the legal doctrine distinguishing direct from collateral consequences, see Chin and Holmes 2002.
5. This legislative attribute distinguishes these sanctions from another category of punishments collectively known as "shaming," in which an offender is required by a sentencing judge publicly to display his offender status. Authorization for particular shaming orders cannot be

traced to the legislative process. One cannot say they reflect the will of the people as expressed through their legislature and approved by their chief executive. Rather, these are orders applied to an individual defendant, or limited class of defendants, by an individual judge. For an excellent discussion of shaming practices and philosophy, see D. Karp, "The Judicial and Judicious Use of Shame Penalties," *Crime & Delinquency,* vol. 44, no. 2 (April 1998).

6. There are notable exceptions. For example, the sex offender registration requirements enacted through the Jacob Wetterling Act were the result of extensive legislative negotiations. See Holly Idelson and Richard Sammon, "The Crime Compromise," *Congressional Quarterly,* August 20, 1994, p. 2452; and David Masci, "The Modified Crime Bill," *Congressional Quarterly,* August 27, 1994, p. 2490.

7. The provision to exclude individuals with drug convictions from eligibility for welfare was debated for two minutes. See G. Rubinstein and D. Mukamal, "Welfare and Housing—Denial of Benefits to Drug Offenders," this volume.

8. Indeed, the courts have held that it is not a breach of the principle of effective assistance of counsel for a defense lawyer to fail to inform his client, for example, that a plea of guilty to a certain offense will expose him to the risk of deportation. This constitutional interpretation stands in contrast to the standards of the American Bar Association that provide: "To the extent possible, defense counsel should determine and advise the defendant, sufficiently in advance of the entry of a plea, as to the possible collateral consequences that might ensue from entry of the contemplated plea." ABA Standards for Criminal Justice, Standard 14–3.2(f) (3rd ed., 1997).

9. For a discussion of the history of these collateral consequences, see Mirjan A. Damaska, "Adverse Legal Consequences of Conviction and Their Removal: A Comparative Study, *The Journal of Criminal Law, Criminology and Police Science,* vol. 59, no. 3, 347, 350–52. See also Nora V. Demleitner, "Preventing Internal Exile: The Need for Restrictions on Collateral Sentencing Consequences," 11 *Stanford Law and Policy Review* 153 (2000) at 154.

10. The American colonies embraced the concept of civil death, generally for sentences of life imprisonment. See Kathleen M. Olivares, Velmer S. Burton, Jr., and Francis Cullen, The Collateral Consequences of a Felony Conviction: A National Study of State Legal Codes 10 Years Later, *Fed. Probation* (1996).

11. For a compendium of these statutes, see Office of the Pardon Attorney, U.S. Department of Justice, Civil Disabilities of Convicted Felons: A State-by-State Survey, appendix B (1996).

12. Bureau of Justice Statistics, Use and Management of Criminal History Record Information: A Comprehensive Report, 1993, prepared by SEARCH.

13. Christopher Uggen, Melissa Thompson, and Jeff Manza, "Crime, Class and Reintegration: The Scope of Social Distribution of America's Criminal Class." Paper presented at the American Society of Criminology meetings in San Francisco, CA, November 18, 2000.

14. In this chapter, I refer to individuals convicted of crimes as "offenders." To call them "exoffenders" would be at odds with the thesis of this chapter, namely that the label "offender," once applied, is not easily removed. Yet the use of any label to reflect past behavior is at odds with the conclusion of the chapter, namely that our society should find ways to recognize the

reintegration of former law violators. Language, reality, and aspiration do not neatly coexist on this topic.

15. See, e.g., Demleitner, op. cit., n. 9; "Unconscionable Bargains: Why Defendants Who Plead Guilty Must Be Informed of All of the Consequences of Conviction." Unpublished paper by Gabriel Bankier-Plotkin (permission of author to cite). There is a distinction between exile and banishment. An exiled offender is sent to a specific place away from his home jurisdiction; a banned or banished offender is barred from certain areas within the jurisdiction. See Ernest van den Haag, *Punishing Criminals: Concerning a Very Old and Painful Question.* New York: Basic Books, 1975, p. 256. Demleitner notes the irony that English convicts transported to the American colonies faced no barriers to full participation in colonial life. Op. cit. at 153.

16. Webb Hubbell, "The Mark of Cain," *San Francisco Chronicle* (June 10, 2001).

17. James B. Jacobs, *New Perspectives on Prisons and Imprisonment.* Ithaca, NY: Cornell University Press, 1983 at 30.

18. National Council on Crime and Delinquency, Annulment of a Conviction of Crime, 8 *Crime and Delinquency,* 97–98 (1962). See also Demleitner, op. cit., at 154 ("collateral consequences act in an exclusionary manner and cause ex-offenders to become society's outcasts.").

19. The Blair government has pledged to overcome the distances created between mainstream society and those who live at society's margins. In this category are included the homeless, runaways, truants, pregnant teenagers, and former prisoners. "Social exclusion" is defined as "what can happen when people or areas suffer from a combination of linked problems such as unemployment, poor skills, low income, poor housing, high crime, bad health, and family breakdown." "Preventing Social Exclusion: Report by the Social Exclusion Unit," March 2001 at 10.

20. President's Commission on Law Enforcement and Administration of Justice. 1967. *The Challenge of Crime in a Free Society.* Washington, D.C.: U.S. Government Printing Office.

21. Demleitner, op. cit., at 155, traces the 20th-century history of collateral consequences of felony convictions. Beginning in the 1950s, a number of reform organizations succeeded in advocating for fewer restrictions on the rights and benefits of ex-offenders, resulting in a decline in "the number and restrictiveness" of these statutes. This trend was reversed in the late 1980s and 1990s. Id. at 155.

22. National Council on Crime and Delinquency, Annulment of a Conviction of Crime: A Model Act, 8 *Crime & Delinquency* 97, 98 (1962).

23. Ibid.

24. President's Commission on Law Enforcement and Criminal Justice, Task Force Report: *Corrections* 88 (1967).

25. National Advisory Commission on Corrections, commentary at 593 (1973).

26. American Bar Association, Standards for Criminal Justice, Chapter 23, Part VIII: "Civil Disabilities of Convicted Persons" (1981).

27. V. S. Burton, F. Cullen, and L. Travis, *The Collateral Consequences of a Felony Conviction,* Federal Probation, 51, 60 (1987). The exceptions to this general conclusion were rights to firearm ownership and parenting rights, both of which had been further restricted.

28. Olivares, op. cit., n. 10.

29. The study found no change in three other categories—disqualification for jury duty, restrictions on public employment, and application of concept of civil death. Olivares, ibid, at 11–14.

30. In 1994, Congress passed the Jacob Wetterling Crimes Against Children and Sexually Violent Offender Registration Act (42 U.S.C.A. § 14071), requiring states to create registries of child molesters and sexually violent offenders. States that fail to comply with the Wetterling Act are subject to a 10 percent reduction in Byrne formula grant funding (The Edward Byrne Memorial State and Local Law Enforcement Assistance Programs [42 U.S.C. § 3750]). In 1996, Megan's Law (104 P.L. 145, 100 Stat. 1345) was passed as an amendment to the Wetterling Act, requiring states to release relevant information on convicted sex offenders. The Pam Lyncher Sexual Offender Tracking and Identification Act of 1996 (42 U.S.C. § 14072) further amended the Wetterling Act by instructing the FBI to develop a national database of names and addresses of sex offenders released from prison.

31. This number comes from the Center for Sex Offender Management, http://www.csom.org/about/more.html (posted 7/3/01; accessed 9/11/01).

32. Bill Hebenton and Terry Thomas, *Criminal Records: State, Citizen, and the Politics of Protection*. Brookfield, VT: Avebury, 1993.

33. In 1991, a report of the Office of National Drug Control Policy found that offenders could lose 462 benefits from 53 federal agencies. Demleitner, op. cit., at n. 86.

34. Ibid. at 384–85.

35. 121 S. Ct. 2271 (2001). For general discussion of these statutes, see Peter H. Schuck and John Williams, "Removing Criminal Aliens: The Pitfalls and Promises of Federalism," 22 *Harvard Journal of Law and Public Policy*, 367, 386 (1999).

36. 42 U.S.C. section 862a.

37. Gwen Rubinstein. 2001. "Getting to Work: How TANF Can Support Ex-Offender Parents in the Transition to Self-Sufficiency," pp 11–12. New York, NY: Legal Action Center.

38. 42 U.S.C. § 13662(c). A 1988 amendment to the 1986 Drug Abuse Act also authorizes the eviction of a family member who was involved in certain drug offenses, even if the case did not result in a conviction. 42 U.S.C. 1437(d)(1)(6) 1999.

39. 42 U.S.C. § 13662(c).

40. 42 U.S.C. § 13663(a).

41. 20 U.S.C. § 1091(r).

42. Dan Curry, "Education Dept. May Relax Provision Denying Student Aid to Those with Drug Convictions," *Chronicle of Higher Education,* August 14, 2001. In the 2000–2001 academic year, about 67,000 of the 7.5 million applicants for student aid said they had been convicted of selling or possessing drugs. About 11,000 left the question blank.

43. PL No. 105–89.

44. 23 U.S.C. § 159. As of 2001, seventeen states, the District of Columbia, and Puerto Rico had enacted legislation conforming with the federal law requiring drivers' license suspensions and revocations. Thirty-three states filed a certification from the governor and resolution by the state legislature expressing opposition to the federal policy. Filing these documents places the state in compliance with the Department of Transportation's policy, so the state is not subject

to loss of federal highway funds. Personal communication from Brian Dover, Department of Transportation (September 19, 2001).

45. The Edward Byrne Memorial State and Local Law Enforcement Assistance Program (42 U.S.C. § 3750) provides formula grants to states to improve the functioning of the criminal justice system with an emphasis on initiatives targeting violent crime and serious offenders. Under the Wetterling Act, states had three years to comply with the provisions (9/13/97) and the option to apply for a two-year extension before losing 10 percent of the state Byrne formula grant. In fiscal year 2000, nearly $500 million was available to states through the Byrne formula grant program. All but fourteen of the fifty-six states and territories applied for the two-year extension.

46. 24 C.F.R. §§ 966.203(b) and 966.4(1)(5)(vii).

47. T. H. Marshall, "Citizenship and Class," in *Class, Citizenship and Social Development* 65, 71 (1964). I am indebted to Demleitner, op. cit., at 154, for this insight.

48. Christopher Uggen and Jeff Manza, 2000, "The Political Consequences of Felon Disenfranchisement Laws in the United States." Paper presented at the annual meeting of the American Sociological Association in Washington, D.C., on August 16, 2000.

49. A number of states have recently relaxed some limitations on voter disqualification of felons. For instance, in May 2001, the governor of Connecticut signed a bill that extends voting rights to felons on probation, adding an estimated 36,000 people to the voter rolls. In New Mexico, the legislature adopted a bill repealing the state's lifetime ban on voting for ex-felons. A Commonwealth Court in Pennsylvania restored the right to vote to thousands of ex-felons, who, as a result, were then able to vote in the 2000 presidential election. "Felony Disenfranchisement Laws in the United States," The Sentencing Project, 2001.

50. I am indebted to Chin for this insight. Op. cit. n. 3.

51. For a discussion of a human and social capital framework for understanding the impact of collateral sanctions, see John Hagan and Ronit Dinovitzer, "Collateral Consequences of Imprisonment for Children, Communities, and Prisoners," in M. Tonry and J. Petersilia, *Prisons 1999* at 121.

52. Researchers have found support for the hypothesis that mass incarceration policies in communities with high enforcement patterns have so diminished the community's mechanisms of informal social control that crime rates have increased after a certain "tipping point" of incarceration is reached. See Todd Clear, Dina Rose, and Judith Ryder, "Incarceration and the Community: The Problem of Removing and Returning Offenders," 47, *Crime and Delinquency,* 336–37, 2001.

53. This consistency in general attitudes toward punishment should be contrasted with the profound shift in public opinion regarding a specific punishment, the death penalty. Over roughly the same period of time, from 1965 to 2000, according to the Gallup polls, the percentage of Americans who said they favored the death penalty increased from 45 percent to a high of 80 percent in 1994, before dropping slightly to 67 percent in 2000.

54. Zimring, Hawkins, and Kamin, p. 178.

55. John Dilulio, Steven K. Smith, and Aaron J. Saiger. "The Federal Role in Crime Control," in

James Q. Wilson and Joan R. Petersilia, eds., *Crime: Twenty-Eight Expert Views*. San Francisco: Institute for Contemporary Study, p. 450 (1994).

56. Frank Newport, "No Single Problem Dominates Americans' Concerns Today," Gallup News Service, May 2, 1998; and Frank Newport, "Surge in Public's View of Energy as Greatest Problem," Gallup News Service, May 17, 2001.

57. Franklin E. Zimring, Gordon Hawkins, and Sam Kamin, *Punishment and Democracy*. New York: Oxford University Press, 2001.

58. Robert Martinson, "What Works?—Questions and Answers About Prison Reform," *Public Interest 35* (2) (1974).

59. Michael Tonry, "The Fragmentation of Sentencing and Corrections in America." In *Sentencing and Corrections, Issues for the 21st Century*, 1, National Institute of Justice Research in Brief (1999).

60. See Zimring, et al., op. cit.

61. These estimates were derived from a study conducted by The Sentencing Project and Human Rights Watch in 1998. The seven states are Alabama, Florida, Iowa, Mississippi, New Mexico, Virginia, and Wyoming, although New Mexico repealed its lifetime ban in 2002. It should be noted that nearly all states have placed restrictions on voting rights for convicted felons. For example, as of 1998, forty-six states and the District of Columbia prohibited inmates serving time for a felony conviction to vote; thirty-two states restrict the voting rights of offenders on probation or parole; and in fourteen states a convicted offender can lose the right to vote for life. See Marc Mauer, *Race to Incarcerate*, 1999.

62. Paper presented by Martin Y. Iguchi, Ph.D., Director, RAND Drug Policy Research Center, at NIDA workshop, "Differential Drug Use, HIV/AIDS and Related Health Outcomes Among Racial and Ethnic Populations," April 26–27, 2001, Bethesda, MD.

63. See Demleitner, op. cit., at 159 for discussion of this shift.

64. David Garland, "The Culture of High Crime Societies: Some Preconditions of Recent 'Law and Order' Policies," *British Journal of Criminology*, Vol. 40 No. 3, Summer 2000, 347, 348.

65. Id. at 350.

66. In thinking of these recommendations, I have benefited from my participation in the American Bar Association's Task Force on Collateral Consequences of Convictions, which was established in 2001 to review the ABA Standards on this issue. Although I cannot speak for the Task Force, I acknowledge the contributions of my fellow members.

67. The ABA Task Force on Collateral Consequences of Convictions recommends that these consequences be called "collateral sanctions and penalties."

68. The Supreme Court recognized this reality in *INS v. St. Cyr*, 121 S. Ct. 2271 (2002), holding that avoiding the collateral consequence of deportation is "one of the principal benefits sought by defendants deciding whether to accept a plea offer or instead proceed to trial."

69. This approach was recently embraced by the Delaware Supreme Court in *State v. Berkley*, 724 A. 2d 558 (Del. 1999), holding that a state law requiring that a convicted person forfeit his drivers' license could not be enforced where the offender did not know it was a consequence of pleading guilty.

CHAPTER 2: WELFARE AND HOUSING—DENIAL
OF BENEFITS TO DRUG OFFENDERS

* The authors wish to acknowledge research assistance provided by Julia Sutherland, Rose Darling, and Steve Gold.

1. Amy E. Hirsch, *"Some Days Are Harder Than Hard"—Welfare Reform and Women with Drug Convictions in Pennsylvania.* Washington, D.C.: Center for Law and Social Policy, 1999, p. 41.

2. Drug Strategies and the Police Foundation, *Drugs and Crime Across America: Police Chiefs Speak Out: A National Survey Among Chiefs of Police.* Washington, D.C.: Drug Strategies, 1996.

3. "Treatment Over Jail Time," ABC News, retrieved from www.abcnews.go.com, June 13, 2001.

4. Peter C. Rydell and Susan S. Everingham, *Controlling Cocaine: Supply Versus Demand Programs.* Santa Monica: RAND Corporation, 1994.

5. Barry R. McCaffrey, "A Way to Beat Illegal Drugs," *Washington Post,* April 17, 2000, p. A21.

6. Albert Woodward, et al., "The Drug Abuse Treatment Gap: Recent Estimates," *Health Care Financing Review,* Volume 18 (1997), pp. 5–17.

7. Christopher J. Mumola, "Substance Abuse and Treatment, State and Federal Prisoners, 1997," *Bureau of Justice Statistics,* January 1999.

8. This term includes (but is not limited to) formal and informal housing, privately and publicly financed housing, halfway houses, transitional housing, and Oxford housing where individuals can learn to live drug-free in the community after release from treatment.

9. "Drug Abuse Violation Arrests by Age, 1970–97," Table on the Bureau of Justice Statistics Web site—www.ojp.usdoj.gov/bjs.

10. U.S. Department of Justice, "Drugs and Crime Facts," 2001.

11. Jodi M. Brown and Patrick A. Langan, "Felony Sentences in the United States, 1996," *Bureau of Justice Statistics,* July 1999, p. 2.

12. Ibid., p. 3.

13. The Sentencing Project, "Drug Policy and the Criminal Justice System," updated 2001. Retrieved from www.sentencingproject.org, September 1, 2001.

14. Lawrence A. Greenfeld and Tracy L. Snell, "Women Offenders." Washington, D.C.: Bureau of Justice Statistics, December 1999, p. 6.

15. Hirsch, op. cit.

16. P.L. No. 104–193 (August 22, 1996).

17. §115.

18. Under the later-enacted Balanced Budget Act of 1997, the ban applies to convictions where both the conduct and conviction occurred after the date of enactment of the law.

19. §408(a)(8).

20. Legal Action Center, "Welfare Reform Community Case Studies." Unpublished data, 1999. Prepared for the Substance Abuse and Mental Health Services Administration.

21. Legal Action Center, *Getting to Work: How TANF Can Support Ex-Offender Parents in the Transition to Self-Sufficiency.* Washington, D.C.: LAC, 2001. Updated January 2002.

22. Legal Action Center, *Steps to Success: Helping Women with Alcohol and Drug Problems Move from Welfare to Work*. Washington, D.C.: LAC, 1999.

23. Joan Loviglio, "DA, Others Urge State to Extend Welfare Benefits to Ex-Felons," Associated Press, June 16, 2001.

24. Legal Action Center, "Welfare Reform Community Case Studies." Unpublished data (1999).

25. Legal Action Center, *Steps to Success,* op. cit.

26. Amanda Noble and Elaine Zahnd, *The Gramm Amendment to Welfare Reform: Problems for Women's Residential Treatment Providers and Their Clients*. Davis: University of California, January 2000.

27. P.L. No. 100–690 (November 18, 1988).

28. Ibid. at § 5101(5).

29. Ibid.

30. P.L. No. 104–120 (March 28, 1996).

31. P.L. No. 105–276 (October 21, 1998).

32. Address Before a Joint Session of Congress on the State of the Union (January 23, 1996).

33. "Meeting the Challenge: Public Housing Authorities Respond to the 'One Strike and You're Out' Initiative," U.S. Department of Housing and Urban Development, September 1997, page v.

34. *Department of Housing and Urban Development v. Rucker,* 122 S. Ct. 1230 (2002).

35. 42 U.S.C. § 1437d(t).

36. In addition to drug offenses, the laws require public housing agencies and providers of Section 8 and other federally assisted housing to deny housing to any household with a member who is subject to a lifetime registration requirement under a state sex offender registration program. 42 U.S.C. § 13663.

37. 42 U.S.C. § 13661(a).

38. 42 U.S.C. § 1437d(l)(6); 24 C.F.R. § 966.4(l)(5)(i). While the standards surrounding eviction specifically target drug-related criminal activity, leases are also required to provide that any criminal activity by a tenant, a member of the tenant's household or guest, or any other person under the tenant's control that threatens the health, safety, or right to peaceful enjoyment of the premises by other tenants is grounds for eviction. 24 C.F.R. §§ 5.859 and 966.4(l)(5)(ii)(A). At the time of the drafting of this chapter, the Supreme Court had agreed to review the Ninth Circuit decision, *Rucker v. Davis* (237 F.3d 1113), which determined that Congress did not intend to authorize the eviction of innocent tenants, during the 2002 term.

39. P.L. No. 104–120, § 9(a) (codified at 42 U.S.C. § 1437d (k) and (l)).

40. 24 C.F.R. § 966.4(l)(5)(i)(B).

41. 24 C.F.R. §§ 5.861, 882.518(c)(3)(i) and 966.4(l)(5)(iii).

42. "Meeting the Challenge," op. cit., p. v.

43. Ibid. at p. 15.

44. 24 C.F.R. §§ 966.203(b) and 966.4(l)(5)(vii).

45. In 1999, state and federal prisons held an estimated 721,500 parents of minor children. Approximately 55 percent of state and 63 percent of federal prisoners reported having a child under the age of eighteen. Among female offenders, 65 percent of state and 59 percent of fed-

eral prisoners had a minor child. Christopher J. Mumola, "Incarcerated Parents and Their Children," *Bureau of Justice Statistics Special Report,* August 2000.

46. P.L. No. 105–89 (codified as amended in scattered sections of 42 U.S.C.).

CHAPTER 3: MASS IMPRISONMENT AND THE DISAPPEARING VOTERS

1. Jamie Fellner and Marc Mauer, "Losing the Vote: The Impact of Felony Disenfranchisement Laws in the United States," Human Rights Watch and The Sentencing Project, October 1998.

2. Alec C. Ewald, "Civil Death: The Ideological Paradox of Criminal Disenfranchisement Laws in the United States," Master of Arts Thesis, University of North Carolina, 2000, p. 1.

3. J. Morgan Kousser, cited in Andrew L. Shapiro, "Challenging Criminal Disenfranchisement Under the Voting Rights Act: A New Strategy," *Yale Law Journal,* Vol. 103, p. 538.

4. Shapiro, p. 541.

5. Ibid.

6. Ewald, p. 91.

7. Ewald, p. 92.

8. See, for example, Michael Tonry, *Malign Neglect* (New York: Oxford University Press, 1995).

9. Christopher Uggen and Jeff Manza, "The Political Consequences of Felon Disenfranchisement Laws in the United States." Paper presented at the annual meeting of the American Sociological Association, Washington, D.C., August 16, 2000.

10. *Washington v. State,* 75 Ala. 585 (1884).

11. *Green v. Board of Elections,* 380 F.2d 445 (2d Cir. 1967), as cited in Ewald, p. 51.

12. Todd F. Gaziano, Testimony before the House Judiciary Committee Subcommittee on the Constitution Regarding HR 906, October 21, 1999, p. 2.

13. Patricia Allard and Marc Mauer, "Regaining the Vote: An Assessment of Activity Relating to Felon Disenfranchisement Laws," The Sentencing Project, January 2000.

14. Fellner and Mauer, p. 6.

15. Ibid., pp. 5–6.

16. Florida Parole Commission, "Clemency Questionnaire."

17. *Richardson v. Ramirez,* 418 U.S. at 78 (Marshall, J., dissenting) (citations omitted).

18. Fellner and Mauer, p. 18.

CHAPTER 4: INCARCERATION AND THE IMBALANCE OF POWER

1. Probation officers, corrections officials, and pretrial services counselors all perform vital functions in the criminal justice system. See James R. Marsha, *Performing Pretrial Services: A Challenge in the Federal Criminal Justice System,* 58 Fed. Probation 3 (1994) (discussing challenges pretrial service officers face in performing pretrial service functions); see also John P. Storm, *What United States Probation Officers Do,* 61 Fed. Probation 13 (1997) (describing duties of federal probation officers such as preparing presentence reports and supervising federal offenders released into the community).

2. Many state and local systems appoint individual lawyers to represent indigent defendants or

hire them on a contract basis. Some use a combination of public defenders and individual court-appointed attorneys. For a thorough description of indigent defense systems, see Marea L. Beeman and Robert L. Spangenberg, *Toward A More Effective Right to Assistance of Counsel Indigent Defense Systems in the United States,* 58 Law and Contemp. Probs. 31 (1995) (detailing state systems for providing legal representation to indigent defendants and methods used by states to fund their systems).

3. Forty-eight states and the District of Columbia prohibit felons from voting while incarcerated. Thirty-two states prohibit felons from voting while on parole, and twenty-eight of these states also prohibit probationers convicted of felonies from voting. In twelve of these states, felony disenfranchisement is permanent. See Jamie Fellner and Marc Mauer, *Losing the Vote: The Impact of Felony Disenfranchisement Laws in the United States,* Human Rights Watch and the Sentencing Project (October 1998).

4. See Marc Mauer, *Race to Incarcerate* 126–40 (1999); Katheryn Russell, *The Color of Crime* 14–46 (1998).

5. There is widespread agreement among criminal law scholars that grand juries generally follow the lead and direction of the prosecutor. See Susan W. Brenner, *Forum: Faults, Fallacies, and the Future of Our Criminal Justice System: The Voice of the Community: A Case for Grand Jury Independence,* 3 Va. J. Soc. Pol'y & L. 67 (1995); Angela J. Davis, *The American Prosecutor: Independence, Power, and the Threat Of Tyranny,* 86 Iowa L. Rev. 393 (2001).

6. Of course, if the prosecutor is an elected official, her constituents could vote her out of office at the end of her term. But since most members of the public ordinarily would be unaware of such a decision, it is highly unlikely that it would become a campaign issue. Angela J. Davis, *The American Prosecutor: Independence, Power, and the Threat of Tyranny,* 86 Iowa L. Rev. 393 (2001).

7. All states and the federal government have mandatory sentencing laws, most often for drug offenses. See *Drug Policy and the Criminal Justice System,* The Sentencing Project (updated 2001).

8. See Denise Watson Batts, "Woman on the Run—Kemba Smith Is Out of Prison and Back Home in Virginia, Trying to Juggle the Duties of Freedom, Celebrity, and Motherhood," June 10, 2001 *Virginian-Pilot & Ledger Star,* A1; Ms. Smith was pardoned by President Bill Clinton on December 22, 2000. Id.

9. Mary Pat Flaherty and Joan Biskupic, "Justice by the Numbers," *Washington Post,* October 7, 1996, A1.

10. The remedy for a violation of the Fourth Amendment's prohibition against unreasonable searches and seizures is exclusion of the evidence that was illegally seized. See *Mapp v. Ohio,* 367 U.S. 643 (1961).

11. See Anne Bowen Poulin, *Prosecutorial Discretion and Selective Prosecution: Enforcing Protection After United States v. Armstrong,* 34 Am. Crim. L. Rev. 1071 n.170 (1997); Angela J. Davis, *Prosecution and Race: The Power and Privilege of Discretion,* 67 Fordham L. Rev. 13, 52–53 (1998); Christopher H. Schmitt, "Why Plea Bargains Reflect Bias," *San Jose Mercury News,* December 9, 1991, at 1A.

12. See Angela J. Davis, *Prosecution and Race: The Power And Privilege of Discretion*, 67 Fordham L. Rev. 13, 35–36 (1998).

13. The Supreme Court has ruled that, in order to prove selective prosecution based on race, the defendant must prove that similarly situated whites could have been prosecuted, but were not. See *Wayte v. U.S.*, 470 U.S. 598, 609 (1985); *U.S. v. Armstrong*, 517 U.S. 456, 470 (1996).

14. *U.S. v. Armstrong*, 517 U.S. 456 (1996).

15. See Bureau of Statistics, Department of Justice, *Felony Defendants in Large Urban Counties* 29 (1992).

16. Flaherty and Biskupic.

17. The standard for indicting a criminal defendant is whether there is probable cause to believe the defendant committed the offense, a much lower standard than the proof beyond a reasonable doubt necessary for a criminal conviction. Stephen A. Saltzburg and Daniel J. Capra, *American Criminal Procedure* 831–32 (6th ed. 2000).

18. See *Berger v. United States*, 295 U.S. 78, 88 (1935); Model Code of Professional Responsibility EC 7–13 ("The responsibility of a public prosecutor differs from that of the usual advocate; his duty is to seek justice, not merely to convict."); Model Rules of Professional Conduct Rule 3.8 cmt. (1983)(describing a prosecutor's responsibilities "to see that [a] defendant is accorded procedural justice and that guilt is decided upon the basis of sufficient evidence"); Standards Relating to the Admin. of Criminal Justice Standard 3-1.2(c)(1992) ("The duty of the prosecutor is to seek justice, not merely to convict").

19. See generally Stephen B. Bright, *Neither Equal Nor Just: The Rationing and Denial of Legal Services to the Poor When Life and Liberty Are at Stake*, 1997 Ann. Surv. Am. L. 783.

20. The Public Defender Service for the District of Columbia is an example of a well-funded office that provides excellent representation for indigent defendants.

21. Bright, at 816.

22. Prosecutors are required to reveal all exculpatory information to the defense. See *Brady v. Maryland*, 371 U.S. 812 (1962). Despite this requirement, courts provide few post-conviction remedies to defendants when Brady violations are discovered. See Angela J. Davis, *The American Prosecutor: Independence, Power, and the Threat of Tyranny*, 86 Iowa L. Rev. 393, 430–31 (2001) (discussing the inadequacy of judicial remedies for Brady violations).

23. Flaherty and Biskupic.

24. Robert L. Misner, *Recasting Prosecutorial Discretion*, 86 J. Crim. L. & Criminology 717, 750–51 (1996).

25. See Erwin Chemerinsky, *An Independent Analysis of the Los Angeles Police Department's Board of Inquiry Report on the Rampart Scandal*, 34 Loy. L.A. L. Rev. 545, 630 (2001) (arguing that judges should do more to assure that there is a factual basis for a guilty plea, including examining the credibility of police reports).

26. See Jose A. Cabranes, "Letter to the Editor: Incoherent Sentencing Guidelines," *Wall St. J.*, Aug. 28, 1992, at A11; Naftali Bendavid, *Breyer's Role as Sentencing Pioneer Still Rankles*, Legal Times, May 16, 1994, at 7; Toni Locy, "2nd Judge Rejects Guidelines for Sentencing in Crack Case: Pressure by DEA Agent Cited as Term Is Reduced," *Wash. Post*, July 21, 1994, at B01;

"A Time for Clinton, Judges to Correct Drug-term Injustice," *San Diego Union Tribune,* December 28, 2000, at B11; Mark Pazniokas, "Judge Questions Tough Sentencing Policies in Drug Cases," *Hartford Courant,* December 2 1995, at A3.

27. Toni Locy, "2nd Judge Rejects Guidelines for Sentencing in Crack Case; Pressure by DEA Agent Cited as Term Is Reduced," *Washington Post,* July 21, 1994, BI.

28. Id.

CHAPTER 5: IMPRISONING WOMEN:
THE UNINTENDED VICTIMS OF MASS IMPRISONMENT

* This chapter is a revised version of a paper entitled "Reinventing Women's Corrections," prepared for Susan Sharp (ed.), *The Incarcerated Woman: Rehabilitative Programming in Women's Prisons.* Upper Saddle River, N.J.: Prentice Hall.

1. Nicole Hahn Rafter, 1990. *Partial Justice: Women, Prisons and Social Control.* New Brunswick, NJ: Transaction Books.

2. Linda R. Singer, 1973. "Women and the Correctional Process," *American Criminal Law Review,* 11: 295–308.

3. Margaret Calahan, 1986. *Historical Corrections Statistics in the United States, 1850–1984.* Washington, D.C.: Bureau of Justice Statistics.

4. Meda Chesney-Lind, 1997. *The Female Offender: Girls, Women, and Crime.* Thousand Oaks: Sage.

5. Calahan (1986).

6. Allen Beck and Jennifer C. Karberg, 2001. *Prison and Jail Inmates at Midyear 2000.* Bureau of Justice Statistics, U.S. Department of Justice.

7. Beck and Karberg (2001); 5.

8. Calahan (1986); Beck and Karberg (2001), 5.

9. Beck and Karberg (2001), 5.

10. Amnesty International, 1999. *Not Part of My Sentence: Violations of the Human Rights of Women in Custody.* Washington, D.C.: Amnesty International.

11. Singer (1973).

12. Rafter (1990).

13. Meda Chesney-Lind and Randall G. Shelden (1998). *Girls, Deliquency and Juvenile Justice.* Belmont: Wadsworth.

14. Barbara Brenzel, 1983. *Daughters of the State.* Cambridge: MIT Press; Rafter (1990).

15. Office of Justice Programs. 2000. *National Symposium on Women Offenders.* Conference Proceedings. Washington, D.C., December 13–15, 1999.

16. Bona Miller, "Different, Not More Difficult." *Corrections Today.* December 1999, pp. 142–144.

17. Caroline W. Harlow, 1999. "Prior Abuse Reported by Inmates and Probationers." BJS Selected Findings. Washington, D.C.: U.S. Department of Justice.

18. Harlow (1999), 1.

19. Harlow (1999), 2.

20. D. Finkelhor and L. Baron, 1986. "Risk Factors for Child Sexual Abuse." *Journal of Interpersonal Violence* 1:43–71.

21. Chesney-Lind and Shelden (1998).

22. Allen Beck, 2000. *Prisoners in 1999.* Bureau of Justice Statistics, U.S. Department of Justice.

23. Tracy L. Snell and Danielle C. Morton, 1994. *Women in Prison.* Washington, D.C.: Bureau of Justice Statistics, Special Report.

24. Tracy Huling, 1991. "Breaking the Silence," Correctional Association of New York, March 4, mimeo.

25. Jane Totman, 1978. *The Murderess: A Psychosocial Study of Criminal Homicide.* San Francisco: R & E Research Associates.

26. Angela Browne, 1987. *When Battered Women Kill.* New York: The Free Press.

27. Kim English, 1993. "Self-Reported Crimes Rates of Women Prisoners." *Journal of Quantitative Criminology* 9:357–382.

28. English (1993), 370.

29. Meda Chesney-Lind and Noelie Rodriguez. 1983. "Women Under Lock and Key." *The Prison Journal* 63:47–65.

30. English (1993), 372.

31. English (1993), 3, 74.

32. Karen Heimer, 2000. "Changes in the Gender Gap in Crime and Women's Economic Marginalization." In *Criminal Justice 2000: Vol. 1, The Nature of Crime. Continuity and Change.* Washington, D.C.: National Institute of Justice.

33. Federal Bureau of Investigation. 2000. *Crime in the United States 1999 Uniform Crime Reports.* Washington, D.C.: U.S. Department of Justice.

34. Barbara Bloom, Meda Chesney-Lind, and Barbara Owen, 1994. *Women in Prison in California: Hidden Victims of the War on Drugs.* San Francisco: Center on Juvenile and Criminal Justice; Richie, this volume.

35. FBI (2000), 217; Beck (2000), 6.

36. Bureau of Justice Statistics. 1988. *Profile of State Prison Inmates, 1986.* U.S. Department of Justice; Beck (2000), 10.

37. Beck (2000), 10.

38. Jamie Fellner, 1997. *Cruel and Unusual: Disproportionate Sentences for New York Drug Offenders.* Human Rights Watch.

39. Myrna Raeder, 1993. "Gender and Sentencing: Single Moms, Battered Women and Other Sex-based Anomalies in the Gender Free World of the Federal Sentencing Guidelines." *Pepperdine Law Review,* Vol. 20, No. 3, pp. 905–990.

40. Raeder (1993), 954; Richie, this volume.

41. Raeder (1993), 939–45.

42. Raeder (1993), 31–32.

43. Raeder (1993), 34.

44. Marc Mauer, 1999. *Drug Policy and the Criminal Justice System.* Washington, D.C.: The Sentencing Project.

45. Libby Copeland, 2000. "Kemba Smith's Hard Time." *Washington Post.* February 13, F01.

46. Sally Anderson, 1994. Comparison of Institutional Admissions. Oregon Department of Corrections.

47. Janet Davidson, 2001. Personal Communication with the Author. December 21.

48. Rafter (1990).

49. Dorinda L. Welle and Gregory P. Falkin, 2001. "Preventing 'Violations' Through Drug Treatment." *Women, Girls, and Criminal Justice.* October/November, pp. 81–82, 95–96.

50. Human Rights Watch. 1996. *All Too Familiar: Sexual Abuse of Women in U.S. State Prisons.* New York: Human Rights Watch.

51. Center for Substance Abuse Treatment. 1997. *Substance Abuse Treatment for Incarcerated Offenders: A Guide to Promising Practices.* Rockville, MD: Department of Health and Human Services, Publich Health Service, draft, p. 2.

52. Substance Abuse and Mental Health Services Administration. 1997. *Substance Use Among Women in the United States.* Rockville, MD: Department of Health and Human Services, Chapter 8, pp. 9, 12.

53. James Inciardi, Dorothy Lockwood, and Anne E. Pottieger. 1993. *Women and Crack-Cocaine.* New York: Macmillian Publishing Company; B. Bloom and S. Covington. 1998. "Gender Specific Programming for Female Offenders: What Is It and Why Is It Important?" Paper presented at the 50th Annual Meeting of the American Society of Criminology, Nov. 11–14. Washington, D.C.

54. Liz Kelly, 1990. "Journeying in Reverse." In L. Gelsthorpe and A. Morris (eds.) *Feminist Perspectives in Criminology.* Milton Keynes: Open University Press.

CHAPTER 6: ENTREPRENEURIAL CORRECTIONS:
INCARCERATION AS A BUSINESS OPPORTUNITY

* Portions of this article first appeared in "Bailing Out Private Jails," *The American Prospect,* September 10, 2001 (Vol. 12, No. 16).

1. Charles Thomas. "Private Adult Correctional Facility Census." Gainsville, FL: Private Corrections Project, http://web.crim.ufl.edu/pcp/ September 4, 2001.

2. Philip E. Fixler. "Behind Bars We Find an Enterprise Zone." *Wall Street Journal.* November 29, 1984.

3. Jim Montgomery. "Correctional Corp. Seeks Lease to Run Tennessee's Prisons—Firm Would Pay $100 Million for 99-Year Term in Plan for Pioneer "Privatization." *Wall Street Journal.* September 13, 1985.

4. Alan Weston. "Would You Stay in One of This Man's Prisons?" *Advantage* magazine. February 1986.

5. Dana Joel. "A Guide to Prison Privatization." *Heritage Foundation Backgrounder.* Washington, D.C.: the Heritage Foundation. 1988.

6. Frank Klimko. "TDC Warden Resigns to Go with Private Firm." *Houston Chronicle.* September 14, 1985.

7. Brian Maffly and Judy Fahys. "Prison Boss Quits 'Pressure Cooker'; McCotter Resigns Job As Prison Boss." *Salt Lake Tribune.* May 10, 1997.

8. Bill Workman. "Pros and Cons of Life at Hidden Valley Ranch." *San Francisco Chronicle.* April 13, 1985.

9. Office of the Corrections Trustee for the District of Columbia. "Report to the Attorney General: Inspection and Review of the Northeast Ohio Correctional Center." Washington, D.C., 1998.

10. Mark Oswald. "Capitol Chronicle: Murder Rate in Prisons Far too High." *Santa Fe New Mexican,* September 4, 1999.

11. Fox Butterfield. "Privately Run Juvenile Prison in Louisiana Is Attacked for Abuse of 6 Inmates." *New York Times,* March 16, 2000.

12. Monica Polanco. "Bartlett Jail Faulted in Escape Study: Criminal Justice Report Cites 16 Problems, Human Error." *Austin American-Statesman,* October 18, 2000.

13. Memo from Patrick Kawai to HCF Warden Nolan Espinosa. "Summary of Identified Security Threat Group (STG) at Florence Correctional Facility (FCC)." Hawaii Department of Public Safety, April 16–20, 2001.

14. Associated Press Newswires. "Ex-Prison Supervisors Told They Will Be Jailed for Beating Inmate." October 27, 2000.

15. Associated Press. "Five Inmates Injured in Jail Melee." *Houston Chronicle.* November 9, 2000.

16. Associated Press. "Torrance County Prison Gets New Warden in Wake of Riot." *Albuquerque Tribune,* December 2, 2000.

17. *William P. v. Corrections Corporation of America.* Civil Action Number 3:98-290-17 Jury Verdict, December 14, 2000.

18. Kevin Dayton. "Arizona Prison in 'Turmoil.' " *Honolulu Advertizer,* July 1, 2001.

19. Nelson Daranciang. "Arizona Private Prison Names New Boss after Deaths." *Honolulu Star Bulletin,* May 12, 2001.

20. Memo from Cheryl Zembik to Ted Sakai. "Briefing Report—Florence Correctional Facility, 4/16–4/20 Monitoring Trip." Hawaii Department of Public Safety. April 30, 2001; John Martinez. Monitoring Report, April 16–20, 2001 Hawaii Department of Public Safetty; Memo from Patrick Kawai to HCF Warden Nolan Espinosa. "Summary of Identified Security Threat Group (STG) at Florence Correctional Facility (FCC)." Hawaii Department of Public Safety, April 16–20, 2001.

21. David Miles. "Prison in Lockdown After Protest." *Albuquerque Journal,* April 25, 2001.

22. Susan Hylton. "Jail Warden Ignores Rehab, Ex-Staffer Says." *Tulsa World,* May 4, 2001.

23. Clifford Meano. "Jail Error Lets Out Another Prisoner." *Tulsa World,* May 30, 2001.

24. Bill Miller. "10 D.C. Guards Charged in Smuggling Sting." *Washington Post,* June 1, 2001.

25. Susan Hylton. "Jail Staff Member Resigns Amid Drug Allegations." *Tulsa World,* June 13, 2001.

26. Ty Tagami. "Riot Rocks Private Prison in Floyd." *Lexington Herald Leader,* July 7, 2001.

27. Associated Press. "Top Two Prison Officials Fired in Wake of Uprising." July 18, 2001.

28. Judith A. Greene. "Comparing Private and Public Prison Services and Programs in Minnesota: Findings from Prisoner Interviews." *Current Issues in Criminal Justice,* Vol. II, No. 2, November 1999.

29. Camille Graham Camp and George M. Camp. *The Corrections Yearbook, 1999.* Middletown, CT: The Criminal Justice Institute.

30. James Austin and Garry Coventry. "Are We Better Off? Comparing Private and Public Prisons in the United States." *Current Issues in Criminal Justice,* Vol. II, No. 2, November 1999.

31. Dennis Cunningham. Presentation at the World Research Group conference, "Privatizing Correctional Facilities." September 25, 2000, in San Antonio, Texas.

32. Kit Miniclier. "Inmate Shortage Has Private Prisons Scrambling." *Denver Post.* May 24, 2000; Carla Crowder. "Colorado Renews Contract with Burlington Prison Facing Continued Problems." *Rocky Mountain News,* July 3, 2000.

33. James McNair. "Wackenhut Prisons Mired in Abuse Scandals." *Miami Herald,* April 6, 2000.

34. Gary D. Robertson. "N.C. to Take Control of Private Prisons." The Associated Press, June 24, 2000.

35. Associated Press. "Private Company Turns Two Units Over to State Prison System." June 30, 2001.

36. Associated Press. "Allen Says Prison Program Is Geared to Needs." *Virginian-Pilot.* October 22, 1997.

37. Associated Press. "Plan to Import Prisoners Will Add to Crowding, a Critic Says." *Virginian-Pilot.* July 7, 1998.

38. Frank Green. "Prison System Wants More." *Richmond Times-Dispatch.* January 27, 2001.

39. Frank Green. "Inmates Boost VA's Revenue." *Richmond Times-Dispatch.* February 25, 2001.

40. Jamie Fellner. "Super-Maximum Security Confinement in Virginia." New York: Human Rights Watch. April 1999

41. Letter from David C. Fathi to John J. Armstrong, Commissioner of Corrections in Connecticut. January 26, 2001.

42. Laurence Hammack. "3,376 Prisoners Statewide Not from Virginia." *Roanoke Times,* May 31, 2001.

43. Staff report. "2 More Inmates Moved to Virginia Prisons." *St. Croix Source,* July 20, 2001.

44. Daniel B. Wood "Private Prisons, Public Doubts." *Christian Science Monitor.* July 21, 1998.

CHAPTER 7: FAMILIES AND INCARCERATION

* I thank the families that participated in this study for sharing their experiences so that others could learn from them. I thank Geoffrey Cohen, Kathryn Dudley, Ryan Goodman, Meda Chesney-Lind, Marc Mauer, Harold Scheffler, Charles Sullivan, Pauline Sullivan, Jenifer Wood, Paul Wood, and the editors at The New Press for their generous help and advice. This research was funded by the National Institute of Justice (Award Number 98-CE-VX-0012), the National Science Foundation (Award Number SBR-9727685), the Wenner-Gren Foundation for Anthropological Research, and the Yale Center for the Study of Race, Inequality, and Politics. This research also could not have been conducted without the cooperation of the District

of Columbia, Virginia, and Maryland Departments of Correction, and the various federal agencies working with District inmates.

1. Eric Lotke, National Center for Institutions and Alternatives, "Hobbling a Generation: Young African American Men in D.C.'s Criminal Justice System Five Years Later (1997)." Figures assume incarceration rates have held constant since statistics were gathered in 1997. The latter figure includes jail, prison, parole, probation, and warrants. It is worth noting that the incarceration rate in the District is similar to the rates of other cities, suggesting that this is fairly typical of other urban areas.

2. Author's estimate, based on year 2000 census population data and geocoded 1999 D.C. Department of Corrections population data, on file with author. Hereinafter referred to as "Study Data Sets."

3. Author's estimate, based on Study Data Sets, supra note 2.

4. The overall rate of incarceration among males in the District is 2.2 percent, while in Baltimore, Maryland, it is 2.3 percent and in New Haven, Connecticut, it is 1.7 percent. Estimates based on census data and data provided by the D.C., Maryland, and New Haven Departments of Corrections.

5. Fifty families of male prisoners participated in the study. Twenty families were part of a preliminary snowball sample, and an additional thirty families were randomly selected from the D.C. Department of Corrections population.

6. Perhaps the most costly regular expense that families complain about are phone charges. Most correctional facilities contract out for phone services, and phone companies compete with one another to give a legal form of kickbacks to the Department of Corrections in each state. Because phone conversations are often time-limited, many families are required to accept several calls to complete a single conversation, with connection charges applying to each call. While there are no publicly available data on overall phone costs for D.C. inmates, the costs are high locally and nationally, as several news accounts have noted. For example:

> In Florida, where the state prison system collected $13.8 million in commissions in fiscal 1997-98, a legislative committee found that big prison systems in ten other states took in more than $115 million in the same budget year. New York topped the list with $20.5 million. In Virginia, MCI gave the state $10.4 million, or 39 percent of the revenue from prison calls. Maryland receives a 20 percent commission on local calls by inmates, which must be made through Bell Atlantic, and gets 42 percent of revenue from long-distance calls, all of which are handled by AT&T. (Paul Duggan, *Captive Audience Rates High: Families Must Pay Dearly When Inmates Call Collect, Washington Post,* January 23, 2000, at A03.)

7. Christopher J. Mumola, Bureau of Justice Statistics Special Report: Incarcerated Parents and Their Children (2000).

8. See, e.g., Bruce Western and Sara McLanahan, *Fathers Behind Bars: The Impact of Incarceration on Family Formation,* in Families, Crime and Criminal Justice 309, at 322 (Greer Litton Fox and Michael L. Benson, eds., 2000) (citing evidence that the incarceration has a "large destabilizing effect" on low-income families). See also, Mark Testa and Marilyn Krogh, "The

Effect of Employment on Marriage Among Black Males in Inner-City Chicago," in *The Decline in Marriage Among African Americans* (1995, M. Belinda Tucker and Claudia Mitchell-Kernan, eds.); and Robert J. Sampson, "Unemployment and Imbalanced Sex Ratios" (same volume), (describing the influence of incarceration on joblessness and sex ratios). These findings logically reverse the causal relationship implicit in many other studies that describe familial environment as influencing rather than being influenced by involvement in the criminal justice system. See, e.g., Robert Joseph Taylor, M. Belinda Tucker, Linda M. Chatters, and Rukmalie Jayakody, "Recent Demographic Trends in African American Family Structure," in *Family Life in Black America* 46 (Robert Joseph Taylor et al. eds., 1997) (reviewing the literature on female headed households and crime).

9. David began selling and using heroin and "love boat" (marijuana laced with PCP), selling and using crack cocaine later, as it became popular in the 1980s.

10. For discussion of behavioral and academic consequences of imprisonment on children, see T. A. Fritsch and I. D. Burkhead, "Behavioral Reactions of Children to Parental Absence due to Imprisonment," 83 *Family Relations* 88, at 30 (1981); L. Ales Swan, "Families of Black Prisoners," in *Survival and Progress* (1981); and A. Lowenstein, "Temporary Single Parenthood: The Case of Prisoners' Families," 35 *Family Relations* 79, passim (1986).

11. Figures are based on Study Data Sets, supra note 2.

12. Of the 6,181 families living in areas with the highest male incarceration rates (averaging 16 percent), 4,842—over 78 percent of those families—were without fathers. Figures are based on Study Data Sets, supra note 2. Unfortunately, the data do not distinguish between biological fathers and stepfathers. However, because women with lower incomes are both more likely to remarry and more likely to live in areas with high incarceration rates, it seems likely that not only are there fewer fathers present in areas with high incarceration rates, but that a disproportionate number of the fathers who are present are stepfathers. See Chandler Arnold, *Children and Stepfamilies: A Snapshot,* Center for Law and Social Policy (1998). The issue is a significant one because, as Cynthia Harper and Sara S. McLanahan have noted, controlling for income and other demographic factors, "while children in single-mother households, particularly those born to single mothers, have higher chances of incarceration, those in stepparent families fare even worse." Cynthia Harper and Sara S. McLanahan, Bendheim-Thoman Center for Research on Child Wellbeing, Working Paper 99-03: Father Absence and Youth Incarceration 33 (1999).

13. According to a recent Senate report, "Children of prisoners are six times more likely than other children to be incarcerated at some point in their lives." S. Rep. No. 106-404, at 56 (2000). See also, Denise Johnston, "Effects of Parental Incarceration," in *Children of Incarcerated Parents,* at 80 (Katherine Gabel & Denise Johnston eds., 995) (noting that "children of offenders are far more likely than other children to enter the criminal justice system").

14. Figures are for men and women over the age of eighteen, and are based on Study Data Sets, supra note 2. Figures were obtained by examining incarceration rates and adult male and female populations by census tract. Incarceration is one of many contributing factors that lead to such a high ratio of women to men, including higher male mortality rates. Unfortunately, at the

time of this writing, separate population data for men and women in the specific age groups most affected by incarceration (ages eighteen to thirty-five) were not available.

15. I say "perceive" because there are no hard numbers on (nor even a consistent definition of) "eligibility" in the District or elsewhere.

16. While David's estimate exaggerates the gender imbalance, the perception of such a large imbalance is as (if not more) important than the statistical reality.

17. The literature describing how informal networks of extended kin and nonkin help support African-American families is extensive. For a recent overview, see Harold W. Neighbors, "Husbands, Wives, Family, and Friends," in *Family Life in Black America* 277, 278 (Robert Joseph Taylor et al., eds., 1997).

18. See Michael Lewis, *Shame, The Exposed Self*, at 200 (1995) ("The impact of stigma is wide: it not only affects those who are stigmatized, but those who are associated with the person so marked. . . . Stigmas are contagious: they impact on members of the family and even the friends of the stigmatized person. Like an infectious disease, the stigma not only affects the victim of the stigma but all those who are associated with him or her.").

19. Erving Goffman, *Stigma* 48 (1963). Goffman writes of this contamination through association:

   [I]n certain circumstances the social identity of those an individual is with can be used as a source of information concerning his own social identity, the assumption being that he is what the others are. [. . .] In any case, an analysis of how people manage the information they convey about themselves will have to consider how they deal with the contingencies of being seen "with" particular others. Id. at 47–48.

20. See Lewis, supra note 18, at 98–118 passim.

21. See Lewis, supra note 18, at 69. See also discussion at Id., 103.

22. Id. at 72. Men, on the other hand, are less likely to blame themselves for failure, and when they do are more likely to experience guilt than shame, given the same circumstances. See Id., at 103 (discussing studies supporting this finding).

23. See Id. at 143–149.

24. See Id., at 103, See, also, Herbert Thomas, *The Shame Response to Rejection*, at 29–34 (1997) (suggesting that deflecting blame in this way enables anger).

25. This may be related to the fact that many relatives of prisoners are unaware of the full extent of incarceration, and of the similar experiences of their neighbors, friends, and fellow church members. For example, when participants were asked if they knew of other incarcerated people in the neighborhood, many did know of one or two out of the many households on the block that had members incarcerated, but did not feel comfortable talking with them about the issue. This type of phenomenon, in which people misjudge the norm, is often described as pluralistic ignorance. Perhaps the most well-publicized example is found in studies of college freshmen who share a pluralistic ignorance of drinking norms, commonly overestimating the extent of drinking among other freshmen. See D.A. Prentice and D.T. Miller, *Pluralistic Ignorance and Alcohol Use on Campus: Some Consequences of Misperceiving the Social Norm*, 64 Journal of Personality and Social Psychology 2, 243-56, (1993).

CHAPTER 8: THE SOCIAL IMPACT OF MASS
INCARCERATION ON WOMEN

1. Bureau of Justice Statistics (1999a). Prior Abuse Reported by Inmates and Probationers. Washington, D.C.: U.S. Department of Justice.
2. Bureau of Justice Statistics (2001). Prison and Jail Inmates at Midyear 2000. Washington, D.C. U.S. Department of Justice.
3. S. Bush-Baskette (1998). The War on Drugs as a War Against Black Women in Crime Control and Women. In S. Miller (Ed), *Crime Control and Women: Feminist Implications of Criminal Justice Policy*. Thousand Oaks, CA: Sage Publications.
4. N. Freudenberg, I. Wilets, M. B. Greene, B. E. Richie (1998). Linking Women in Jail to Community Services: Factors Associated with Re-arrest and Retention of Drug-Using Women Following Release From Jail. *Journal of American Medical Women's Association,* 53: 89–93.
5. Freudenberg, 1998; United States Department of Housing and Urban Development (1999). *State of the Cities—1999.* Washington, D.C.: U.S. Government Printing Office.
6. Bureau of Justice Statistics (1999b). Women Offenders. Washington, D.C.: U.S. Department of Justice.
7. M. Mauer, C. Potler, and R. Wolf (1999). Gender and Justice: Women, Drugs and Sentencing Policy. Washington, D.C.: The Sentencing Project.
8. B. Richie (1996). *Compelled to Crime: The Gender Entrapment of Battered Black Women.* New York: Routledge; Owen (1998). *In the Mix: Struggle and Survival in a Women's Prison.* Albany: SUNY Press.
9. Bureau of Justice Statistics (2000). Incarcerated Parents and Their Children. Washington, D.C.: U.S. Department of Justice.
10. R. E. Dobash and R. P. Dobash (1992). *Women, Violence and Social Change.* New York: Routledge; National Research Council (1996).
11. R. J. Gelles and J. W. Harrop (1989). Violence, Battering and Psychological Distress Among Women. *Journal of Interpersonal Violence,* 4(4), 400–420.
12. National Victims Center (1992).
13. National Institute of Justice (1998). *Prevalence, Incidence and Consequences of Violence Against Women: Findings from the National Violence Against Women Survey.* Washington, D.C.: U.S. Department of Justice.
14. M. Ratner (1993) (Ed.). *Crack Pipe as Pimp: An Ethnographic Investigation of Sex-for-Crack Exchanges.* New York: Lexington Books; P. Tjaden and N. Thoennes (1998). Stalking in America: Findings from the National Violence Against Women Survey, Research in Brief. Washington, D.C.: U.S. Department of Justice.
15. Anti-Violence Project/National Coalition of Anti-Violence Programs (1998). *Report on Lesbian, Gay, Bisexual and Transgendered Domestic Violence.* New York: AVP/CNAVP.
16. National Institute of Justice (1998); R. L. Hampton and R. L. Gelles (1994). Violence Towards Black Women in a Nationally Representative Sample of Black Families. *Journal of Comparative Family Studies.* 25(1): 105–119; Salomon (1996).

17. I. W. Hutchinson, J. D. Hirschel, and D. E. Pesackis (1994). Family Violence and Police Utilization. *Violence and Victims.* 9, 299–313; Richie (1996); Sullivan (1994).

18. V. Kanuha (1997). Domestic Violence, Racism and the Battered Women's Movement in the U.S. In J. Edelson and Z. Eisikovitz (Eds.) *Future Interventions with Battered Women and Their Families.* Thousand Oaks, CA: Sage; C. E. Rasche (1995). Minority Women and Domestic Violence: The Unique Dilemmas of Battered Women of Color. In N. Sokoloff and B. Rafel Price (Eds.) *The Criminal Justice System and Women: Offenders, Victims and Workers.* New York: McGraw Hill; P. T. Reid and R. Kelly (1994). Research on Women of Color: From Ignorance to Awareness. *Psychology of Women Quarterly.* 18: 477–486.

19. Bureau of Justice Statistics (1999a); A. Browne (1999). Harvard University. Personal Communication.

20. S. Osthoff (1999). National Clearinghouse for the Defense of Battered Women. Personal Communication.

CHAPTER 9: CHILDREN, COPS, AND CITIZENSHIP:
WHY CONSERVATIVES SHOULD OPPOSE RACIAL PROFILING

* Irene Hahn and Brad Hays provided valuable research assistance on this article.

1. Marc Mauer, *Race to Incarcerate* (New York: The New Press, 1999) pp. 15–23.

2. See, e.g., Katheryn K. Russell, *The Color of Crime* (New York: NYU Press, 1998), pp. 38–44; Statement of Robert L. Wilkins, "Racial Profiling within Law Enforcement Agencies," Hearing before Senate Committee on the Judiciary, Subcommittee on Constitution, Federalism and Property Rights, March 30, 2000; David Cole, *No Equal Justice: Race and Class in the American Criminal Justice System* (New York: The New Press, 1999), pp. 16–62; Lori Montgomery, "New Police Policies Aim to Discourage Racial Profiling," *Washington Post,* June 28, 2001, p. A1.

3. Morgan Reynolds, "Profiling Not All About Race," *Washington Times,* April 15, 2001. Reynolds, the director of the Criminal Justice Center at the conservative National Center for Policy Analysis, attributes the disproportionate traffic stops of innocent black motorists to the war on drugs.

4. Lieutenant Arthur Doyle, "From the Outside Looking In: Twenty-Nine Years in the New York Police Department," in *Police Brutality,* Jill Nelson, ed. (New York: W. W. Norton, 2000); Cole, *No Equal Justice,* p. 23.

5. Henry Louis Gates, Jr., *Thirteen Ways of Looking at a Black Man* (New York: Random House, 1997), p. 110.

6. Paul Butler, "Encounters with the Police on My Street," *Legal Times,* November 10, 1997, p. 23.

7. Timothy Lynch, "We Own the Night: Amadou Diallo's Deadly Encounter with New York City's Street Crimes Unit," Cato Institute Briefing Papers, No. 56, March 31, 2000, p. 6.

8. See, e.g., Charles Murray, *Losing Ground: American Social Policy 1950–1980* (New York: Basic Books, 1984).

9. Ken Ringle, "The Hard Heart of Poverty: Bush's 'Compassionate Conservative' Guru Sees Culture as Culprit," *Washington Post,* April 3, 2001, p. C1.

10. Myron Magnet, *The Dream and the Nightmare: The Sixties' Legacy to the Underclass* (San Francisco: Encounter Books, 1993), p. 74.

11. Id.

12. James Q. Wilson, "Crime, Race and Values," *Society,* November/December 1992, p. 92.

13. This is the central thesis of Stephen and Abigail Thernstrom, *America in Black and White* (New York: Simon & Schuster, 1991).

14. Id., at p. 511.

15. Magnet, *The Dream and the Nightmare,* p. 157.

16. Quoted in Jerome Miller, *Search and Destroy: African-American Males in the Criminal Justice System* (Cambridge, England: Cambridge University Press, 1996), p. 98.

17. Ta-Nehisi Coates, "Black and Blue: Why Does America's Richest Black Suburb Have Some of the Nation's Most Brutal Cops," *Washington Monthly,* June 2001.

18. Jill Nelson, "Shall We Dance?" *Savoy,* August 2001, p. 48.

19. Quoted in Coates, "Black and Blue."

20. Butler, "Encounters with the Police on My Street."

21. Stephen Mastrofski, "Policing for People," Police Foundation, March 1999, pp. 3–4.

22. Kennedy, *Race, Crime and Law,* p. 153.

23. William D. Eggers and John O'Leary, "The Beat Generation: Community Policing at Its Best," *Policy Review,* Fall 1995, pp. 1–3.

24. Jane Jacobs, *The Death and Life of Great American Cities* (New York: Vintage, 1961), pp. 31–32.

25. Timothy Lynch, "We Own the Night," p. 5.

26. Id.

27. Quoted in Harris, "Racial Profiling within Law Enforcement Agencies," Hearing before Senate Committee on the Judiciary, Subcommittee on Constitution, Federalism and Property Rights, March 30, 2000.

CHAPTER 10: BLACK ECONOMIC PROGRESS
IN THE ERA OF MASS IMPRISONMENT

* We gratefully acknowledge Marc Mauer's comments on an earlier draft. Research for this paper was supported by grant SES-0004336 from the National Science Foundation and a grant from the Russell Sage Foundation.

1. These ratios were calculated using figures from the U.S. Census and Table 1, p. 22, in Alfred Blumstein and Allen J. Beck (1999), "Population Growth in U.S. Prisons, 1980–1996," in *Prisons: Crime and Justice, a Review of Research,* vol. 26, edited by Michael Tonry and Joan Petersilia, pp. 17–62. They include both men and women and do not include jail inmates.

2. Becky Pettit and Bruce Western (2001), "Inequality in U.S. Prison Incarceration," paper presented at the annual meeting of the American Sociological Association, Anaheim, California.

3. This analysis is reported in Bruce Western and Becky Pettit (1999), "Incarceration, Employ-

ment Rates, and Black-White Earnings Inequality." Russell Sage Foundation Working Paper No. 150.

4. Results from an employer survey are reported by Harry Holzer (1996), *What Employers Want: Job Prospects for Less-Educated Workers*. New York: Russell Sage Foundation, p. 59. Employment restrictions resulting from a felony conviction are surveyed by the Office of the Pardon Attorney (1996), *Civil Disabilities of Convicted Felons: A State-by-State Survey*. Washington, D.C., U.S. Department of Justice.

5. The idea that incarceration can generate social connections to illegal rather than legal employment is suggested by John Hagan (1993), "The Social Embeddedness of Crime and Unemployment," *Criminology*, vol. 31, pp. 465–91. On gang recruitment in prison, see John M. Hagedorn (1998), *People and Folks: Gang, Crime, and the Underclass in a Rustbelt City*. Chicago: Lake View Press. Also, Martin Sánchez-Jankowski (1991), *Islands in the Street: Gangs and American Urban Society*. Berkeley: University of California Press.

6. The research is reviewed by Bruce Western, Jeffrey R. Kling, and David F. Weiman (2001), "The Labor Market Consequences of Incarceration," *Crime and Delinquency*, vol. 47, pp. 410–427.

7. Daniel Nagin and Joel Waldfogel (1998), "The Effect of Conviction on Income Through the Life Cycle," *International Review of Law and Economics*, vol. 18, pp. 25–40; Shawn David Bushway (1996), *The Impact of a Criminal Record on Access to Legitimate Employment*, Ph.D. dissertation, Carnegie Mellon University.

8. Mercer Sullivan (1989), *"Getting Paid:" Youth Crime and Work in the Inner City*, Ithaca, N.Y.: Cornell University Press.

9. The effect of incarceration on employment is lower for blacks than for whites, according to the estimates of Bruce Western and Katherine Beckett (1999), "How Unregulated Is the U.S. Labor Market? The Penal System as a Labor Market Institution," *American Journal of Sociology*, vol. 104, pp. 1030–60. Research on the effects of spatial concentrations of economic and social disadvantage is summarized by Ronald B. Mincy (1996), "The Underclass: Concept, Controversy, and Evidence," in *Confronting Poverty*, edited by Sheldon Danziger, Gary Sandefur, and Daniel Weinberg. New York: Russell Sage Foundation, pp. 119–122.

CHAPTER 11: THE PROBLEM WITH "ADDITION BY SUBTRACTION": THE PRISON-CRIME RELATIONSHIP IN LOW-INCOME COMMUNITIES

1. D. R. Rose and T. R. Clear. 1998a. Incarceration, Social Capital and Crime: Examining the Unintended Consequences of Incarceration. *Criminology*, 36 (3), 441–479.

2. D. R. Rose and T. R. Clear. 1998b. Who Doesn't Know Someone in Jail? The Impact of Exposure to Prison on Attitudes of Formal and Informal Control. Paper presented to the American Society of Criminology, Toronto, Canada (November).

3. D. R. Rose, T. R. Clear, E. Waring, and K. Scully. 2000. Coercive Mobility and Crime: Incarceration and Social Disorganization. Unpublished manuscript.

4. D. R. Rose, T. R. Clear, and J. A. Ryder. 2000. Drugs, Incarceration and Neighborhood Life:

The Impact of Reintegrating Offenders into the Community. Final Report to the National Institute of Justice. NY: John Jay College (September).

5. Thomas P. Bonczar and Allen J. Beck 1997. Lifetime Likelihood of Going to State or Federal Prison. Bureau of Justice Statistics, U.S. Department of Justice (March).

6. J. P. Lynch and W. J. Sabol. 1992. Macro-Social Changes and Their Implications for Prison Reform: The Underclass and the Composition of Prison Populations. Paper presented to the American Society of Criminology, New Orleans (November).

7. CASES. 2000. *The Community Justice Project.* NY: Center for Alternative Sentencing and Employment Services.

8. Rose, Clear, Waring, and Scully, 2000.

9. Albert J. Hunter. 1985. Private, Parochial and Public Social Orders: The Problem of Crime and Incivility in Urban Communities. In Gerald D. Suttles and Mayer N. Zald (eds.), *The Challenge of Social Control: Citizenship and Institution Building in Modern Society.* Norwood, NJ: Aldex Publishing Co., pp. 230–242.

10. Travis Hirschi. 1969. *The Causes of Delinquency.* Palo Alto: Stanford University Press.

11. Clifford R. Shaw and Henry D. McKay. 1942. *Juvenile Delinquency and Urban Areas.* Chicago: University of Chicago Press.

12. Robert J. Sampson, Stephen W. Raudenbush, and Felton Earls. 1997. Neighborhoods and Violent Crime: A Multilevel Study of Collective Efficacy." *Science* 277:918–24.

13. Hunter, 1985.

14. Mark Granovetter. 1973. The Strength of Weak Ties. *American Journal of Sociology.* 81:1287–1303.

15. Ibid.

16. Shaw and McKay, 1942.

17. Wesley Skogan. 1990. *Disorder and Decline: Crime and the Spiral of Decay in American Neighborhoods.* NY: The Free Press.

18. Rose, Clear, and Ryder, 2000.

19. T. Meares. 1997. Charting Race and Class Differences in Attitudes Toward Drug Legalization and Law Enforcement: Lessons for Federal Criminal Law. *Buffalo Criminal Law Review,* 1, 137–174; Liquan Cao, James Frank, and Francis T. Cullen. 1996. "Race, Community Context and Confidence in the Police. *American Journal of Police.* 15:1; 3–22; Sandra Lee Browning, Francis T. Cullen, Liqun Cao, Renee Kopache, and Thomas J. Stevenson. 1994. "Race and Getting Hassled by the Police: A Research Note. *Police Studies.* 17:1; 1–11.

20. Thomas Tyler. 1990. *Why People Obey the Law.* New Haven: Yale University Press.

21. Robert J. Sampson and Dawn Jeglum-Bertusch. 1998. "Legal Cynicism and (Subcultural?) Tolerance of Deviance: The Neighborhood Context of Racial Differences." *Law and Society Review.* 33:777–804.

22. Rose and Clear, 1998b.

23. Rose, Clear, and Ryder, 2000.

CHAPTER 12: BUILDING A PRISON ECONOMY IN RURAL AMERICA

1. Tracy Huling, producer. Filmed interview with Ted Flegel, 5/5/97, in *Yes, in My Backyard* (1999), Galloping Girls Productions and WSKG Public Broadcasting.

2. Farmers are defined here as those owning small family farms—gross sales less than $250,000—in accordance with the popular conception of American farmers and the definition of small family farms used by the National Commission on Small Farms and the Economic Research Service, U.S. Department of Agriculture. This definition excludes large, very large, and non-family farms. Nine out of ten U.S. farms are small family farms. See America's Diverse Family Farms, Agriculture Information Bulletin 769, Economic Research Service, U.S. Department of Agriculture, May, 2001.

3. According to the U.S. Bureau of the Census, a "metropolitan statistical area" is a central city of at least 50,000 people or an urbanized area consisting of 50,000 people or more in a city (or cities) and the surrounding counties that are economically tied to it. "Non-metropolitan" America is all that which is not included in such metropolitan statistical areas. See Calvin Beale, "Prisons, Population, and Jobs in Non-Metro America," Rural Development Perspectives, vol. 8, no.3, 1993; Calvin Beale, "Rural Prisons: An Update," Rural Development Perspectives, vol. 11, no. 2, February, 1996; Calvin Beale, presentation at conference, Crime and Politics in the 21st Century, sponsored by the Campaign for an Effective Crime Policy, Bethesda, Maryland, November 12–14, 1998.

4. Calvin Beale, "Cellular Rural Development: New Prisons in Rural and Small Town Areas in the 1990s," paper prepared for presentation at the annual meeting of the Rural Sociological Society, Albuquerque, New Mexico, August 18, 2001.

5. Calvin Beale's figures include prisons only and do not include regional jails built in rural communities. Beale's figures on rural prisons should also be considered conservative because they do not include prisons built in some rural communities nevertheless designated by the Census Bureau as metropolitan areas because of the high numbers of people who live in these communities commuting to work in cities. How many additional rural prisons this might entail is currently unknown.

6. *Rochester Democrat and Chronicle,* "Romulus Considers Courting a Prison," undated.

7. Telephone interview with Ernest Preate, June 15, 2001.

8. Caroline Glassic, "Brush Valley Chosen," *News-Item,* August 17, 2001.

9. Jonathan Franklin, "Jails Go Up, Yes, in Their Backyards," *Boston Globe,* July 31, 1994.

10. Tracy Huling, "Prisons as a Rural Growth Industry: An Exploratory Discussion of the Effects on Young African-American Men in the Inner-Cities," paper presented at Consultation of the U.S. Commission on Civil Rights, April 15, 1999, in *The Crisis of the Young African Male in the Inner Cities,* U.S. Commission on Civil Rights, Washington, D.C., July, 2000.

11. Ruth Wilson Gilmore, *Golden Gulag,* Berkeley, CA: University of California Press, 2002.

12. Sheryl McCarthy, "Malone Got a Lock on Prisons, Then . . . ," *Albany Times Union,* April 15, 2000.

13. Beale, op cit.

14. Steve Raher, "Things to Consider When Looking at a Correctional Facility," *Brush News-Tribune,* August 8, 2001.

15. Douglas Clement, "Big House on the Prairie," *Fedgazette,* Federal Reserve Bank of Minneapolis, Vol. 14, No. 1, January, 2002.

16. Gilmore, op cit.

17. Katherine Carlson, "What Happens and What Counts: Resident Assessments of Prison Impacts on Their Communities," *Humboldt Journal of Social Relations,* Volume 17, 1991.

18. Tracy Huling, producer. Filmed interview with prison guard supervisor, Greene Correctional Facility Inmate Work Crew, 4/1/97, in *Yes, in My Backyard* (1999), Galloping Girls Productions and WSKG Public Broadcasting.

19. Gilmore, op cit.

20. Raher, op cit.

21. Ibid.

22. Associated Press, "Vacant Prison Turns Expected Boom to Bust for Small Town," *St. Louis Post Dispatch,* June 23, 2001.

23. Douglas Clement, "Busted?" *Fedgazette,* Federal Reserve Bank of Minneapolis, Vol. 14, No. 1, January 2002.

24. Gilmore, op cit.

25. McCarthy, op cit.

26. Francis X. Donnelly, "Ionia Finds Stability in Prisons," *Detroit News,* 2001.

27. Kelsey Kauffman, *Prison Officers and Their World,* Cambridge, Mass.: Harvard University Press, 1988.

28. Ted Conover, *Newjack: Guarding Sing Sing.* New York: Random House, 2000.

29. www.tedconover.com.

30. Richard Purdue, letter, September 9, 1997.

31. Kelsey Kauffman, *The Brotherhood: Racism and Intimidation Among Prison Staff at the Indiana Correctional Facility–Putnamville.* Russell Compton Center for Peace and Justice, DePauw University, April 2000.

32. Kelsey Kauffman, "Confronting White Supremacy Among Prison Employees." Speech given at National Conference of the National Association of Blacks in Criminal Justice, July 23, 2001, Cincinnati, Ohio.

33. Sanjay Pinto, "Behind the Wire," *Intelligence Report,* Issue No. 100, Fall, 2000, Southern Poverty Law Center, Montgomery, Alabama.

34. Kauffman, supra 31.

35. Phil Campbell, "That'll Teach 'Em," theStranger.com, 5/18/2000, www.thestranger.com.

36. Jennifer Vogel, "White Guard, Black Guard: Racism in Washington Continues," *Seattle Weekly,* March 11, 1999 and *Prison Legal News,* May 1999.

37. Kauffman, supra 31.

38. Tracy Huling, "Prisoners of the Census," MoJo Wire, *Mother Jones,* May 10, 2000.

39. Ibid.

40. Ibid.

41. Nicholas Kulish, "Crime Pays: Since Census Counts Convicts, Some Towns Can't Get Enough—Federal and State Funds Tied to Total Population Help Florence, Ariz., Rebuild—Annexing the Penitentiary," *Wall Street Journal,* August 9, 2001.

42. Nancy Cook Lauer, "Prisons Playing Role in Politics," *Tallahassee Democrat,* August 4, 2001.

43. Taren Stinebrickner-Kauffman, "Census Count of Inmates Can Skew Voting Outcomes," *Indianapolis Star,* August 29, 2001.

44. Huling, supra, 38.

45. Daniel Feldman, "20 Years of Prison Expansion: A Failing National Strategy," in *Public Administration Review,* Vol. 53, No. 6, November/December, 1993.

CHAPTER 13: THE IMPACT OF MASS INCARCERATION ON IMMIGRATION POLICY

* I would like to thank the following colleagues for their encouragement and expertise as I stumbled through uncharted territory in my quest for understanding: Irwin Stotzky, professor of law, University of Miami; Joanne Macri, managing attorney, Prisoners' Legal Services of New York (Buffalo); Rebecca Dalpe, research assistant and third-year law student, University at Buffalo School of Law; Gerald Seipp, partner, Serotte, Reich & Seipp; Karen Spencer, Archives and Special Collections librarian, University at Buffalo School of Law; Sophie Feal, project coordinator, Volunteer Lawyers Project of Buffalo; and Kevin C. Johnson, professor of law, University of California at Davis School of Law. Each in their own way has enriched this chapter immeasurably.

1. Non-U.S. citizens also represent a growing segment of the United States *prison* population, as more aliens are being prosecuted—and receiving longer sentences—for violating federal immigration laws.

2. William G. Paul, America's Harsh and Unjust Immigration Laws. *USA Today Magazine,* July 1, 2000.

3. Mike Clary and Patrick McDonnell, Sentenced to a Life in Limbo, *Los Angeles Times,* Wednesday, September 9, 1998, p.A1; Cheryl Little, *INS Detention in Florida,* 30 Univ. of Miami Inter-American Law Rev. 551 (Winter-Spring 1999).

4. Testimony of Joseph Greene, Acting Deputy Executive Associate Commissioner, and Edward McElroy, INS District Director for New York, before the House Judiciary Committee's Subcommittee on Immigration and Claims, December 19, 2001.

5. Helen Morris, *Zero Tolerance: The Increasing Criminilization of Immigration Law,* 74 Interpreter Releases 1317 (August 29, 1997).

6. Donald Kerwin, *Throwing Away the Key: Lifers in INS Custody,* 75 Interpreter Releases 649 (May 11, 1998).

7. Wendy Young, *U.S. Detention of Women and Children Asylum Seekers: A Violation of Human Rights,* 30 University of Miami Inter-American Law Rev. 577 (Winter–Spring 1999).

8. In 1996, IIRIRA eliminated the distinction between "exclusion" of aliens seeking admission to the United States and "deportation" of those already within the country, by describing all in-

stances in which non-U.S. citizens are forcibly removed from the country by the government as "removal." To avoid confusion, the author uses the more broadly recognized term "deportation" throughout this chapter.

9. Michael Welch, *The Immigration Crisis: Detention as an Emerging Mechanism of Social Control,* 23 Social Justice 169 (September 22, 1996); Ultimately, immigration policy provides for the physical banishment of these aliens through deportation while the criminal justice system symbolically banishes prisoners from civil society through lengthy sentences, harsh conditions of parole and civil disability that greatly narrow the ability of ex-offenders to participate in political, social, and economic spheres.

10. Donald Kerwin, *How Our Immigration Laws Divide, Impoverish and Undermine American Families,* 76 Interpreter Releases 1213 (Aug. 26, 1999).

11. Michael Welch, *The Role of the INS in the Prison-Industrial Complex,* 27 Social Justice 73 (Fall 2000).

12. ACLU Immigrants' Rights Project, *Justice Detained: Conditions at the Varick Street Immigration Detention Center* (1993).

13. Id.; Welch, supra note 9.

14. ACLU Immigrants' Rights Project, supra note 12.

15. Testimony of Doris Meissner, Commissioner of the INS, before the Subcommittee on Immigration, U.S. Senate Judiciary Committee, September 16, 1998, 1998 WL 18089535.

16. The theory of the "new penology" was first proposed by Jonathan Simon and Malcolm Feeley in M. Feeley and J. Simon (1992) "The New Penology" in *Criminology, 30,* 449–474.

17. Welch, supra note 9.

18. Id.

19. Daniel Kanstroom, *U.S. Immigration Policy at the Millennium: Deportation Social Control and Punishment: Some Thoughts About Why Hard Laws Make Bad Cases,* 113 Harvard Law Review. 1889 at 1891, n.3, (June 2000).

20. *Zadvydas v. Davis,* 533 US 678 (June 28, 2001).

21. INA, § 235(b). See Juan P. Osuna, ed., *Understanding the 1996 Immigration Act: The Illegal Immigration Reform and Immigrant Responsibility Act of 1996* (Washington, D.C.: Federal Publications Inc., 1997), pp. 5–2.

22. Gerald Seipp, *The Aggravated Felony Concept in Immigration Law: Traps for the Onwary and Opportunities for the Knowledgable,* Immigration Briefings, no. 02-1 (West Group) January 2002.

23. IIRIRA §321(b); INA §10(a)(43).

24. Kerwin, supra note 10.

25. Id.

26. Lena Williams, A Law Aimed at Terrorists Hits Legal Immigrants. *New York Times.* Wednesday, July 17, 1996, at A1.

27. Indeed after AEDPA was passed, both INS policy makers and immigration advocates agreed that mandatory detention provisions and the expansion of grounds for deportation to include any drug offense and crimes of moral turpitude—no matter how minor—failed to sufficiently distinguish between the seriousness of crimes, take into account how long ago the crime was

committed or consider time served in prison already. David Martin, legal counsel for the INS, even urged Congress to ameliorate some of the harsher provisions of AEDPA, particularly the elimination of the discretion of immigration judges to waiver deportation, characterizing the deportation of "longtime residents who have paid their debt to society" as a result of a single drug possession "disproportionate." Id.

28. Uniting and Strengthening America by Providing Appropriate Tools Required to Intercept and Obstruct Terrorism (USA PATRIOT) Act of 2001, Pub. L. 107-56, 107.

29. It should be noted, however, that provisions of the proposed USA PATRIOT Act specifically authorizing prolonged detention were expressly dropped in committee in order to expedite consensus on the legislation. A decisive factor in the decision to ultimately omit provisions in the act for prolonged detention was the U.S. Supreme Court's recent decision in *Zadvydas*, declaring that indefinite detention by the INS is unconstitutional.

30. From 1984 to 1994, the number of federal prosecutions increased by about 2 percent annually. Drug prosecutions increased at about 7 percent annually in the same period of time. The number of noncitizens prosecuted, however, increased by about 10 percent annually, with a corresponding increase of 13 percent annually for noncitizens prosecuted for drug offenses. By 1994, drug-related offenses accounted for a whopping 45 percent of the criminal prosecutions of noncitizens, while immigration violations accounted for 34 percent and violent crimes 1.4 percent. Helen Morris, supra note 5.

31. Marc Mauer, The Sentencing Project, *Race to Incarcerate* (New York: The New Press, 1999), at 60.

32. Id.

33. As early as 1964, conservatives used the issue of crime as a critique of the welfare state. Barry Goldwater argued on the campaign trail in 1964 that welfare programs actually increased lawlessness and crime:

If it is entirely proper for the government to take away from some to give to others, then won't some be led to believe that they can rightfully take from anyone who has more than they? No wonder law and order has broken down, mob violence has engulfed great American cities, and our wives feel unsafe in the streets.

Katherine Beckett, *Making Crime Pay: Law and Order in Contemporary American Politics* (Oxford University Press, 1997), p. 35 (citing Piven and Cloward, *Poor People's Movements: Why They Succeed and How They Fail* [New York: Vintage Books, 1979], at 338).

Currie states the conservative argument this way: "It's often said that though we've spent 'trillions' of dollars on antipoverty programs since the 1960s, crime has risen anyway, and that, accordingly, public spending on the poor is not the solution and may indeed be the problem." Elliott Currie, *Crime and Punishment in America* (New York: Metropolitan Books, 1998), p. 131.

Moreover, Scott Christianson notes with irony that many of the same arguments made against welfare can be made against imprisonment. It can be argued that both make the recipient worse off than before, thereby achieving the opposite goal of what was intended. Both imprisonment and welfare are revolving door systems that continue from one generation to the next. Scott Christianson, *With Liberty for Some: 500 Years of Imprisonment in America* (Boston: Northeastern University Press, 1998), p. 297.

34. Christian Parenti, *Lockdown America: Police and Prisons in an Age of Crisis* (New York: Verso Press, 1999), at 167–68.

35. Id. at 168.

36. Mauer, supra note 31.

37. Robert Bach, The Progress of Immigration Reform, in *In Defense of the Aliens,* Volume 21 (New York: Center for Migration Studies, 1999), pp. 7, 12 (Lydio F. Tomasi, ed., 1999).

38. Brad Whorton, *The Transformation of Refugee Policy: Race, Welfare, and American Political Culture, 1959–1997,* p. 21 (1997). Unpublished PhD dissertation, University of Kansas (on file with the University of Kansas Library).

39. A "second wave" of 75,000 middle-class Cubans and blue-collar workers arrived between 1962 and 1965, and a "third wave" of mainly working-class Cubans arrived between 1965 and 1973. Id. at 22.

40. Id.

41. Felix Masud-Piloto, *From Welcomed Exiles to Illegal Immigrants: Cuban Migration to the U.S., 1959–95* (London: Rowman & Littlefield Publishers, Inc., 1996), at 85.

42. Id. at 92.

43. Id. at 100; Mark S. Hamm, *The Abandoned Ones: The Imprisonment and Uprising of the Mariel Boat People* (Boston: Northeastern University Press, 1995), at 58.

44. Three hundred fifty, to be more precise. Less than one-half of 1 percent of all the Cubans who came to the United States came via the Port of Mariel, Hamm, at 58.

45. Norman L. Zucker and Naomi Flink Zucker, *Desperate Crossings: Seeking Refuge in America* (New York: M. E. Sharpe, Inc., 1996), at 66.

46. Id. at 64.

47. Masud-Piloto, supra note 41 at 115.

48. Id.

49. Zucker and Zucker, supra note 45 at 65.

50. 8 U.S.C. § 1159(a) (1988).

51. Zucker and Zucker, supra note 45 at 66.

52. David M. Reimers, *Unwelcome Strangers: American Identity and the Turn Against Immigration* (New York: Columbia University Press, 1998), p. 84; Alan M. Kraut, *Silent Travelers: Germs, Genes and the "Immigrant Menace"* (New York: Basic Books, 1994), p. 260–61.

53. Kraut, supra note 52.

54. James R. Zink, *Comment: Race and Foreign Policy in Refugee Law: A Historical Perspective of the Haitian Refugee Crises,* 48 DePaul L. Rev. 559, at 605. Citing Patrick Buchanan—*In His Own Words,* FAIR, February 26, 1996 (quoting *This Week with David Brinkley,* ABC television broadcast, Jan. 8, 1991).

55. Id. at 28.

56. Jess Bravin, et al., Justice Department Moves to Use New Authority in Detaining Aliens. *Wall Street Journal,* September 26, 2001, at A6.

57. Jonathan Peterson and Patrick J. McDonnell, Tightening Immigration Raises Civil Liberties Flag. *Los Angeles Times,* September 23, 2001, at A12.

58. Aliens that cannot be repatriated to their home countries due to statelessness or home country opposition.

59. *Zadvydas v. Davis,* 533 U.S. 678 (June 28, 2001).

60. *INS v. St. Cyr,* 533 U.S. 289 (June 25, 2001).

61. David Firestone and Christopher Drew, Al Qaeda Link Seen in Only a Handful of 1,200 Detainees. *New York Times,* November 29, 2001, at A1.

62. Tamar Lewin, For Many of Those Held in a Legal Tangle, Little Is Revealed. *New York Times,* November 1, 2001, at B5.

63. Uniting and Strengthening America by Providing Appropriate Tools Required to Intercept and Obstruct Terrorism (USA PATRIOT) Act of 2001, Pub. L. 107-56, 107.

64. Seth Stern, Lawyers See Potential Abuse of Visa Laws to Hold Suspected Terrorists. *Christian Science Monitor,* October 18, 2001, at 18.

65. Amanda Carufel, *Anti-Terrorism Legislation Passed: New Law Sparks Civil Liberties Concerns* (October 26, 2001) http://www.ailf.org/911/102601a.htm.

66. Peter Slevin and Mary Beth Sheridan, Justice Department Uses Arrest Powers Fully: Scope of Jailings Stirs Questions on Detainees' Rights to Representation and Bail. *Washington Post,* September 26, 2001, at A10.

67. Elisabeth Bumiller, Bush Announces a Crackdown on Visa Violators. *New York Times,* October 30, 2001, at A1.

68. Amy Goldstein and Dan Eggen, U.S. to Stop Issuing Detention Tallies: Justice Dept. to Share Number in Federal Custody, INS Arrests. *Washington Post,* November 9, 2001, at A16.

CHAPTER 14: THE HOUSE OF THE DEAD:
TUBERCULOSIS AND INCARCERATION

1. L. Wacquant. *Les prisons de la misère.* Paris: Raison d'Agir, 1999, p. 88. Note that the process of privatization described by Wacquant—increasingly, government prisons and holding facilities are transferring prisoners to private security corporations—is not unrelated to the processes of medical privatization described in the volume edited by J. Y. Kim, J. V. Millen, A. Irwin, and J. Gershman (eds). *Dying for Growth: Global Inequality and the Health of the Poor.* Monroe, ME: Common Courage Press, 2000.

2. R. Greifinger, N. Heywood, and J. Glaser. Tuberculosis in prison: balancing justice and public health. *Journal of Law, Medicine & Ethics* 1993; 21(3–4):332–41.

3. Although careful studies are lacking, tuberculosis incidence in prisons in Kazakhstan and other newly independent states of the former Soviet Union may well exceed one hundred times that in surrounding communities (from data presented at the conference, "Public Health Implications of Tuberculosis in Prisons and Jails in Eastern Europe and Central Asia," Budapest, Hungary, 4–7 June 1998. Many of the papers presented in the Budapest conference later appeared in the volume edited by Stern and Jones 1999). H. Reyes and R. Coninx. Pitfalls

of tuberculosis programmes in prisons. *British Medical Journal* 1997; 315:1447–50. Greifinger, Heywood, and Glaser 1993 also offer data on this association. It's important to add here that nameless millions live in a preantibiotic time warp, since they, whether in or out of detention, continue to die from this disease: worldwide, tuberculosis remains the single leading infectious cause of adult deaths.

4. P. E. Farmer, J. Bayona, M. Becerra, et al. Poverty, inequality and drug resistance: meeting community needs in the global era. *Proceedings of International Union Against Tuberculosis and Lung Disease North American Region Conference.* 1997. P. E. Farmer, J. Y. Kim, C. Mitnick, et al. "Responding to outbreaks of MDRTB: introducing 'DOTS-Plus'." In: L. B. Reichman, E. S. Hershfield (eds). *Tuberculosis: a comprehensive international approach.* 2nd edition. New York: Marcel Dekker Inc., 1999; pp. 447–69.

5. The U.S. Department of Justice reports that, in 1998, 14,528,300 people were arrested and detained in a jail or prison; of these, 675,900 were for violent offenses and 1,805,600 were for property crimes (U.S. Department of Justice and Federal Bureau of Investigation 1999).

6. Reyes and Coninx 1997, p. 1449.

7. The literature on tuberculosis and prisons is of mixed quality. The term "resistance," for example, is misused in several ways. Some social scientists pour resources—material and intellectual—into celebrations of prisoners' refusal to take medications as acts of "resistance." For a review, see P. E. Farmer. Social scientists and the new tuberculosis. *Social Science Medicine* 1997d; 44(3):347–58. Physicians and public-health specialists, in turn, often attempt to ignore drug resistance in the hopes that it will go away.

8. Compare Reyes and Coninx (1997, pp. 1447, 1449) to Greifinger, Heywood, and Glaser (1993, p. 339). Note, of course, that the former refer primarily to resource-poor countries, while the latter refer to U.S. institutions.

9. These figures are from The Sentencing Project, 2001. New prison population figures show slowing of growth but uncertain trends.

10. See, for example, L. Garrett. *The Coming Plague: Newly Emerging Diseases in a World Out of Balance.* New York: Farrar, Straus, and Giroux, 1994. "Studies showed that some 80 percent of all MDR-TB index cases in 1989–90 (not including the secondary HIV-positive cases) were injecting drug and crack users, many of whom, as a result of federal and local crackdowns, drifted in and out of the jail and prison system" (1994, p. 524).

11. M. M. Braun, B. I. Truman, B. Maguire, et al. Increasing incidence of tuberculosis in a prison inmate population: association with HIV infection. *Journal of the American Medical Association* 1989; 262:393–7.

12. Centers for Disease Control and Prevention. Prevention and control of tuberculosis in correctional institutions: recommendations of the Advisory Committee for the Elimination of Tuberculosis. *Morbidity and Mortality Weekly Report* 1989; 38(18):313–25.; Centers for Disease Control and Prevention. Famine-affected, refugee, and displaced populations: recommendations for public health issues. *Morbidity and Mortality Weekly Report* 1992; 41(RR-13):1–76.

13. Laurie Garrett puts it best: "The emergence of novel strains of multiply-drug-resistant TB

came amid a host of clangs, whistles, and bells that should have served as ample warning to humanity. But the warning fell on unhearing ears" (1994, p. 508).

14. A. Skolnick. Some experts suggest the nation's "War on Drugs" is helping tuberculosis stage a deadly comeback. *Journal of the American Medical Association* 1992; 268(22):3177-78.

15. Greifinger, Heywood, and Glaser 1993, p. 335.

16. By 1992, "New York has had the highest reported prevalence of HIV infection among inmates: 12 percent of incoming males and 20 percent of incoming females" (Greifinger, Heywood, and Glaser 1993, p. 334). In 1997, 10.3 percent of the male population and 20.7 percent of the female population in New York prisons were HIV positive—compared to a national percentage of only 2.2 percent for males and 3.5 percent for females (L. M. Maruschak. HIV in prisons 1997. *Bureau of Justice Statistics Bulletin* 1999; 1–12).

17. For a penetrating analysis of the rise of incarceration as a key plank in the "neoliberal" agenda regnant in the United States, see the trenchant analysis by Loïc Wacquant, *Prisons of Poverty*, Minneapolis: University of Minneapolis Press, expanded edition, 2002 (translated from *Les prisons de la misère*. Paris: Raison d'Agir, 1999). The War on Drugs is interpreted in a similar light in the exploration by A. Chien, M. Connors, and K. Fox. "The drug war in perspective." In: J. Y. Kim, J. V. Millen, A. Irwin, J. Gershman (eds). *Dying for Growth: Global Inequality and the Health of the Poor*. Monroe, ME: Common Courage Press, 2000; pp. 293–327.

18. M. Mauer. *Race to Incarcerate*. New York: The New Press, 1999.

19. The racial disparity in rates of incarceration increased dramatically between 1988 and 1996: while the white rate increased from 134 to 188 per 100,000 population, an increase of 28 percent, the black rate jumped 67 percent, from 922 to 1547 per 100,000 population (Human Rights Watch. *Punishment and Prejudice: Racial Disparities in the War on Drugs*. New York: Human Rights Watch, 2000). "For the first time, the number of persons admitted for drug offenses was greater than the number admitted for property offenses, violent offenses, or public-order offenses" (Greifinger, Heywood, and Glaser 1993, p. 333). For an important study of race and class in the U.S. criminal justice system, see David Cole's *No Equal Justice: Race and Class in the American Criminal Justice System*. New York: The New Press, 1999. "This downward spiral cannot go on forever," concludes Cole (p. 178). "Unless we begin to think about what criminal justice policy would look like if we could not rely on double standards and disparate impacts, we will continue to be plagued by persistent crime. For pragmatic as well [as] moral reasons, the future of criminal justice depends upon reducing the race and class disparities that society has thus far found so 'useful.' "

20. Greifinger, Heywood, and Glaser 1993, p. 333.

21. For example, John Raba, formerly medical director of the Cook County jail, was quick to link the "war on drugs" to outbreaks of MDRTB: "The result is that we are now seeing outbreaks including a number of cases of highly lethal multidrug-resistant TB. We're continuing the nation's program of incarcerating drug users despite the absence of any demonstrated individual or social benefit" (cited in Skolnick 1992, p. 3177).

22. Many patients later shown to have HIV-associated active tuberculosis were AFB smear-negative; many had atypical chest radiographs and disseminated disease.

23. D. E. Snider, Jr., L. Salinas, and G. D. Kelly. Tuberculosis: an increasing problem among minorities in the United States. *Public Health Report* 1989; 104(6):647.

24. Centers for Disease Control and Prevention. Tuberculosis mortality in the United States: final data, 1990. *Morbidity and Mortality Weekly Report* 1991; 40:SS23–SS27.

25. P. Bifani, B. Pjikaytis, V. Kapur, et al. Origin and interstate spread of a New York City multidrug-resistant *Mycobacterium tuberculosis* clone family. *Journal of the American Medical Association* 1996; 275(6):452–7.

26. Garrett 1994, p. 520.

27. *New York Post* reporter Ann Bolinger was herself infected with *M. tuberculosis* while covering the Rikers Island outbreak. See Skolnick 1992.

28. Greifinger, Heywood, and Glaser 1993, p. 335.

29. Notes Robert Cohen, former medical director of the Rikers Island jail, "Court-ordered inmate population caps have been the only thing that has kept correctional institutions in many jurisdictions from collapsing into total chaos" (cited in Skolnick 1992, p. 3178).

30. Garrett 1994, p. 523.

31. Cited in Skolnick 1992, p. 3178.

32. Wacquant 1999, p. 12.

33. Taylor, Besse, and Healing 1994, p. 968.

34. See L. Garrett. "TB Surge in Former East Bloc." *Newsday.* 25 March 1998: A21.

35. Reyes and Coninx 1997, p. 1450; they cite A. Khomenko and Médecins sans Frontières. Note that in spite of the magnitude of the U.S. problem, deaths from tuberculosis remained relatively rare, and did not inflect the country's overall mortality curves. In a sense, the Russian patients have been transported to the "preantibiotic time warp" inhabited by the southern-hemisphere poor.

36. Interview with Ivan Nikitovich Simonov, former chief inspector of prisons, and now with the Chief Board of Punishment Execution, Ministry of Internal Affairs, Russian Federation (June, 1998).

37. B. Kazionny, G. Wells, H. Kluge, et al. Implications of the growing HIV-1 epidemic for tuberculosis control in Russia. *Lancet* 2001; 358; 1513–1514.

38. Interview with Valery Sergeyev of Penal Reform International, Moscow Bureau (June, 1998). It should be noted that U.S. prisons are not as crowded as their Russian counterparts because of a meteoric rise in private prison building: privately owned facilities have increased their holding capacities from 15,300 inmates in 1990 to 145,160 by December 1999 (C. W. Thomas. Correctional privitization in the United States: an examination of its modern history and future potential. 2000 Mental Health in Corrections Symposium, Kansas City, Missouri, June 22, 2000).

39. Interface, January 5, 2002. Available at ⟨http:/www.interfax.ru/show_one_news.html? lang=EN&group_id=28&i d_news=5551321&tz=0&tz-format=MSK&reg=pris⟩, accessed on 1/7/02.

40. See Stanley A. "Russians Lament the Crime of Punishment." *New York Times* 8 January 1998: A1.

41. Alexandra Stanley (1998) recounted a very similar story—that of teenager Dima Shagina, arrested along with other boys for stealing a car. It took almost three years for Shagina's case to come to trial, by which time he too was sick with active tuberculosis. His mother hopes that his next stop will be a TB penal colony—she "hopes so" because many tuberculosis patients die in the Matrosskaya Tishina jail.

42. The prison also lacked syringes, masks, and other supplies. As a result, staff morale was low, if not as low as some would expect. "We regard this as an especially terrible problem," remarked the facility's medical director. "We have professionals who want to work, but don't have the necessary resources."

43. Interview with Valery Sergeyev of Penal Reform International, Moscow Bureau (June, 1998).

44. Stanley 1998, p. 1A.

45. Our own experience in Peru shows that a majority of patients sick with even highly resistant strains of MDRTB can be cured. See P. E. Farmer, J. Bayona, S. Shin, et al. Preliminary results of community-based MDRTB treatment in Lima, Peru. *International Journal of Tuberculosis and Lung Disease* 1998; 2(11 Suppl. 2):S371. See also G. S. Turett, E. E. Telzak, L. V. Torian, et al. Improved outcomes for patients with multidrug-resistant tuberculosis. *Clinical Infectious Diseases* 1995; 21:1238–44.

46. Reyes and Coninx 1997, p. 1448.

47. Reyes and Coninx 1997, p. 1448. The irony, here, is that we're willing to go to war over weapons inspections but throw our hands up in the face of relatively minor challenges, such as quality control in prison laboratories.

48. Reyes and Coninx 1997, p. 1449.

49. Cited in Reyes and Coninx 1997, p. 1447; emphasis mine.

50. "Since the outbreak in New York, other outbreaks have been reported in correctional systems in Connecticut, Washington, Ohio, Alabama, and California. Following the reports of cases in these states, resources were provided for an appropriate public health response. *In contrast, there has been scant funding for TB control outside the prison walls.* This is unfortunate, because TB in prison is solely a symptom of a broader public health problem" (Greifinger, Heywood, and Glaser 1993, p. 336).

51. J. Willett and R. Manheim (eds), *Bertolt Brecht Poems,* London: Eyre Methuen, Ltd, 1976.

52. Reyes and Coninx 1997, p. 1447.

53. M. Foucault. *Surveiller et punir: naissance de la prison.* Paris: Gallimard, 1975, p. 22, translation mine.

54. *Estelle v. Gamble,* 429 U.S. 97 (1976).

55. The court ruled that the "resulting threat to well-being of the inmates is so serious, and the record so devoid of any justification for the defendant's policy, that, under the standard of *Bell v. Wolfish,* this practice constitutes 'punishment' in violation of the Due Process Clause" (cited in Greifinger, Heywood, and Glaser 1993, p. 338).

56. *Austin v. Pennsylvania Department of Correction,* 1992, WL 277511 (E.D.Pa.).

57. For example, in late March 1998, a parolee sued a county jail, a prison, and the Colorado De-

partment of Health after developing tuberculosis while in prison for theft. See K. Abbott. Parolee with tuberculosis sues county jail, state prison. *Rocky Mountain News* 2 April 1998: A31.

CHAPTER 16: THE INTERNATIONAL IMPACT OF U.S. POLICIES

1. I would like to thank Vivien Francis and Femke van der Meulen, researchers at the International Centre for Prison Studies, for their assistance in writing this article.
2. Address to EU Conference, Crime Prevention: Towards a European Level, 12 May 1997.
3. World Prison Brief on www.prisonstudies.org—only the United Kingdom, Spain, and Portugal exceed 100. Finland, Sweden, Norway, and Denmark are below 65.
4. Delegation of the European Commission to the United States, European Union in the U.S., News Release, No. 53/00, 15 September, 2000.
5. Felix G. Rohatyn, America's Deadly Image, *Washington Post,* 20 February 2001.
6. Policies such as life imprisonment, imprisonment for minor drug possession, three-strikes and you're out.
7. Select Committee on Home Affairs, Third Report, Alternatives to Prison Sentences, the Stationery Office, London, 1998, para 15.
8. Execution Policy, Dutch Ministry of Justice, 9 May 2000, see at: www.minjust.nl.
9. See "Prison population" at the Danish Prison and Probation Service Web site at www. kriminalforsorgen.dk, July 2001.
10. The French National Front at www.front-national.com.
11. The British National Party at www.bnp.org.uk.
12. Corrections Population Growth, Second Progress Report for the Federal/Provincial/Territorial Ministers for Justice, Solicitor General Canada, Regina, Saskatchewan, 1998, p. 1.
13. Bill C-41. (1996). Canadian Criminal Code.
14. Roy Walmsley, World Prison Population List, Research Findings no. 88, Home Office Research, Development and Statistics Directorate, London, p. 3.
15. World Prison Brief on www.prisonstudies.org.
16. Walmsley, World Prison Pop., p. 3.
17. World Prison Brief on www.prisonstudies.org.
18. Public Education, Speakers Kit, Module 5, Incarceration, Web site of the Correctional Service of Canada. www.csc-scc.gc/ca.
19. Notes made by the present author at the meeting.
20. Final Report of the Third Meeting of Ministers of Justice or Ministers or Attorneys General of the Americas, March 1–3 2000, Secretariat of Legal Affairs, Organisation of American States.
21. See www.coe.int for a list of all the members and dates of joining.
22. See for example Prison overcrowding and prison population inflation—Recommendation No. R (99) 22 and report (2000); European rules on community, sanctions and measures—Recommendation No. R (92) 16 and explanatory memorandum (1994); the European Prison Rules—Recommendation No. R(87)3, adopted by the Committee of Ministers of the Council of Europe on 12 February 1987, Council of Europe, Strasbourg.

23. Newsletter Penal Reform Project in Eastern Europe and Central Asia, Penal Reform International (PRI) and the International Centre for Prison Studies (ICPS), No. 11, Winter 2000, London, p. 1.

24. The *Times*, 3 January 2001, London.

25. Newsletter, Penal Reform Project in Eastern Europe and Central Asia, Penal Reform International and the International Centre for Prison Studies, No. 11 Winter 2000, London, p. 6.

26. Newsletter, Penal Reform Project in Eastern Europe and Central Asia, Penal Reform International and the International Centre for Prison Studies, No. 12 Spring/Summer 2001, London, p. 9.

27. Newsletter, Penal Reform Project in Eastern Europe and Central Asia, Penal Reform International and the International Centre for Prison Studies, No. 11, Winter 2000, London, p. 10.

28. Ibid, p. 11.

29. Newsletter, Penal Reform Project in Eastern Europe and Central Asia, Penal Reform International and the International Centre for Prison Studies, No. 10 Autumn 2000, London, p. 11.

30. RFE/RL newsline, Vol. 4, No. 166, Part 1, 29 August 2000.

31. Walmsley, World Prison Pop., pp. 5–6.

32. Roy Walmsley, World Prison Population List, Research Findings no. 116, Home Office Research, Development and Statistics Directorate, London, pp. 5–6.

33. See Human Rights Watch, Cold Storage, Super-Maximum Security Confinement in Indiana, New York, 1997; and Katherine Beckett and Theodore Sassoon, The Politics of Injustice: Crime and Punishment in America, Thousand Oaks, 2000, pp. 186–187.

34. 1999 Report of the Auditor General of Canada—Chapter One—Correctional Service of Canada, Reintegration of Offenders, paras 1.25–1.46, Ottawa.

35. Véronique Vasseur, Médecin-Chef a la Prison de la Santé, Le Cherche Midi Editeur: Paris, 2000.

36. See Country Reports on Human Rights Practices 2000, France, U.S. Department of State Bureau of Democracy, Human Rights and Labor, February 2001 at www.state.gov.

37. Amélioration du Contrôle Extérieur des Etablissements Pénitentiaires, Rapport de la Commission á Madame le Garde des Seceaux, French Ministry of Justice, 2000, p. 151.

38. See Projet de loi pénitentiaire at the French Ministry of Justice, July 2001, available at: www.justice.gouv.fr.

39. See Ministry of Justice Factsheet, Punishment in the Netherlands, December 1996 at www.minjust.nl.

40. Prison Populations in Europe and North America, HEUNI, Helsinki, 1997.

41. World Prison Brief on www.prisonstudies.org.

42. See Dutch Correctional Service at www.dji.nl/pdf/jaarverslag/missie.pdf.

43. Introducing Restorative Justice in Belgian Prisons, Katholieke Universiteit Leuven—Onderzoeksgroep Penologie en victimologie, Belgium, 1999, p. 1.

44. Personal communication, Katholieke Universiteit Leuven—Onderzoeksgroep Penologie en victimologie, Belgium, to author in March 2001.

45. Information provided to the author by the Japan Federation of Bar Associations.

46. See EU/China: EU sends human rights warning to Beijing, European Report, 24 January 2001.

47. Personal information given to author by the ICCLRCP.
48. Amnesty International Annual Report 2001, section on Iran, available at www.web.amnesty. org.
49. Iran Prison Chief urges sharp cut in jail terms, Reuters, 7 June, 2001.
50. PRI Newsletter No. 46–47, January 2002, Penal Reform International, London p. 3.
51. Annual Report 2000, International Centre for Prison Studies, King's College, London, 2001.
52. Ibid. and Newsletter Penal Reform Project in Eastern Europe and Central Asia, Penal Reform International and the International Centre for Prison Studies, No. 12 Spring/Summer 2001, London, page 4–6.
53. Annual Report 2000, International Centre for Prison Studies, Kings College, London, 2001, and Hunger strikes and prison interventions in Turkey: Publication of observations by Council of Europe Anti-Torture Committee delegation at www.coe.int.
54. Newsletter, Penal Reform Project in Eastern Europe and Central Asia, Penal Reform International and the International Centre for Prison Studies, No. 12 Spring/Summer 2001, London, pp. 1–2.
55. Prison conditions in Africa: report of a pan-African seminar, Kampala, Uganda, 19–21 September 1996, PRI, Paris, 1997.
56. Vivien Stern, Alternatives to prison in developing countries—some lessons from Africa, Punishment & Society, Sage, Vol. 1 (2) October 1999, London, 231–241.
57. Penal Reform International Annual Report 2000, London, 2001, pp. 6–7.
58. Vivien Stern, Alternatives to prison in developing countries, ICPS, London, 1999, pp. 28–32.
59. PRI Newsletter, No. 44, March 2001, Penal Reform International, London, p. 6.
60. Vivien Stern, A Sin Against the Future, Penguin, Harmondsworth, 1998, pp 292–93.
61. David Biles and Vicki Dalton, Deaths in Private Prisons 1990–99: A comparative Study, Trends and Issues in Crime and Criminal Justice, Australian Institute of Criminology, No. 120, June 1999, pp. 1–3.
62. Stern, A Sin Against the Future, pp. 294–96.
63. Prison Privatisation Report International, Prison Reform Trust, No. 37, September/October 2000, London, pp. 1–3.
64. Prison Privatisation Report International, Prison Reform Trust, Jan./Feb. 2001, London, p.1.
65. See Scottish Prison Service at: www.sps.gov.uk/research/prisons/Kilmarnock.
66. Prison Privatisation Report International, Prison Reform Trust, No. 34, March/April 2000, London, p. 1.
67. See Recent Privatisation Trends, OECD, 2000, p.1.
68. Stern, A Sin Against the Future, pp. 277–306.
69. Rod Morgan, England and Wales, in Dirk van Zyl Smit and Dunkel Freider, *Imprisonment Today and Tomorrow*, Kluwer Law International, The Hague, 2001, p. 220.
70. Prison Privatisation Report International, Prison Reform Trust, No. 25, Nov./Dec. 1998, London, p. 5.
71. Prison Privatisation Report International, Prison Reform Trust, No. 38, Jan./Feb. 2001, London, p. 11.

72. Prison Privatisation Report International, Prison Reform Trust, No. 23, September 1998, London, p. 2.

73. Prison Privatisation Report International, Prison Reform Trust, No. 40, April/May 2001, London, p. 1.

74. Si Kahn, Grassroots leadership community assets campaign 2000: stopping for-profit private prisons, Prison Moratorium Project at www.nomoreprisons.org; and the newsletter, Prison Privatisation Report International, has been an indispensable tool for anti-privatisation activists.

75. Roy Walmsley, An overview of world imprisonment: global prison populations, trends and solutions: A Paper presented at the United Nations Program Network Institutes Technical Assistance Workshop, Vienna, Austria, May 10, 2001, at www.prisonstudies.org.

76. Roy Walmsley, World Prison Population List, Research Findings no. 88, Home Office Research, Development and Statistics Directorate, London, p. 4.

77. Number of prisoners: 206,011 in mid-2000, 20th Asian and Pacific Conference of Correctional Administrators and World Prison Brief, available at www.prisonstudies.org.

78. Stern, A Sin Against the Future, pp. 280–81.

79. David Faulkner, *Crime, State and the Citizen,* Waterside Press, Winchester, p. 126.

80. Ibid., p. 181.

81. Ibid.

82. Stern, A Sin Against the Future, p. 169.

83. Home Office, Prison Statistics, England and Wales 1997, Government Statistical Service, 1998.

84. Figure for 20 July 2001 from www.hmprisonservice.gov.uk.

85. House of Commons, Official Report, London, 27 Jun. 2001: Column 654.

86. Alan Travis, Special Report: Drugs in Britain, *Guardian,* London, 2 July 2001.

87. Anne Perkins, Lilley calls for soft drug legalisation, *Guardian,* London, 6 July 2001.

88. John van Kesteren, Pat Mayhew, and Paul Nieuwbeerta, Criminal Victimisation in Seventeen Industrialised Countries; key findings from the 2000 International Crime Victims, Ministry of Justice, Netherlands, 2000, p. 87.

89. Michael Tonry, Why Are U.S. Incarceration Rates So High? In *Overcrowded Times,* Vol. 10, No. 3, June 1999.

90. See U.S. State Department, Bureau for International Narcotics and Law Enforcement Affairs, Mission Statement at www.state.gov/www/global/narcotics.

91. Personal communication to author.

92. World Prison Brief, www.prisonstudies.org.

93. Elias Carranza, Prison Overcrowding in Latin American and the Caribbean, Situation and Possible Responses, ILANUD, unpublished paper, June 2001.

94. See Nils Christie, Crime Control as Industry: Towards GULAGS, Western-Style, Routledge, London, 2nd edition, 1994, and Zygmunt Baumann, Globalization, Cambridge, 1998, and Anthony Giddens, The third way, Cambridge, 1998; John Gray, False dawn: the delusions of global capitalism, London, 1998, and Herbert J. Gans, *The Underclass and Antipoverty Policy,* New York, 1995.

95. David Garland, *The Culture of Control: Crime and Social Order in Contemporary Society,* Oxford University Press, Oxford, 2001, p. ix.

96. Ibid., p. xi.

97. Ibid., p. 10.

98. Ibid., p. 11.

99. Ibid., p. 201.

100. Government of Ontario, Canada, see Web site www.gov.on.ca.

About the Authors

DONALD BRAMAN is a doctoral candidate at Yale University in the department of anthropology. He has spent the last three years conducting fieldwork investigating the impact of incarceration on families and communities in the District of Columbia. He is currently writing a book on that subject.

MEDA CHESNEY-LIND is professor of women's studies at the University of Hawaii, and adjunct professor of criminal justice at the University of Illinois. Her books include *Girls, Delinquency and Juvenile Justice* (with Randall Shelden), *The Female Offender: Girls, Women, and Crime*, and *Female Gangs in America* (with John Hagedorn). She is an outspoken advocate for the needs of girls and women in the criminal justice system.

TODD R. CLEAR is Distinguished Professor, John Jay College of Criminal Justice, City University of New York. His most recent books are *What Is Community Justice?* (Thousand Oaks, CA: Sage), *The Community Justice Ideal* (Boulder, CO: Westview), and *Harm in American Penology* (Albany, NY: SUNY Press). He is also editor of *Criminology and Public Policy*, published by the American Society of Criminology.

ANGELA J. DAVIS is a professor of law at American University Washington College of Law, where she teaches criminal law, criminal procedure, race, crime, and politics, and other related courses. She has written scholarly articles on racism in the criminal justice system and the abuse of prosecutorial discretion. Professor Davis is a former director of the Public Defender Service for the District of Columbia.

PAUL FARMER is a medical anthropologist whose work draws primarily on active clinical practice: He divides his clinical time between Brigham and Women's Hospital (Division of Infectious Diseases) and a charity hospital in rural Haiti. His work in anthropology and in social medicine has focused on diseases disproportionately afflicting the poor, and the Program in Infectious Disease and Social Change at Harvard

Medical School, which Farmer runs along with his colleagues in the Department of Social Medicine, has pioneered novel, community-based treatment strategies for sexually transmitted infections (including HIV), drug-resistant typhoid, and tuberculosis in resource-poor settings. Farmer has also written extensively about health and human rights, and about the role of social inequalities in the distribution and outcomes of readily treatable diseases.

JAMES FORMAN, JR., is a fellow at the New America Foundation. He is a graduate of Brown University, Yale Law School, and a former law clerk for Supreme Court Justice Sandra Day O'Connor. Mr. Forman helped to found the Maya Angelou Public Charter School, an education and job-training project for District of Columbia teens.

JUDITH A. GREENE is a criminal justice policy analyst and recipient of a Soros Senior Justice Fellowship. She has previously directed the State-Centered Program for the Edna McConnell Clark Foundation and served as director of court programs at the Vera Institute of Justice. Her articles on sentencing issues, police practices, and correctional policy have appeared in a broad range of publications.

JOSH GUETZKOW is a graduate student in the department of sociology at Princeton University. His research focuses on the political and cultural sociology of the criminal justice system.

TRACY HULING is a public policy analyst, writer, and award-winning filmmaker. Her work has been published by the U.S. Commission on Civil Rights, The Sentencing Project, National Center on Institutions and Alternatives, Human Rights Watch, *Mother Jones,* and the *Chicago Tribune,* among many others. She is the producer of *Yes, in My Backyard* (1999), the first documentary film portrait of a rural prison town, which aired on public television 1999–2002.

MARC MAUER is the assistant director of The Sentencing Project and the author of *Race to Incarcerate* (The New Press), which was named a semifinalist for the Robert F. Kennedy Book Award. He has served as a consultant to the Bureau of Justice Assistance and the National Institute of Corrections, and has frequently testified before Congress and addressed a broad range of national and international audiences.

TERESA A. MILLER is an associate professor of law at the University at Buffalo, where she teaches and researches the legal regulation of prisoners. She became interested in immigration policy after observing disturbing similarities between incarceration and immigration detention. She is currently investigating prisoners' civil disabilities, the civil penalties imposed as a consequence of felony convictions that prolong criminal punishment by stigmatizing ex-offenders long after their sentences have ended.

DEBBIE MUKAMAL is a staff attorney in the Legal Action Center's New York office. Her work centers around legal barriers faced by individuals with criminal records. She has researched and analyzed local housing policies affecting individuals with criminal records in jurisdictions nationwide.

BECKY PETTIT is an assistant professor of sociology and faculty affiliate of the Center for Studies in Demography and Ecology, University of Washington. Her research focuses on the relationship between demographic processes and inequality.

BETH E. RICHIE is a professor in the departments of criminal justice and women's studies at the University of Illinois at Chicago. Her research interests center on battered African-American women and the relationship between violence against women and women's participation in crime. She also serves as a consultant to various organizations, including the Social Science Research Council and the National Institute of Corrections.

GWEN RUBINSTEIN is director of policy research in the Washington, D.C., office of the Legal Action Center. She is a nationally recognized expert on the critical policy issues at the intersection of TANF, Medicaid, and addiction.

VIVIEN STERN is senior research fellow at the International Centre for Prison Studies, Kings College London, and author of *A Sin Against the Future: Imprisonment in the World* (1998), *Bricks of Shame: Britain's Prisons* (1993), and *Alternatives to Prison in Developing Countries* (1999). She edited *Sentenced to Die? The Problem of TB in Prisons in Eastern Europe and Central Asia* (1999). She is a member of the Upper House of the British Parliament, and Honorary Secretary-General of Penal Reform International.

PETER Y. SUSSMAN was an editor at the *San Francisco Chronicle* for nearly thirty years. In the 1980s and 1990s, he published in the *Chronicle* the works of federal prison writer Dannie Martin, and he spearheaded a First Amendment lawsuit when Martin was punished for his newspaper writing. Martin and Sussman are coauthors of *Committing Journalism* (W. W. Norton, 1993). Sussman has won many national awards for his advocacy of media access to prisoners, including the Wells Memorial Key, the highest honor granted by the Society of Professional Journalists.

JEREMY TRAVIS is a senior fellow at the Urban Institute in Washington, D.C., developing research and policy agendas on crime in community context, sentencing, and prisoner reentry. He previously served as the director of the National Institute of Justice from 1994 to 2000, as the deputy commissioner for legal matters of the New York City Police Department, and with the Vera Institute of Justice. He has taught classes at Yale University and New York University, and has published extensively on criminal law and criminal justice policy.

BRUCE WESTERN is professor of sociology and faculty associate of the Office of Population Research at Princeton University. His research focuses on the influence of public policy and labor relations on patterns of earnings and employment.

Index